THE LAST HEATHEN

The

LAST

CHARLES MONTGOMERY

ENCOUNTERS WITH

GHOSTS AND ANCESTORS

IN MELANESIA

HEATHEN

Douglas & McIntyre
VANCOUVER/TORONTO

Douglas & McIntyre Ltd.
2323 Quebec Street, Suite 201
Vancouver, British Columbia
Canada v5T 4s7
www.douglas-mcintyre.com

National Library of Canada Cataloguing in Publication Data
Montgomery, Charles, 1968–
The last heathen : encounters with ghosts and ancestors
in Melanesia / Charles Montgomery.

ISBN 1-55365-072-7

1. Melanesia—Description and travel.
2. Montgomery, Charles, 1968– —Travel—Melanesia. 3. Melanesia—
Religion. 4. Missions—Melanesia—History—19th century.
5. Montgomery, Henry I. Title.
DU490.M66 2004   919.5   2004-902818-9

Editing by Saeko Usukawa
Cover and text design by Jessica Sullivan
Front cover inset photograph © Craig Tuttle/CORBIS/MAGMA
Printed and bound in Canada by Friesens
Printed on acid-free, forest-friendly (100% post-consumer
recycled) paper processed chlorine-free

We gratefully acknowledge the financial support of the Canada
Council for the Arts, the British Columbia Arts Council,
and the Government of Canada through the Book Publishing Industry
Development Program (BPIDP) for our publishing activities.

The epigraph for Chapter 10 is reproduced with permission from
Solomon Islands ed. 3 © 1997 Lonely Planet Publications.

CONTENTS

What indeed do we not owe to the influence of the departed?
They are not dead. Thousands of them live for us,
they still speak to us out of every century, and from far down
the ages, till we have reached the furthest bounds of history.
Somehow they seem all round us.

HENRY MONTGOMERY, *Life's Journey*

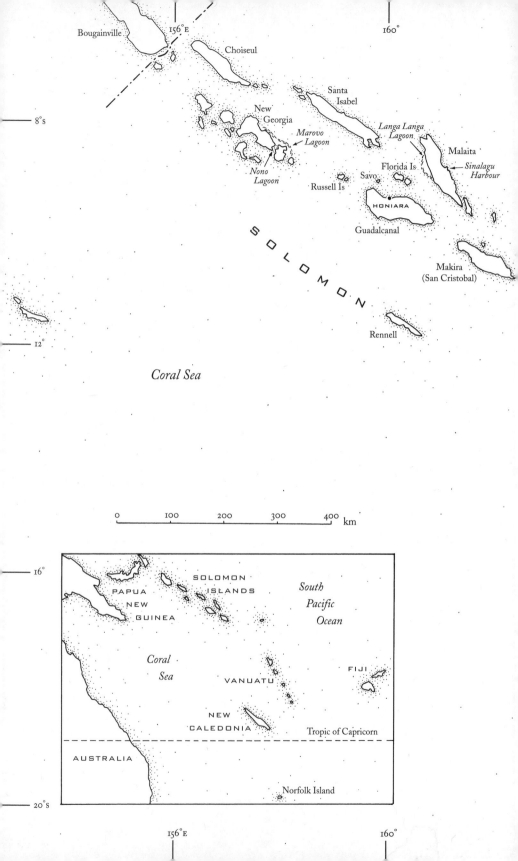

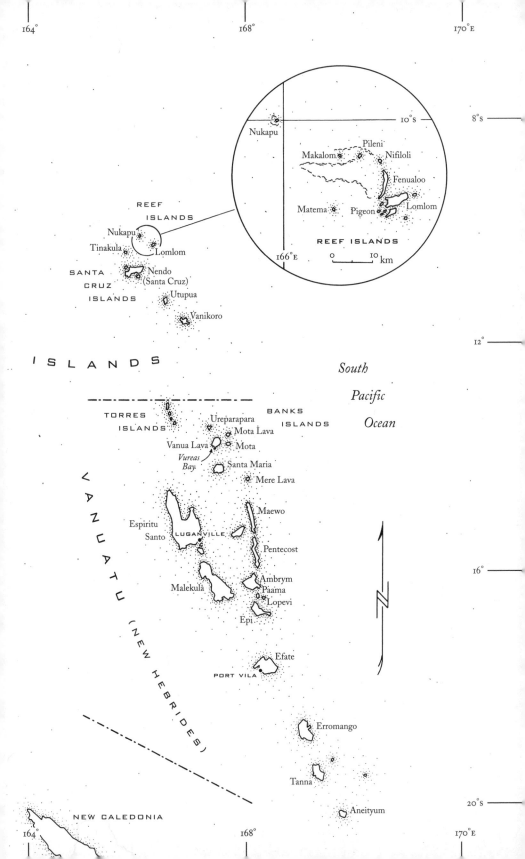

164°   168°   170° E

8° S

Nukapu

Pileni

Makalom   Nifiloli

Fenualoo

Matema   Pigeon   Lomlom

REEF
ISLANDS

Nukapu

Tinakula   Lomlom

REEF ISLANDS

166° E

0   10 km

SANTA   Nendo
CRUZ   (Santa Cruz)
ISLANDS   Utupua

Vanikoro

12°

I S L A N D S

South

Pacific

Ocean

TORRES   BANKS
ISLANDS   Ureparapara   ISLANDS
    Mota Lava
Vanua Lava   Mota
*Vureas
Bay*   Santa Maria
    Mere Lava

V A N U A T U (N E W H E B R I D E S)

Maewo

Espiritu   LUGANVILLE
Santo

Pentecost

16°

Ambrym
Malekula   Paama
    Lopevi

Epi

Efate
PORT VILA

Erromango

Tanna

20° S

NEW CALEDONIA   Aneityum

164°   168°   170° E

THE LAST HEATHEN

1

A PACKET OF SAND

Hunters for gold or pursuers of fame, they all had gone out on that stream,
bearing the sword, and often the torch, messengers of the might
within the land, bearers of a spark from the sacred fire. What greatness had not
floated on the ebb of that river into the mystery of an unknown earth!

JOSEPH CONRAD, *Heart of Darkness*

THE STORY should begin in Oxford.

Oxford, in the muted light of early spring, not far from the pin-cushion spires of the old Bodleian Library, past the long sandstone wall and the constellation of early spring narcissus, through the marble rotunda and the oak-panelled anteroom, up the creaking staircase to the attic—that's where I found the envelope that set the journey in motion.

I remember the oath—you can't just wander into the attic of Rhodes House or any other part of the Bodleian Library without taking the oath, which includes a promise not to set fire to the books. It's understood that you will not touch the older manuscripts with your fingertips, since oil from human skin is like acid to the wrinkled flesh of old parchment. I raised my hand and swore.

But the envelope. I found it in file C/NZ/MEL2, a cardboard box full of tattered letters, newspaper clippings and journal extracts. Inside it was a postcard from Egypt, stamped at Port Said: Jan. 30, 1884. There was no image on the front of the card, just the address of one Reverend Prebendary Plant, the vicar of Weston-on-Trent. The envelope also contained a sheet of cream-coloured paper folded many times over and sealed with red wax. The seal was broken.

I made a little fortress of books and albums so the archivists could not see me, then I carefully unfolded the paper. Inside it was another piece of paper, folded to the dimensions of a matchbook. It had also been sealed with wax, and this seal was broken too. I opened it and peered inside.

It contained perhaps a spoonful of sand and splinters, as though someone had taken a walk on a beach, then scraped the sole of his shoe and swept the remains into that little packet. I reached in and ran my finger through the grit. The splinters were so dry they crumbled on touch. I turned the paper over. Handwritten on the back of it: "Sand and wood from the spot where Bishop Patteson died."

A story: John Coleridge Patteson, the first Bishop of Melanesia, had been welcomed ashore on the tiny atoll of Nukapu on a sunny afternoon in 1871. He was led to a palm-thatched hut and offered a grass mat, on which he lay down to rest. The bishop closed his eyes, as if to ready himself for the blow that would shatter his skull, as if he was waiting to die and be resurrected as the martyr-hero of the western South Pacific. The blow came. Everyone agrees on that one detail. Dozens of versions of the story eventually emerged, and they once captivated England as thoroughly as those of the martyrdom of Livingstone in Africa, but the circumstances surrounding the bishop's murder are still shrouded in mystery.

I took a pinch of the sand and rolled the grains between my thumb and forefinger. Nukapu. I imagined the reef, the island and the murder that was a transforming moment in the history of the South Pacific, a moment that tied together the dreams of an ancient culture, the crimes of a generation of rogues and the aspirations of hundreds of spiritual adventurers.

I WAS TEN YEARS OLD when the first piece of the story came to me. My parents had bought a farm on Vancouver Island, on the west coast of Canada, and then my father died. A few months after the funeral, my mother discovered my father's dispatch box in a corner of the attic. She hauled the black tin trunk down to the dining-room table and began to sift through it. I remember watching her and seeing the worry on her brow. I know now that she was terrified my father was receding, sinking into the mud of memory, threatening to disappear forever. She wanted to imprint my brother and me with something of our father's character—something that would remind us that we were part of a story that did not end with his death, a story that would bind us to him, or at least to his name.

The box didn't offer much. My father was a sailor. He had left home at fifteen. He had served on troopships in the Atlantic and Indian oceans during World War II, dodged German submarines in the Mediterranean. He had fed dinner leftovers to sharks off the coast of Sicily. One letter, posted in Cape Town, described a showdown with a water buffalo in Mozambique. What else? He once had a girlfriend in Greece. He bought a Super 8 camera in Tokyo. He spent decades at sea, but the scraps in his box didn't begin to fill in the blanks. It was as if he had not wanted his story to be told.

But there were other stories in the box. Diaries. Bits of paper. Newspaper clippings. A family tree. Photos of stone mansions in Ireland and India, soldiers on tanks, tea parties on vast lawns, buggies drawn by camels. There were books about God: volume after volume of theological musings and pious advice for Christians, palm-sized booklets with titles like *Visions* or *Life's Journey,* and guides for young missionaries headed for distant colonies. The covers of some were stamped with the same nautical scene: a square-rigged ship sailing towards an island populated with diminutive natives. The sea was rough but the sun smiled down on the ship, whose sole passenger stood at the bow, waving an open Bible towards shore.

These were my great-grandfather's books. Unlike my father, the Right Reverend Henry Hutchinson Montgomery did want his story known. You could tell by looking at him. The bishop may have been buried in 1932, but he had been a part of our household for as long as I could remember. There he was, floating in a cloud of crimson brushstrokes above the dining-room table. A royal blue cloak printed with exquisite thistle bouquets hung from his shoulders. A pancake-sized medallion and a gold cross dangled from his neck. The face was weathered, the cheeks hollowed with age, but the bishop's white beard was tidy, trimmed and as dignified as his long nose. He looked down over that nose, not at you, but into—what was it, a prayer book? He wore a high cap shaped like a cone. He seemed utterly satisfied. We never cursed in front of him.

It was under that portrait that we sifted through the black trunk to discover the story that would make me forget all about my father's mystery years. It didn't look like much on the outside: a pocketbook bound with blue cotton and frayed at the crown. The cover, polished by years of jostling among other unread volumes, reflected the lamplight. The title was stamped across it in gold, as brilliant as the day it was printed:

The Light of Melanesia.

The pages were the colour of smoke, and brittle. Some were decorated with floral motifs, thistles and mermaids. The text was faint. But the photos were mesmerizing. Faded monotones showed muscular black men clutching spears or dozing on sleek outrigger canoes. Those men were naked but for the feathers that poked from their frizzy hair like peacock plumage, curls of—was it shell? bone?—that hung from their earlobes and noses, and shocking phallic sheaths that shot up from their loins. Bare-breasted women emerged like shadows from still lagoons. A gang of magnificent, barrel-chested men carried a long pole adorned with rings of feather money. Then, beyond a village of grass huts, past an explosion of jungle, a ship with three masts waited at anchor.

The writing was difficult. I didn't read it all, just enough to understand that this was an account of a journey made more than a century ago; that back in the days when the world was a wild and treacherous place, when white men in top hats and ties confronted cruel savages on the rocky shores of remote islands, when black magic and powerful spirits still ruled the backwaters of the world, the bishop had a very big adventure somewhere on the far side of the Pacific Ocean—an adventure sanctioned by God Himself. The story I fashioned from the raw material of those pages went like this:

By 1889, the British Empire was nearing the apex of its power. It controlled a fifth of the world, but much of that domain was still lacking in spiritual guidance. The Archbishop of Canterbury consecrated the forty-

two-year-old Henry Montgomery as Bishop of Tasmania and sent him off
to the empire's distant fringe. The bishop was happy in the antipodean
colony. He had a comfortable manor house and a great stone cathedral in
which to preach. He had a wife and four children. But after three years, he
left them all. He caught a steamer to New Zealand, where he set sail for
the Tropic of Capricorn aboard the mission schooner *Southern Cross*. The
objective: to bring the word of God to the heathens of the Melanesian archipelago, a chain of hundreds of islands shrouded in violence, fear and—
equally shocking to the Victorian missionaries—nakedness, promiscuity
and sloth.

It was perilous work. Dozens of traders and evangelists had already
been murdered on the shores of Melanesia. Some, like Patteson, were
clubbed to death. Some were pierced with arrows tipped with human
bone. Others were held underwater until their bodies stopped shaking.
The most unlucky were cooked and eaten.

The natives weren't behaving well towards each other, either. An epidemic of headhunting and black magic had spread east from New Guinea
through the Solomon Islands. Entire villages had been wiped out. A hundred miles of coastline on the island of Santa Isabel were left desolate by
the skull-collecting chiefs of New Georgia. On San Cristobal, lowland
villagers were buying children from mountain tribes because old women
on the coast were killing their own grandchildren.

It was clear to the bishop that Satan had reached the islands long before the missionaries and imbued his servants with the most sinister of
powers. Black magic was rampant. A sorcerer could kill a man by shaking
a handful of cobwebs at him. People worshipped sharks, stones, invisible
spirits and the dead, all of whom demanded constant blood sacrifice. The
jungles of Melanesia echoed with the chanting of their followers.

As if the brew of black magic, infanticide and assassination were not
enough, the scum of European civilization had also beaten the missionaries to the islands, hungry for the sandalwood that grew throughout the
archipelago. The aromatic wood was in such high demand in China that
white traders would do anything to get it. They stole what they could
and paid for the rest with axes and muskets, which only increased the
headhunters' efficiency. Then the white traders started harvesting the

Melanesians themselves—they knew the islanders would make hardy labourers for sugar cane plantations in Queensland and Fiji. When young men didn't want to leave their islands, they were lassoed from their canoes like wild horses, dragged aboard the labour-recruiting vessels and locked below deck. Sometimes the blackbirders—as the labour recruiters came to be called—simply shot villagers who wouldn't co-operate. Occasionally, they dressed up as missionaries to win the natives' trust. The survivors took their revenge on the next white faces they saw, which, as often as not, were missionaries.

To my adolescent mind, Melanesia seemed a fabulously sinister place. Good and evil were indeed clashing in the South Pacific, and in 1892, goodness needed a new champion: Bishop Patteson's replacement had succumbed to the ravages of tropical disease and retreated to England. The archipelago had been left without a bishop. There was no choice for my great-grandfather, really, but to sail across the miles and face the great darkness head on, so the martyrs would not have died in vain.

Henry Montgomery wrote to his children from the deck of the *Southern Cross*. "Remember," he told them, "that your father visited all these islands, and that his heart went out to the dwellers among these lonely scenes, praying ever that they might be brought to know their Father in His son Jesus Christ." He reminded his children that they were special. "You have all been taught that we must be true and pure and upright because we are Christ's disciples; but next after that reason there is no incentive to live nobly which is so powerful as the possession of a great family tradition. You come from a family of 'gentlemen'; you know that word does not signify mere outward refinement: it tells of a refined and noble mind, to which anything dishonourable or mean or impure is abhorrent and unworthy."

This was the kind of story and these the sort of words my mother had wanted me to find. I left my great-grandfather's diaries in the tin trunk but held on tightly to his story and his counsel. After hours spent shovelling manure I would kick off my gumboots on the porch and pad quietly into the dining room, and I would just stand and look at the old man, and know that here was proof that I was connected to something grand, noble and far, far away from the stumps, muck and drudgery of our farm.

I didn't think much about religion, or that there might be anything less than heroic about the bishop's journey. I just imagined his schooner at full sail, that vast, beckoning ocean and a hundred thousand cannibals beneath the palms, waiting. And I let the bishop's story ebb and flood through my dreams, as vivid and enduring as *The Jungle Book* or *Treasure Island* or *Star Wars*. It remained like that for two decades, long after I had stopped bothering with church, long after I had relegated the bishop's god to the pantheon of imagined heroes, as fictional as Mowgli or Hercules or Yoda.

BUT SOMETIMES A STORY returns to demand your attention, and you must decide whether to let it live or fade. I found *The Light of Melanesia* again when I was thirty-two. I read it all this time, slowly. I studied it with fascination and a growing sense of doubt. The bishop didn't seem so right any more: not his convictions and especially not his crusade to export his God to the other side of the world. I searched for clues about his motivation, his contradictions and, I suppose, the dark side of his mission.

Melanesia became an obsession. I harassed Oceanists, theologians, mission historians, anyone who might tell me the story, not just of my great-grandfather and his Victorian peers but of the islands they had set out to change. The more I learned, the more I was captivated by that archipelago of bloody ritual and bubbling volcanoes, and the more ambiguous the missionaries' legacy became. I flew to England to search for their diaries and letters. I thought that if I completed the story I might be able to put it aside for good.

I began in London, inside the buckling brick walls of the Archbishop of Canterbury's fortress on the south bank of the Thames. In the chill of Lambeth Palace Library, I pored over hundreds of pages of ecclesiastical correspondence from the late nineteenth century. The Victorian bishops might have revealed something if their scribbles weren't so damn illegible.

I took the train to Oxford and uttered the Bodleian Oath. There, in the creaking attic of Rhodes House, I was rewarded. I found crates and crates of notes, reports from the Melanesian Mission, logbooks from the *Southern Cross* and a dozen accounts of Patteson's murder. There was a shoebox full of sketches: faded line drawings of spears, canoes and carved paddles. There were diaries too: accounts of misty mornings, sunsets and slaughter on creamy sand beaches. There were woeful notes about the sins into which some missionaries had fallen: "The temptations on a desert island," mourned one cleric.

Digging through it all was like peering into the mist of my own unconscious memory. Every photo, every story, seemed strangely familiar, as if they had grown from the story I had been telling myself for years. The more I read, the more the dust seemed to stir, and the bricks and slate and shattered windows came together to form a great tower of memory amid the rubble, like those films of building demolitions shown in reverse. But it wasn't quite the shape I remembered.

Anglicans like to say their great Melanesian enterprise was an accident that heaped the white man's burden on a fraternity of English gentlemen. It began in 1841, when the Eton-educated George Augustus Selwyn was sent from England to serve as the first bishop of the colony of New Zealand. Selwyn's diocese should have extended north to 34 degrees south of the Equator, just past the tip of New Zealand's North Island. But someone slipped in the word "north" where Selwyn's letters patent should have read "south." The clerical error extended his territory thousands of miles through Melanesia, past the equator and the Tropic of Cancer to well beyond Hawaii. Selwyn embraced the mistake with evangelical glee. He chartered ships and hitched rides north with the Royal Navy, leapfrogging ahead of the Catholic and Presbyterian missionaries who were already trickling across the Pacific from Tahiti and Tonga to be slaughtered in the archipelagos west of Fiji.

Selwyn's progress was slow. Few white volunteers were keen to fend for themselves on islands whose reputation for savagery had made headlines from Birmingham to Brisbane. The bishop needed help if he was going to save Melanesians from the Devil, not to mention the misguided influence of Scottish Presbyterians and French Catholics. If Selwyn wanted his far more sensible doctrine to take hold, he needed to innovate. He needed a new kind of missionary.

So, just as the blackbirders were beginning to hunt among the islands for plantation labourers, Selwyn set out to harvest his own crop of young Melanesians. He befriended chiefs, charming them with gifts of fish hooks, axes and calico, then convinced them to let him carry away the most promising of their youngsters to his Christian training camp in New Zealand. Most of the recruits were after more axes and fish hooks. (In fact, the trade was so central to the bishop's persona that islanders confused his title with the word "fish hook." They called him "bish-hooka.") The strong boys, the ones who didn't drop dead from the flu, dysentery or homesickness, were moulded into an army of black apostles and sent back to the islands, where to preach was to invite ostracization and, occasionally, assassination.

In 1855 Selwyn returned to England to drum up donations for his mission. His sermons inspired a fellow Eton graduate with a talent for both cricket and linguistics. The latter skill would be useful: Selwyn's potential converts spoke more than a hundred different languages. John Coleridge Patteson was not yet thirty when he accompanied Selwyn back to New Zealand aboard the *Southern Cross*. In 1861 Selwyn handed the entire mission over to Patteson and consecrated him the first Bishop of Melanesia.

Patteson was even more ambitious than his mentor. Every year he ventured farther into the archipelago. At each new island he swam to shore from the ship's whaleboat, with a vocabulary notebook tucked inside his hat and presents tied around his neck. He picked up dozens of local languages, and in them tried to explain to the islanders that they had got the nature of the cosmos all wrong. He told them that if they learned to obey his god, they could live on after death; but if they did not obey, they would go on to endless pain and sorrow. Like Selwyn, he gave them fish hooks and axes. And like Selwyn, he took their children away.

In New Zealand, then later at the mission's new base on Norfolk Island, the boys were instructed in the dignified rituals of the Anglo-Catholic liturgy. While the students learned how to button their shirts and tie their shoelaces, how to use knives and forks, how to read, pray, sing hymns and play cricket, they told their teachers about the world they had left behind. One missionary, the erudite Oxonian scholar Robert Henry Codrington, paid keen attention to their stories. I found Codrington's sketches and notes in Oxford and drifted through them into a world vibrating with supernatural power, where ghosts and spirits moved among men and miracles happened constantly.

The boys told Codrington about an invisible force they said flowed through the atmosphere of life, through objects, people and actions. They called it *mana*. Everyone had a little *mana* in them. In New Georgia, islanders were sure it was concentrated in people's heads. That's why the New Georgians chopped off the heads of their enemies and carried them home. It was a gruesome harvest, but quite logical, if you thought about it: *mana* was the most useful treasure of all. It could be attracted, concentrated and directed for good as well as evil.

The Melanesians had no supreme being, but their islands were thick with spirits who attached themselves to stones, places, animals or even words. Sometimes the spirits screamed and howled through dark nights. Sometimes, amid hidden groves of tangled banyan, they revealed their mysteries to the members of secret societies who asked for their help. Some spirits were so old and powerful that they resembled gods, but none of them had the gall to claim to be lord of all the universe. The boys told Codrington about Qat, the hero of a dozen islands, who had made pigs, rocks and people, and who was always ready to come to the aid of seafarers. "Qat!" men shouted from their canoes. "May it be. Let the canoe of you and me turn into a whale, a flying fish, an eagle; let it leap on and on over the waves, let it go, let it pass out to my land." And Qat would calm the sea, speeding the travellers home.

Some islands positively bustled with the ghosts of ancestors who inhabited the bodies of sharks, alligators, octopuses, snakes and birds. With secret knowledge, a man could win the favour of a shark ancestor, and that shark would come when called; it would herd schools of fish into his net. It would also devour his enemies. The ancestors rewarded allegiance with the same fierce loyalty as the Lord of the Old Testament. Just as God had smashed the enemies of Moses, so the ancestor spirits helped Melanesians in their own battles.

There wasn't just one holy ghost in Melanesia; there were thousands of them. And Melanesian spirituality was egalitarian. With the right technique, anyone could harness the power of curses, magic cures and helpful spirits. Anyone could collect and direct *mana*. The ethereal realm wasn't in heaven. It was all around you. It was in you.

But those spirits, as powerful and plentiful as they were, began to retreat even as Codrington wrote down their names. His Melanesian students became ashamed of their dances, their secret societies and their ghosts. In the pidgin English picked up from traders, they began to call their ancestors by the name white men had given them: *devil-devils*. When the students returned home with the new teaching, they destroyed shrines, trampled sacred spaces and cast *devil-devil* stones into the sea.

One by one, the islands of Melanesia were claimed by the competing mission societies. Sometimes the missionaries squabbled over God's new kingdom, but eventually deals were cut, islands were traded back and forth, and palm-thatched cathedrals rose on the shores of every major island between New Zealand and New Guinea. By the time Henry Montgomery arrived, the Church of England's Melanesian Mission oversaw a far-flung network of 381 Melanesian "teachers." Wherever the missionaries went, dysentery and smallpox followed in their wake, but the Church grew, and so did European control of the islands. Traditional chiefs and priests lost their power to white administrators and the newly appointed black clergy. The shark spirits and ancestors who had watched over Melanesians for thousands of years receded in the shadow of the new god. In the century following my great-grandfather's voyages, Christianity would reach every island in the archipelago, even as his Church at home was diluted by the northern drizzle.

NOW I HAD MY GRAINS of sand and the name of my island. Nukapu, the place where old Melanesia had made its last stand, was real. Its sand was gritty and undeniably solid. It was an island that could be found. And if Nukapu was the place where myths intersected, it might also be the place where they could be measured. I folded the packet and placed it back in its envelope.

I caught the train back to London, trudged down to the Thames and banged on the wooden door of Lambeth Palace one last time. There was no answer. Of course. It was Sunday. I turned to the river. The wind was battering the year's first crocuses and raising a chop on the grey water, which was churning darkly upon itself. If only Joseph Conrad could see his great stream now. The river that had sent so many gunboats and mission ships to bring the British version of light to the world was now so confused by wind and tide that it didn't seem to know which way it was flowing. The sky hung low and sombre. Rain began to spit.

I crossed Lambeth Bridge and pushed west past Parliament. Tourists milled around the entrance to Westminster Cathedral, and also outside the plain church that stood in its shadows. This was St. Margaret's, where my great-grandfather had served as curate before sailing to the South Seas. I wandered into its great hall of sculpted arches, chandeliers and padded benches. There was Jesus hanging from his cross amid immense sheets of Flemish stained glass. King Henry VIII, of all people, knelt at his feet. It was hard not to feel sorry for Jesus and for the rector who gave a dull sermon about giving up coffee for Lent. The church was nearly empty. The sparse congregation reeked of mildew and Chanel No. 5. A baby cried. Its screams echoed from the arched roof.

I watched as row by lonely row the Christians stepped forward to kneel before the altar to consume the body and the blood of Christ, in the hope that that their souls would be washed pure and that Jesus might dwell in them, and they in him. I lingered on my bench and thought about the cannibals, the sacred dances, the ancestors who didn't rise up from their graves and fly to heaven but who lived on after their deaths, inhabiting rocks, sharks, sacred groves and violent storms.

What had become of the archipelago my great-grandfather set out to transform? Who had won the battle for souls now that the sacred fire had dimmed here at the heart of the proselytizing empire? Had the island spirits survived? Was there yet some shore where gospel and empire had never taken hold, where hollow drumbeats still marked the survival of the universe that the missionaries had sought to destroy? Or better, a forgotten stretch of palm trees where barefoot mystics had taken the new god, chipped away at its image, melted it down and stirred the remains together with the spirits who had always prowled their world, to create something beyond bloody superstition and the incredible fantasy of the Old Testament.

Although I knew this was the worst kind of romantic primitivism, and though I was certain that Melanesian myths were just as illusory as the Christian ones to which my ancestors had clung, my heart raced, and I was gripped by the urgency of the moment, the thought of secrets disappearing beneath the waves of time, and the idea that *The Light of Melanesia* was only the beginning of a story.

I did not realize that I was already under the ancestors' influence when I decided to cross the ocean to look for their legacy in Melanesia. I did know the power of their myths, but I did not expect them to seduce me, to dare me to move among them and to carry the torch of their truths. I just imagined myself wading ashore through the foam of spent waves, stepping across the sand, peering into those jade shadows, shivering and ready for the primal howl, the flash of magic, the story that would change everything.

2

THE BUSINESS

OF PORT VILA IS GOD

Good-bye. I vanish from civilization,
hoping to return a wiser man.

HENRY MONTGOMERY, letter, 1892

M Y PLAN was simple, which is how adventures begin, but not how they end. I would follow the route of the *Southern Cross*. I would travel by ship, launch, canoe and on foot, as the missionaries had, and I would find my damned pagans if I had to dig their bones out of the sand.

There was a map in *The Light of Melanesia*. The names on it were so minute and so faded that I could read them only with a magnifying glass. There were four distinct groups of islands:

On the lower right corner, a collection of nebulous blotches: the New Hebrides.

Above, a handful of spilt coins: the Banks Islands.

Inching towards the frayed left-hand corner like a family of slugs: the Solomon Islands.

And there, midway between the Banks and Solomon Islands, like crumbs floating on the water, was the Santa Cruz Group, and among them, one especially lonely fleck next to a smudged word that might have read: Nukapu.

Nukapu.

The map had no scale, but a faint arrow pointed towards its bottom left-hand corner, and along that arrow was printed: TO SYDNEY: 1500 MILES.

You imagine places before you search for them. It has always been that way with Melanesia. The first explorers, who migrated to the islands from Asia, must have been led by faith. After all, they could only paddle so far east past Papua New Guinea and through the Solomons before the horizon appeared to run out of islands. So, while the central Solomons were probably settled as long as twenty thousand years ago, it took another 170 centuries for the canoe voyagers to launch their exploration of the atolls that were scattered like constellations across the South Pacific. The ocean argonauts learned to read the waves and the stars. But it was imagination that told them there was more land out there beyond the edge of the world.

There is less room for imagination nowadays. We have the Internet to guide us.

The Internet told me that the New Hebrides had been renamed Vanuatu, a republic which billed itself as "the South Pacific's Premier Tax Haven." There were golf courses and reliable banks. The Santa Cruz Group had amalgamated with the Solomon Islands, which, it was announced over and over again, were "the Happy Isles." There was much smiling and scuba diving, and a large white satellite telecommunications dish of which Solomon Islanders were very proud. That information came from the government's Web site. South Pacific news media tended to focus instead on how Solomon Islanders were apt to burn villages and shoot each other with machine guns. "Death on the altar" was one notable headline. The Happy Isles had fallen into civil war. I decided to start in Vanuatu and ease my way towards the darkness.

The Internet is, of course, a collage of fact, fantasy and propaganda. So is history. But not this story. I'll prove it by being honest about Le Meridien Resort and Casino.

This is how travel writers work: they contact a country's national tourism bureau, they promise to write happy stories about golf and cold beer and people who never stop smiling, and then they ask for free flights, hotels, meals and booze. Especially booze. Yes, and then they spend weeks lounging in crisp linen sheets, watching BBC World and drinking guava punch. It's called a reciprocal relationship.

I did not care about linen sheets, but I did like the idea of flying for free, so I wrote to Vanuatu's National Tourism Office, making promises and asking for help. Then I caught a 747 from Los Angeles to Fiji. I had to wait three days for the weekly shuttle to Port Vila, capital of Vanuatu, on Efate Island. That was a two-hour flight, and free as well. But you are not really free when you make these deals. It can take days to extricate yourself from the cloistered confines of the resort world.

It was dark and humid when I stepped off the plane in Port Vila. An official from the tourism bureau intercepted me at customs, bundled me into her car and drove me away from the lights of the airport, through a forest, over a hill, and into the arms of Le Meridien Resort and Casino. I was greeted by a pair of giggling teens bearing hors d'oeuvres and Champagne. My bungalow overlooked a lagoon. The bathtub was bigger than a car and it had six jet engines. I fell onto a king-size prairie of linen, turned on BBC World and tickled myself.

At dawn, I jogged around the golf course, following the high fence that kept the riff-raff away from the realm of linen sheets. I hit the breakfast buffet and sat among the Australian bankers and their families. The bankers were fat and exhausted. The wives were hideously thin. The bankers stuffed their children with sausages. The wives sipped mineral water. Flies wandered across their shoulder blades, waiting, I suppose, for them to collapse in the heat. We ate steamed plums and chocolate croissants. The music of *La Traviata* wafted through the palms.

Later, the woman from the tourism office called me with a plan. There was golfing to be done. And a harbour cruise. And shopping. Anything she could do to help, she said. Anything at all. I broke out in a sweat.

"Heathens," I said. "I'm looking for heathens."

"Ah, yes, we have the photos at the cultural centre," she said.

"Living heathens," I said.

"Don't be ridiculous," she said. "This is a Christian island."

I hung up the phone and, neglecting to turn off the air conditioner, slipped away, past the laundry girl and the groundskeepers and the resort guards. I ran out the gate and all the way into town.

Port Vila proper was a discordant place, an eager collection of post-colonial cement blocks, duty-free shops and French supermarkets. It wanted to be Tahiti, or perhaps Waikiki. It had the turquoise harbour full of yachts and pink paragliders, and a smattering of tiny patisseries, where tiny French princesses with tiny white purses kissed each other on both cheeks. But down in the market, husky Melanesian matrons still followed the dress code introduced by missionaries a century before: Mother Hubbard–style dresses that billowed in the breeze above bare feet or hung from ample breasts like drapery.

I was vaguely surprised by their appearance. I'd expected their hair to be long and flowing and their skin lightly tanned, like the tangerine beauties on Paul Gauguin's South Pacific canvasses. But these women had skin the colour of copper or dark roasted coffee. Their hair was frizzy enough to style into pumpkin-sized afros. I should not have been surprised: the word "Melanesia"—or Melanésie, according to its first user, French explorer Dumont D'Urville—was constructed specifically to refer to the parts of the Pacific inhabited by dark-skinned people. *Melas* and *nesos* are Greek for "black" and "islands." Unlike Polynesians (who populated the many—*poly*—islands to the east), the people whom D'Urville encountered from New Guinea to Fiji were so dark that he imagined they were transplanted from Africa.

The streets were full of wild-looking young men who lounged curbside or hooted at each other from the open boxes of pickup trucks. They braided their hair into loose dreadlocks. They twisted their beards into artful knots. They furrowed their brows fiercely in the sunlight. They were sinewy and strong. At first I decided they were rough, but then I saw their faces melt into generous smiles. The men held hands in the shade. They giggled like schoolboys or Hobbits. Small carved crosses dangled from their necks.

The shops and the gigglers were merely a backdrop to the real business of Port Vila, which was religion. The town was crawling with American and Australian missionaries. There were Mormons in pressed white shirts and ties, severe Seventh-day Adventists, burger-gulping members of the Assemblies of God, tongue-speaking Pentecostals and charismatic holy rollers in business suits. Men shouted the gospel from street corners.

I was standing on Kumul Highway, the town's main street, trying to get my bearings, when the flow of mini-buses parted to make way for an acne-scarred white man in his twenties. The foreigner wore jackboots and a white robe, and he carried a flag with a Christian cross stitched on it. With his Aryan aesthetic and severe countenance he might have been leading a Ku Klux Klan procession, but this white hood was followed by a hundred brown children. They handed out greeting cards depicting a hedgehog in vestments. "I forgive you," said the cartoon hedgehog. The children sang: *"Jesus hem i numbawan. Hem i luvim yumi."—Jesus is number one. He loves you and me.*

THE SCENE WOULD HAVE warmed the hearts of the earliest Europeans to find Melanesia. As much as they were hunters of fortune and treasure, the explorers were also evangelists who imagined the Pacific as a new kingdom for their God. First were the Spanish, who were the most zealous and the cruellest. Emboldened by their purification of South America's Inca, the conquistadors were hungry for new glory. They were sure that if they sailed far enough west from Peru, they would find the land of Ophir, the biblical source of the gold that King Solomon used to build his temples in Jerusalem. It was a fantasy that would change the map of the world.

In 1567, the Viceroy of Peru sent his nephew, Alvaro de Mendaña, out into the Pacific Ocean to search for land and treasure. On board was the cosmologer Pedro Sarmiento de Gamboa, who was convinced that the Inca had once sailed a fleet of reed boats across the Pacific to islands inhabited by a fabulously wealthy black race. Sarmiento wanted their gold. Mendaña just wanted to give the natives Catholicism.

It took them nearly a year to find an island big enough to fit Sarmiento's imagined kingdom. Mendaña called the island Santa Ysabel and claimed all the surrounding shores for his king and his god. The locals did not appreciate Mendaña's efforts to save them, and they refused to share their yams with his starving crew. Relations reached a low point when ten of Mendaña's men paddled to shore on Guadalcanal to obtain water. Only one survived. "The dead were cut into pieces," wrote chief purser Gomez Catoira. "Some without legs and without arms, others without heads, and the ends of all their tongues were cut off, and their eye-teeth drawn, and those whose heads were left had had the skulls cut open and the brains eaten."

Sarmiento duly marched inland, burned hundreds of houses and killed at least twenty men. Mendaña ordered the native dead to be drawn, quartered and left at the spot where his own men had been massacred. He then headed home to report he had found the fabled islands of King Solomon, though he had found no gold, silver or spices, nor had he converted any heathens. But Sarmiento was convinced that the discoveries proved the existence of Terra Australis Incognita, a great southern continent which he imagined stretching from Java all the way to Tierra del Fuego.

Twenty-seven years passed before Mendaña could gain support for a second voyage. In 1595, the old man set sail again, this time with his wife and the Portuguese navigator Pedro Fernandez de Quirós. En route, they landed in the Marquesas, where they slaughtered more than two hundred people before continuing west. Mendaña was determined to colonize his new world and tried to build a permanent settlement on Santa Cruz, but he fought with the natives constantly and died of malaria. Quirós evacuated the survivors and sailed for the Philippines. But he was now a man obsessed.

In 1605, Quirós set off again from Peru with two ships and three hundred Spanish sailors. Midway through the following year, he drifted into a vast bay surrounded by mountain ranges, and announced he had found Sarmiento's lost continent. He called it La Austral del Espiritu Santo and he established a city: New Jerusalem. He gave his men robes of blue taffeta and charged them with the salvation of the native population. On the day of Corpus Christi, they paraded along the beach behind the holy sacrament, flags flying. Then they headed off to burn a village. Like Mendaña, Quirós never stopped fighting with his intended converts. Ravaged by fever, fish poisoning and war, he abandoned his New Jerusalem after just thirty-seven days.

The fantasy of Quirós's Australian paradise was integrated into European geographers' images of the southern continent until 1766, when the Frenchman Louis Antoine de Bougainville sailed between Espiritu Santo and Malekula, proving it was not the southern continent at all, but merely an island in what is now Vanuatu.

Melanesia was no kinder to the evangelists who began to flock to the islands in the nineteenth century. John Williams, Melanesia's first modern evangelist, arrived in the New Hebrides in 1839. His London Missionary Society had converted most of Polynesia; Williams thought Melanesia would be just as easily won. He rowed to shore on Erromango with an assistant, full of confidence. In most accounts the two men were clubbed to death as they splashed in the shallows. Accordingly, the society began to use Polynesian teachers as cannon fodder in this spiritual war of attrition. Dozens of Samoans died from disease or treachery on Erromango before the society gave up and a pair of Nova Scotian Presbyterians took over. George and Ellen Gordon landed in 1851. They managed to convert a handful of people in the course of a decade, but then they made a fatal error. When an epidemic of measles killed hundreds of Erronmangans, the Gordons announced Jehovah had brought his wrath down upon them for remaining heathen. The Gordons were accordingly blamed for the epidemic, hacked down with axes and eaten.

The Erromangans were clearly onto something. Indigenous populations in the New Hebrides plummeted in the nineteenth century from the effects of labour recruitment and diseases introduced by Europeans. This made it easier for European traders and planters to gain a foothold, sometimes acquiring paper title to thousands of acres of land in exchange for a few bolts of calico or bottles of gin. Soon it was Europeans who were fighting each other for land. When French plantation owners asked their government to annex the islands, Presbyterian missionaries, incensed by the prospect of French (meaning Catholic) rule, demanded that England take over instead. Neither government had the resources or inclination to do so, but neither was inclined to concede territory to the other, so they agreed to share the islands.

France and Britain proclaimed the New Hebrides Condominium in 1907. The deal gave the islands two heads of state, two bureaucracies, two police forces and two separate legal systems, with two separate national courts, as well as a joint court presided over by a Spaniard, who was fluent in neither English nor French. The system was soon dubbed "the Pandemonium" for the anarchy it spawned. The governments didn't stop white planters from appropriating land or flogging and swindling their native labourers. But the colonizers did create a town at Port Vila, where the British commissioner and French consul flew their respective flags across the harbour from each other, hosted cocktail parties and desperately tried to uphold an atmosphere of sophistication. They banned horse races in the town centre and forbade Melanesians to remain out after dark—except when planters happened to be using their black labourers as collateral in poker games. The Condominium lurched along until 1980, when islanders gained independence and began to call themselves Ni-Vanuatu.

THE SCHIZOPHRENIA of the Condominium era seemed to have lived on. Port Vila was now supposed to be Melanesian: after all, the prime minister was native. And look at all those dark faces, all those dreadlocks, all those shacks serving nightly rounds of *kava*, the ancestors' favourite narcotic drink. Then again, perhaps Vila was French. Cappuccino and quiche were just as easy to come by as coconuts and yams. Or maybe it was English. Pubs showed Aussie rules football matches with English-language play-by-play, even if the commercials were voiced over in Papua New Guinea pidgin. The Ciné Hickson played American films dubbed in French. White plantation owners rumbled into town to scour Au Bon Marché, the French supermarket, for camembert and Chardonnay, then they left in their pickups, the cabs loaded with imported escargots and the boxes crowded with dusty black hitchhikers.

And then there were the tribalists: eyebrows pierced violently, noses caked white with zinc, hair bleached freakish shades of blonde, arms tattooed with thorn garlands. They invaded precisely at noon, disgorged from Australian cruise ships. They descended on Vila with the ferocity of Anzacs at Gallipoli and the steely sense of purpose common to suburbanites on safari. I watched them from the shade of the Cannibal House, where they paid $10 each for the opportunity to take photos of their children standing in a waist-high stew pot, surrounded by spear-clutching "warriors" in loincloths. The warriors hammed it up, pinching their Australian customers under their arms, exclaiming playfully: "Mmm, nice and fat!"

One is supposed to be mortified by this kind of thing. And I would have been but for the Ni-Vanuatu, who were most eager to keep the cannibal mystique alive. It was good for business. Albert, a boat pilot from nearby Lelepa Island, boasted shortly after we met that his people had been among the last to be converted. "My great-grandfather was born in the darkness time, before the Christians came," he told me proudly. "The first missionaries on Lelepa were from England, a husband and wife. They brought their twelve-year-old son with them. My ancestors killed those missionaries and ate them. Ha! Ha! Not the boy, though. They wanted to adopt him, but that boy just would not stop crying. It was awful! They couldn't bear it. So they tied a rock around his neck, took him out and dropped him in the middle of the bay." Now Albert gave tours of the harbour where the boy had drowned. The tourists enjoyed hearing about cannibalism, he said, especially if the victims were missionaries.

Apparently, Vila's heathen past had been reduced to caricatures and souvenirs. The missionaries had won. But if all the locals were Christian, why were missionaries still flocking to Vanuatu? Why the hallelujah processions down Kumul Highway? Why the sense of evangelical urgency in the scrubbed faces lined up for burgers at Jill's American Way Café?

"Because people here still live with so much wrong thinking! We are just trying to offer them what they need: a purer, more powerful gospel message," said my first friend in Port Vila. That was Kay Rudd. She lived with her husband, Jack, in the manicured hillside compound of the Joy Bible College. Kay wore a dress printed with tiny flowers. Her cheeks were thick and rosy. Jack wore a khaki leisure suit. They were as warm and proscriptive as grandparents. They were missionaries. When I told them I was hunting for heathens, they invited me to their bungalow for ice cream.

"Oh, Vanuatu might call itself a proper Christian country. People might *claim* to be Christian," Kay told me. "But voodoo, black magic, spirits ... folks still live in utter fear of all these things. And you know, dear, a true Christian doesn't have to be afraid."

"Because ghosts and magic don't exist," I said. "You are helping people overcome their superstitions."

Kay sighed and gave me a look of strained patience. "I didn't say that. Evil is real. But we Christians have the power to break its spell. If we can get Bibles into people's hands, in their own language, they will see they have the power to beat the black magic. They don't have to fear it."

"But everyone I've met in Vila is a Christian already," I said.

"Well, we are still fighting the battle out on the islands."

The sun had disappeared beneath the banyans. Cicadas screamed from the trees. Fluorescent lights flickered on through distant windows. Kay put away the ice cream and told me an Inspirational Story. It was about Tanna Island, at the south end of the archipelago.

A very bad thing had happened on Tanna in the 1940s. Just when the Tannese seemed to have given up their ghosts and other devils, just when the missionaries thought they had won the island for Christ, along came a false prophet. The fellow called himself John Frum and made himself out to be some kind of messiah. He promised the islanders that if they abandoned the Church and went back to their heathen ways, he would return one day on a great white ship loaded with goodies from America. The islanders bought the story hook, line and sinker, said Kay. They nailed shut the church doors and ran the priests out of their villages. Except for a few tenacious congregations, Tanna had been gripped by John Frum fever—and lost to Christianity—for more than half a century.

But then, in 1996, the white ship from America finally appeared. On board was a friend of Jack and Kay's. His name was John Rush. Tanna's beleaguered Christian pastors decided Rush was the saviour they had been waiting for. After all, he was American, he had arrived on a great white ship, and—best of all—he was named John. The circumstances were too close to the Frum myth not to be put to use.

"You get it, right?" said Jack, rubbing his hands together. "John *from* America: John—*Frum*—America! When that ship pulled in, it was like a prophecy fulfilled, and the pastors knew it."

"They figured John could go to the John Frum chiefs and tell them to stop waiting. Tell them that America was not going to come solve all their problems," interrupted Kay.

"He didn't want to do it. He really didn't want to be mistaken for John Frum," said Jack. "But the pastors begged him. So he went down to Sulphur Bay, the main Frum village, and would you believe the John Frum people were waiting for him? They rolled out the red carpet. They lined the path with flowers and gave him a big feast."

"John's visit was the beginning of the end for John Frum," said Kay. "That cult is finished now. The Presbyterians have rebuilt the church in

Sulphur Bay. God is in. Frum is out. But our John won't take any credit for the good work. He says it was all because of the wise chief who let the Christians in."

"Chief One was his name. Isaac One," said Jack. "They call him that because he never repeats himself. Chief One. Isn't that cute?"

Isaac One. I scribbled that name in my notebook, and I mourned secretly. One more cult down the drain. But the Rudds were so full of down-home cheeriness they were hard not to like. Kay glowed with perspiration and good intentions. I let her hug me good-bye, and then I marched down to the harbour.

I wandered along the darkened waterfront, where shadows moved among shadows, murmuring indecipherably and erupting into laughter. Somewhere a loudspeaker creaked and hissed, and occasionally let forth the sad squeal of a Chinese violin. Lights from yachts, canoes and distant villages shone on the surface of the harbour, as though it was the edge of the universe, beyond which swirled some terrible struggle between good and evil, white and black magic, unseen and formless but still clashing endlessly just beyond the horizon, singeing every life it touched. Or it might be the edge of nothing at all, an emptiness that could be filled only by the force of imagination.

I decided to begin my search on Tanna. I wanted to find this Isaac One and ask him why he had turned his back on magic.

3

TANNA:

A CONFLAGRATION

OF BELIEF

*Partly because of empire, all cultures are involved in
one another; none is single and pure, all are hybrid, heterogeneous,
extraordinarily differentiated and unmonolithic.*

EDWARD SAID, *Culture and Colonialism*

HEN YOU READ the accounts of Victorian adventurers, it is easy to be convinced that life at sea is exhilarating and romantic. The open horizon, the salt spray, the implied danger and possibility of all that heaving ocean. What could be more inspiring?

My great-grandfather wrote lovingly about his months aboard the *Southern Cross*. The 300-ton schooner was fitted with an engine, but she generally relied on her three masts, the foremost of which was square-rigged. The ship cut languidly through the waves. The Melanesian converts spent the intervals between prayers dangling from the rigging or stretched asleep on the ship's dolphin striker. There was no sweeter moment for the bishop than dusk, when the *Southern Cross* had anchored in a quiet bay and a sense of peace settled on his mind. "At such times," he wrote, "it was permissible even to sit on deck in those suits, light and not

elegant, which men find useful as 'garments of the night' in the tropics."
Now and then, from some village hidden among the coconut palms, he
would hear the tinkling of a bell, the whistle of a conch shell horn or the
bang of a drum, and he would know that the converts were being called to
prayer, and he would be touched.

The world has changed.

The ocean is no longer romantic. Not when you are aboard a cargo
ship and you have left the calm of the harbour and the swell is up and
the vomiting has begun. The ocean is not a gentle mother, not a buck-
ing stallion, not an adversary you can grapple with. The ocean is a great
rotting blanket that won't be still. It is a pool of rancid milk. A gurgling
toilet. Something to be endured. This is what I learned on my voyage
to Tanna.

The MV *Havanna* had been making the 480-kilometre run between
New Caledonia and Port Vila—with a stop at Tanna—for three months,
and was said to be the finest ship in the archipelago. She created a stir
wherever she went. She had *seats,* the agent who sold me my passage told
me excitedly. But the *Havanna* seemed more like a floating warehouse
than the ferry I expected. She had an enclosed main deck with room for a
dozen shipping containers, and a passenger compartment welded on top,
like an afterthought. Her bow fell open like a broken jaw onto the government wharf. Two hundred of us charged into the maw the moment the
ship's crew let their guard down.

We sailed at dusk. Once we left the harbour, there was nothing to see.
There was no squall. There was no lightning. But the spray rose like
ghosts each time the *Havanna*'s blunt nose plunged into the undulating
shadow of the southeast swell. The ship twisted and rolled unnaturally,
and the night was filled with the hollow boom of waves striking the bow,
the groan and flex of the hull and a screeching that sounded like 20-foot
containers sliding across the steel floor of the hold. We did not use our
cushioned chairs. We clung to the floor like lovers and vomited into plastic bags, purses and open palms.

At the first hint of dawn I stumbled out onto the ship's deck. Men
stood doubled over the railing. Drool trailed from their chins until it was
caught by the wind and flung into the sea. A half-caste woman waved me

over and offered me a spongy white ball, which at first I took for a muffin. In fact, it was the fibrous centre of an overripe coconut.

"*Mais* this will take that 'orrible taste *long* mouth *blong yu*," the woman said. There was a bit of French and a swath of English. But the finale of her overture was Bislama, Vanuatu's de facto national language. What she had said was: "But this will take that horrible taste from that mouth of yours."

Bislama has been called a pidgin, which is to say it is an amalgamation, a simplification and a bastardization of other languages by island people. My great-grandfather despised it. He wished Melanesians would learn proper English or at least stick to their own languages rather than using what he called the "vilest of compounds that ever polluted the purity of speech."

But the more I learned about Bislama, the more I realized it was one of the great triumphs of Vanuatu. The moniker originated from *bêche-de-mer*, the name the French gave to the sea slugs they bought from islanders and sold in the markets of Hong Kong. Bislama got its beginnings in the first half of the nineteenth century, when South Sea islanders worked as crew on whaling ships and developed a simple jargon to communicate with Europeans. It is full of nautical references and sailorly slang. When the sun goes down, they say, "*Sun hem i draon,*" as though the sun is drowning in the sea. When something is broken, "*Hem i bagarup.*" Say it out loud: "Him, he buggered up."

The jargon developed further between 1863 and 1911, when more than fifty thousand Ni-Vanuatu were sent to work as indentured labourers on plantations in Australia, Fiji and Samoa. Those workers who spoke the same language were separated so they couldn't organize against their employers. Separating the *wantoks* (one-talks), or common-language speakers, was easy: there were more than a hundred distinct languages in the New Hebrides alone. Workers had no choice but to speak to each other using the only words they had in common—English and French—though they used Melanesian grammar and syntax. Then they took the new language home with them.

Bislama may have been the bane of arbiters of proper grammar, but it gave the Ni-Vanuatu the common tongue they needed to achieve independence. Government documents may be written in English or French, but parliamentary debates are conducted in Bislama.

Everything is a *fala* (fellow), even a tree, a shark or a girl. A boy who admired a girl told me, *"Hem i wan gudfala gel. Mi likem hem tumas."* Then I understood that *tumas* did not mean "too much" but "a hell of a lot."

Things are defined by their relationship with other things. The word *blong* (belong) is everywhere—but the word *long* is a preposition, not an adjective. So if you ask a Ni-Vanuatu when colonial rule ended, he will tell you, *"Kantri blong mifala, hem i winim independens long 1980."* That was the same year the New Testament was translated into Bislama and people began reading the *gud nius blong Jisas Krais.* If you ask a woman where she is going, she might say, *"Mi go nao blong swim long sanbij,"* and you would know she was now off to the beach to wash (*swim* means "wash").

Bislama can be poetic in its literalness. A *pijin blong solwata* is the bird we all associate with salt water: a seagull. A telescope is a *glas blong look-look big.* A condom is a *rubba blong fakfak.*

French words have also slipped into the language. To know is to *savve* (from the third-person singular *save* of the verb *savoir*). There are Polynesian words: children are *pikinini,* food is *kai-kai.* Now phrases are being traded back and forth between various pidgin-speaking countries. The Ni-Vanuatu borrow from Papua New Guinea when they tell you good-bye: *lookim yu bakagen.* But the strongest word of all is pan-Oceanic. If something or someplace is *tabu,* it is forbidden. You stay the hell away from it.

THE STARS FADED and Tanna appeared like an ink stain across the horizon. The silhouette gradually grew into a series of folded mountainsides. Blue smoke curled from thatched roofs. Surf fringed the shoreline, exploding occasionally into bouquets of white spray. Sunlight broke across a ridge serrated by rows of palms. There was no harbour. We manoeuvred past a reef and eased alongside a cement jetty which jutted out from a tongue of coral stone at Lenakel, Tanna's main village.

I tossed my pack on the grass and waited. I had sent a message ahead to Port Resolution, which was within striking distance of the fabled John

Frum stronghold at Sulphur Bay. The villagers at Port Resolution claimed to run a yacht club. They knew someone with a truck. They would come and fetch me.

"Port Resolution? They will certainly not come to collect you. They are *rubbish* men," advised a stern Tannese man who installed himself on the grass next to me. His name was Kelsen. He had come to claim his new wheelbarrow from the *Havanna*. It shone. Kelsen had an untidy beard, which he tugged on constantly, and a ponderous brow, which at first I mistook for a mark of wisdom. He sat with me as I waited by the sea. I told him I was looking for former John Frum cult members.

"The John Frum people are all going to hell, that much is certain," said Kelsen.

I was heartened. "So then some people here still believe in John Frum?"

"Yes, the fools believe. But *nogud yu stap* with John Frum people. They are dirty. They have nothing to eat. They are fighting each other. You should stay in a proper hotel."

Kelsen said he lived at the base of Yasur volcano. He promised to tell me a magic story about the volcano that I would never forget. Nobody else could tell me the story. Just Kelsen. He owned it. The story had been passed down for generations. He was considering writing it down and selling it.

"I could help you write it down," I said.

But Kelsen already had a plan. If I wanted to hear his story, I would have to forget about the sinners at Port Resolution and come stay with him. Kelsen had built a hotel of his own at the base of the volcano.

The day was getting on. I didn't have much choice. Kelsen threw my pack in his new wheelbarrow and led me along a row of tin-roofed stores. The road was lined with cement poles. Electric power had come to Lenakel three months before my arrival—just in time for World Cup soccer, said Kelsen. We lay in the grass at a road junction. After an hour, a pickup truck appeared. Kelsen flagged it down. We climbed in the box and rumbled east on a dirt road, up through the palms into the mountains.

Tanna was so thick with life it was a caricature of paradise: the black volcanic soil exploded with banana, taro, manioc, flowering poinsettia, orange groves and tree ferns. Melon-sized papaya hung from house-high stems. Banyan trees cast shadows the size of baseball diamonds, their canopies balanced atop hundreds of roots which twisted down from the branches like strands of macramé.

As we passed in and out of the shadows, Kelsen explained to me that it wasn't just the John Frummers who were going to hell. It was most of the people on Tanna, including many of the Christians. "These people disobey the Bible every day," he grumbled. "They break the rules that Moses wrote down in Leviticus. They eat unclean food: pigs, flying foxes, sharks, crabs. They smoke. They drink *kava*. All forbidden! Worst of all, they go to church on Sunday, when we know that *Saturday* is the true Sabbath. They will be punished in time."

Kelsen knew these rules because his family had converted to Seventh-day Adventism in 1922. They had never fallen for the John Frum message or any other false teaching, he assured me proudly.

The forest on the east side of Tanna was caked in grey dust, and the trees began to resemble stone carvings. The road became like a sandbox. Then we rounded a bend and entered the devastation. It was as though the jungle had been buried and sealed under a layer of scoured earth. Bucket-sized boulders were strewn across the ash plain like spilt marbles. The volcano rose directly in front of us like a great Saharan dune, a perfect, pristine and not particularly threatening heap of sand. This was Yasur, the volcano whose fireworks had guided Captain James Cook into Port Resolution—named for his ship—in 1774. Yasur was sacred in those days. Each time Cook attempted to climb it, his Tannese guides led him in circles back to the sea.

The mountain was quiet now, but our driver didn't slow for the view. He sped over a spur of the volcano towards a gap in the forest on the far side of the plain. We were halfway there when the afternoon was shattered by a deafening explosion. The driver swerved for a moment, then continued on, even as a salvo of rocks exploded from the peak like pebbles thrown up by some giant hand. I dove to the floor. Kelsen laughed. The mountain belched a black mushroom cloud of smoke, then fell quiet.

We entered the forest again and followed a rutted track to a clearing and a collection of thatch huts on stilts. This was Kelsen's grand hotel. It was crude and beautiful. There were flowering trees and dozens of potted plants. Chickens clucked. Children dashed back and forth. Somewhere in the forest, a pan flute played *Amazing Grace.* It reminded me of the post-apocalyptic idyll depicted in the pamphlets that Jehovah's Witnesses hand out on street corners. Nothing bad ever happens here, I thought. But then a terrific sucking noise ripped through the valley—like a tsunami rolling across a pebble beach—then another appalling roar, and then a momentary vibration, not of the earth but of the air, which caused the huts to tremble and pressed my shirt against my skin. More smoke boiled above the treetops. I noticed there was no grass in Kelsen's village, only a thick layer of ash on the ground. The garden, the huts, the trees, they could all be burnt and buried in an afternoon.

Kelsen's wife was too shy to look at me, but she brought me a plate of *laplap,* a root vegetable pudding baked and served in coconut leaves. The pudding was cold and rubbery. It had been cooked on Friday. Today was Saturday, the *true* Sabbath, and work was forbidden.

The days passed and Kelsen failed to tell me his volcano story. He took me for walks instead. We tramped through the jungle, following scant trails from village to village. The forest floor was punctuated by crude holes and littered with coconut husks: the work of wild pigs. At one village I heard the banging of coconut shells and singing, coming from a tiny lean-to. There was an old woman inside, surrounded by children.

"What are they singing about?" I asked.

"The grandmother has her own religion. She teaches it to all the little kids," said Kelsen.

"Can we talk to her?"

"No, no, of course not. She's a woman."

At the edge of another village, we walked into a clearing beneath a banyan tree. A man stood there, wearing a *lavalava,* a light scarf, wrapped around his waist. He dropped the *lavalava* the moment he saw me. I was embarrassed for us all, until I realized he had done it on purpose. Kelsen called to him, encouragingly. The man approached, and I saw that he wasn't quite naked. His penis was wrapped in what looked like hundreds of strands of grass or bark, the ends of which dangled artfully about his bare testicles. The bulk of the contraption, the penis part, was held erect by a grass belt wrapped around his waist. This was a *nambas,* which was the only thing most men in the region had worn for centuries. (The first Europeans to see *nambas* were scandalized by them. E. Vigors, an early visitor, cloaked his horror in Latin, proclaiming that the men were "destitute of all clothing *si excepias penem quem decorant* MODO *dissimilis indigenes Tannae ube membrum virile semper erectum tenent, sub singulo ligatum.*")

The *nambas* man beamed at me. Kelsen barked at him in a language I did not understand, and the man performed something like a slow pirouette, as if to prove to me that yes, indeed, his behind was bare. They spoke some more, then the man charged off into the forest.

We marched through two more villages. At each of them, Kelsen issued more orders and pointed at me, now with a growing tone of urgency and irritation. I was beginning to dislike Kelsen, when we entered a clearing, grander than all the rest and flanked by two banyan so huge they made the space feel like an auditorium. Kelsen sat me down on a little bench.

"Now do you want to see the heathens dance?" asked Kelsen.

"Maybe," I said, baffled.

"You will pay them, of course."

After a few minutes I heard chatter in the shadows, and then chanting. One by one, a troop of familiar faces emerged from a gap in the roots of the biggest banyan: an old man with a patchy beard, then a sculpted young version of himself, another fellow with tidy dreadlocks, three giggling teenaged boys and finally our friend from the first village. They had all shed their town clothes and were naked except for their *nambas.* They formed a circle and began to dance. They clapped their hands and stamped the earth, peering over their shoulders to see if I was taking pictures. I was, of course, but mostly out of politeness, since it was an uninspiring spectacle. The *nambas* gang was bored. The whole exercise was a racket, a roadside attraction orchestrated by Kelsen, heathenism's greatest detractor. But I thought if I was polite I might at least be able to talk to the old man when they finished.

"You are Christians like Kelsen," I said to the chief when the dancing stopped.

He shook his head. "Ha ha! No, we don't believe in Church," he said in Bislama. "We believe in *kava* and pigs."

"But didn't the missionaries ever come and talk to you, to change you?"

"Yes, they have heard the good news," interjected Kelsen in English. "But they don't want to listen. They are going to hell."

"The missionaries came," said the chief. "They told us not to make our *kastom*. But we were born with *kastom* and we won't forget it. My grandfather and my great-grandfather, they followed *kastom*. So I will too. Life here is easy. We eat, sleep and drink *kava* for free. Christians have to work so hard. They have to pay for everything," he said, eyeing Kelsen slyly.

Kastom. I would learn that the word meant many things to Melanesians. To translate *kastom* as "culture" was to chart only a part of its power. *Kastom* was Melanesian history, tradition, ritual and magic, but it also referred to traditional systems of economics, social organization, politics and medicine. If you said something was *kastom*, you were attaching it to the traditions of the ancestors. You were sanctifying it. But sometimes the word was simply used to excuse a practice from scrutiny. (Why aren't women allowed to drink *kava*? *Kastom*. Why can't women be pastors? *Kastom*. Why don't *kava* bowls get washed between servings? *"Hem i kastom blong mifala nomo."*)

"We solve every problem we have using pigs and *kava*," the chief said. "For example, if we make a fight with another village, we can kill a *pik-pik* to make it better. If we have other kinds of problems, we drink *kava*, then we talk to the spirits. A spirit could be in the hollow of the banyan tree. It could be somewhere else too, but it comes when we ask it to."

Kelsen nodded approvingly, but mumbled in English: "Idolatry."

"Friend, let me ask you a question," said the chief. "Suppose Kelsen goes to church and asks his Jesus for rain. Will it rain? No. Well, if I want rain I go to the banyan, drink my *kava* and make a prayer to my papa or my mama. They are dead, but if I need rain they will bring it. If I have lost a *pik-pik* in the forest, they will bring that back to me too."

"Foolish heathens," said Kelsen. "Jesus can make it rain too."

It was impossible to talk to the chief about religion without running the gauntlet of Kelsen's commentary. I changed the subject.

"The *nambas*. Does it hurt?"

"No, not at all," said the chief. "We have been circumcised. Our penises are very strong."

Kelsen jumped in again to explain that all Tannese boys were circumcised before adulthood. Even his own boys would be circumcised.

"But why would you do it, Kelsen?" I asked.

"Because it's *kastom*."

That word again.

"But Kelsen, you are Christian!"

"Yes, but *kastom* doesn't mean *not* Christian. And besides, if you don't get circumcised, you smell bad."

The chief touched my hand to get my attention, then made a fist and punched the air. "We have strong, strong penises! Even very old men on Tanna can make children. Friend, suppose you ever have a problem making babies on your own island, you just come back here and our *kastom* doctor can give you medicine for your penis."

I thanked the chief and asked him about John Frum.

"Don't worry about John Frum," Kelsen said. "John Frum is for crazy people. John Frum has no power—"

"You must go to Sulphur Bay," interrupted the chief. "The John Frum dance is Friday night."

This agitated Kelsen to no end. "Time for go now," he said, then asked me for 500 vatu—about $5—to give the chief.

I paid and we retreated through the forest, me feeling strangely glum, knowing the chief and his boys would be climbing back into their regular clothes as soon as we disappeared.

"Five hundred vatu: a very good deal," Kelsen explained. "That's how much they charge the tourists over in Yakel village. And those heathens wear grass skirts, not *nambas*. Sometimes you can even see they have shorts on under their skirts. More naked should mean more money, yes?"

I swear Kelsen was skipping now.

"You see," he said. "I know the heathens. I am your best guide. You are very lucky to have found me."

Kelsen was a tragic case. He ridiculed pagan *kastom*, but he clearly suffered without it. For one thing, he was fighting with his brother over the money that guests paid to stay in their village. Since the two men were both Adventists, they could not hold a *kastom* pig-killing ceremony to settle the dispute. The brothers could not rely on their ancestors or island myths to guide them. They would be parted like Cain and Abel, Kelsen had told me—though he insisted that he would be the one to keep the money. He quivered with greedy longing. It was my first taste of the illness that had metastasized into an all-out civil war in the Solomon Islands.

Kelsen begged me not to go to Sulphur Bay. There was nowhere to stay, he said. John Frum's followers had all left the stronghold of their faith and run off into the hills where I would never find them. He assured me that if I stayed with him just one more night, he would tell me his volcano story. But he had been promising that for days.

I FOLLOWED THE CART TRACK back towards Yasur, this time on foot. At midday, I reached the ash plain, where I spotted a trio of Mormon missionaries. Their white shirts blazed in the sunlight. Their ties flapped in the wind. We shook hands. I told them I thought they deserved great credit for keeping their shirts clean no matter how rough the mission field might be. They told me I shouldn't be so cheery, especially since I was headed for Sulphur Bay.

"There is a false prophet on this end of the island," one said gravely. "He has led hundreds of people astray."

"John Frum," I said.

"No. The false prophet's name is Fred. He is very dangerous. He has been throwing babies into the volcano."

They gave me directions to Sulphur Bay anyway. I crossed the ash plain, mesmerized by the black mushroom clouds that periodically issued from the summit of Yasur. There was a single set of footprints in the ash, zigzagging up a spur to the summit ridge.

Babies in the volcano. Honestly.

But Fred . . . that name was familiar. Then I remembered. Back in Port Vila, I had met a Canadian man who had just served a six-month stint as Tanna's only doctor. Fockler was his name. He told me that Tanna intrigued and baffled him. Like the time the national police had summoned him to Sulphur Bay to check on a man named Fred who had established a new village on a shoulder of the volcano.

"Rumour had it that this guy had gone off the deep end," the doctor said. "He was having all kinds of visions and he had been accused of all sorts of crimes—you know, ritual child abuse, or something like that. Oh, they also said that Fred had leprosy."

Fockler had dutifully trucked across the island with his rubber gloves and a bag full of antipsychotic drugs. He had barely begun to hike up the mountain when he came face to face with Fred, who was a big man with very messy hair. It was clear that Fred had, indeed, suffered from leprosy. His eyebrows and hands were slightly misshapen. But the condition was clearly inactive and not contagious. Fockler pretended to examine the prophet's skin while actually conducting a quick mental status assessment.

"I asked him if he saw visions, you know, or heard any messages, and he said, 'I can't tell you that, it's the source of my power.' Well, that pretty much shut down my psychological assessment. But he didn't seem overtly psychotic."

The doctor figured that the police were looking for an excuse to lock Fred up, but he decided it was not his job to do their dirty work. He told the assembled crowd that he would let them keep their prophet. They cheered. The doctor returned to the hospital in Lenakel, and Fred remained on the mountain with his visions.

I followed a track into the forest and down along a ravine. The slopes on either side of the ravine had been scoured right down to bare rock. That puzzled me: the creek that trickled through the gorge could never have done such damage. The devastation widened to several hundred metres as I neared the sea. Then the track veered away from the creek and ended in a wide field surrounded by huts. This was Sulphur Bay. And this, I thought, was the field where John Frum's followers must once have gathered. But the village was empty and the field had been thoroughly excavated by pigs, two of which watched me silently from their craters. There was an old cement cistern. Its tap yielded only dust.

I heard the sound of voices coming from the creek. I followed them and found dozens of women bathing, singing and slapping their laundry, which steamed in the afternoon heat. Some of them were topless, which was not exactly in keeping with Presbyterian teaching. I walked on to talk to their husbands, who were bathing upstream.

I had scarcely mentioned the name Isaac One when a young man leaped forward, grabbed my hand and tugged me away from the creek.

"Not here," he said adamantly. "Not Sulphur Bay."

He pulled my pack from my back and strode off with it, heading further upstream. I had little choice but to follow him. After a few minutes, we entered a clearing much like the ones I had seen on my walks with Kelsen: an oval of earth pounded hard by bare feet, this one shaded by a grove of breadfruit trees. Their spiny fruit hung from the branches like green piñatas. The clearing was full of people: old men in filthy *lavalavas* and ski jackets, young men in surf shorts. Boys and mongrels lurked shyly around their heels. The men were tending little fires and puttering with great dirty clumps of roots. They turned to gaze at me silently.

"Isaac One," I said. An old man stepped forward.

I pulled a bag of rice and three tins of tuna from my pack, intending to hand them to the chief, but thought better of it when he scowled and turned away. I placed them on a grass mat instead. The chief did not acknowledge my gifts. He murmured something to my guide, who took my pack and disappeared into the forest. I was nervous. The sky turned purple over the volcano. Dusk settled on the *nakamal*—for that is where I had arrived: the traditional *kava*-drinking ground beside almost every village on Tanna.

"The chief is very drunk," said the man who brought me. *"Kava."*

Isag Wan (as I discovered his name was really spelled) was beguiling. The chief was as thin and bent as the smouldering twig he clutched in one hand, at the ready to relight the cigarette which never left his mouth. He had the bloodshot eyes of a *kava* addict. But those eyes were still quick. His beard was peppered grey, and he wore a khaki jacket with "U.S. Army" stamped on the chest. He was forever kicking the mongrels that followed him around the *nakamal*.

I tried to introduce myself, to explain why I had come, but the chief just waved me silent with a bony hand, then proceeded to fuss over a grass mat, which he spread on the dirt for me.

"Long moning yu kam long ofis blong mi," he said, then turned away.

Come to his office? Here? I hadn't seen so much as a tin roof in a week.

The night's *kava* session had already begun, and the chief would not be distracted. The scene was familiar—I had read accounts of the ritual by the earliest Presbyterian missionaries, who noted that the Tannese followed each gulp of the drink with an invocation of a spirit or a prayer meant to activate the power of a magic stone. The missionaries did not like that at all. They banned *kava* consumption for several decades before John Frum came to challenge the Church.

No women were permitted in the *nakamal*. I watched the men whittling away at clumps of *kava*. They half-heartedly scraped off the dirt and woodiest skin from the root, which looked like ginger, only bigger. Then they cut up the root into bite-sized portions and handed them to teenaged boys, who waited like dogs for table scraps. The boys chewed and the men fed them more bits of root, until their cheeks ballooned like singing frogs. Then one of the boys spat the contents of his mouth onto what looked like a hankie (which seemed appropriate, given the way he cleared his nose and horked once his chewing was done). The blob of masticated root looked like a cow-pie. Isag Wan held the cloth and chewed root over a coconut shell bowl. Someone poured water over the fibrous mass, then the chief wrapped the cloth around it and squeezed until juice dripped into the bowl. They kept pouring and squeezing until the bowl was full of mud-grey slurry.

The chief drank his shell in three quick gulps. Then he turned and spat a great bouquet of spray towards the forest. As he was spitting, he made a sound somewhere between a groan and a yawn.

"The chief is saying his *tamavha*: he is praying," whispered a young man who had settled in next to me. His name was Stanley. A single knot of dreadlocks sprang from the back of Stanley's head. He wore a T-shirt with a cartoon mouse on it. The mouse was drinking tequila.

"And now it is your turn," Stanley said.

Everyone in the *nakamal* turned to watch me. I rose and was approached by a lad with red paint smeared across his face. He looked like a character from *The Lord of the Flies*. Snot oozed from his nostrils in vibrant shades of green and yellow. He cleared his nose and swallowed, then he handed me what I considered to be an unfairly large coconut shell that was close to overflowing with the muddy brew.

"Just like the chief did," said Stanley. "All in one go, and then you say your *tamavha.*"

The *kava* looked like dirty dishwater, tasted of mud and cloves, and acted like anaesthetic. My tongue went numb even as I chugged my unfairly large shell. I spat into the forest, barked "God help me," then peered into the shadows. After two more shells, the numbness spread to my stomach and my head. All was well. The world hummed quietly, and I tried to place the source of this newfound feeling of transcendence.

Scientists have been researching the pharmacology of the *Piper methysticum* shrub for more than a hundred years. Researchers in the 1980s found that the pepper shrub's root contains compounds with anticonvulsant, muscle relaxant and local anaesthetic effects. There may also be psychoactive constituents, but nobody seemed to agree whether or not *kava* contains enough to get drinkers good and high, in the clinical sense.

Kava is consumed in pockets right across the South Pacific, from New Guinea to the Marquesas. But nowhere is the drink said to be as powerful as on Tanna. That could be because Tanna is the only place where the root is prepared by chewing, rather than pounding or grating. Researchers have suggested that the root's active ingredients, whatever they are, have low rates of water solubility, so that saliva might act as an emulsifying agent. All that chewing by all those snot-nosed virgins might actually release the *kava*'s true power.

The night air was wrapping itself around me like strands of gauze. I sat on my grass mat and proclaimed the goodness of it all to Stanley. "Everything is purple. Life is purple, really," I told him cheerily. "Don't you think?"

Stanley glanced around the clearing and shook his head sternly. "Quiet, quiet. Only whisper now." The *nakamal* was not like a bar where you could yell at your neighbour, he said.

So I whispered: "Do you believe in John Frum?"

"I believe," Stanley said.

Stanley lived in Port Resolution but had hiked over the mountain to celebrate the John Frum Sabbath with Chief Wan. Tomorrow, he said, there would be dancing.

"But what happened to Sulphur Bay? Why is it so empty? Why doesn't the chief live there any more?" I asked.

"It's all because of Fred," he said. The leper prophet again. "Didn't you see what Fred did over by the volcano? There was once *wan bigfala* lake on the ash plain. Two years ago Fred used magic to drain it. He made a flood. It destroyed the river and killed some houses in Sulphur Bay. Fred told everyone that God did this, but we know it was Fred using *kastom* magic. Isag Wan had to protect his people from Fred. That's why he moved out of Sulphur Bay to this village, Namakara."

"Yes, Fred is a bad man," I said, wishing Stanley's words would match the rhythm of his lips, which seemed to be moving in slow motion.

"Now he tells everyone he is the Messiah and he will take them to heaven. People have been coming from all over Tanna to live with Fred up on the volcano. It's very sad."

I had so many questions, but Stanley's voice was now trailing off into an indecipherable mumble. He was sitting next to me, but his words seemed to issue from far beyond the edge of the clearing where they mingled with the whirring of thousands of cicadas and the murmuring of the forest. The stars, however, looked close enough to touch. So did the fires that glowed like jewels in the dirt, and the ends of cigarettes that moved like fireflies, and the eyes of the pigs and dogs that flashed in the shadows. Tranquillity settled like a fog on my thoughts. My knee rested against Stanley's knee, and it was warm.

A boy took my hand and led me through the trees into a hamlet of darkened huts. A warm light shone from one of them. The boy removed a thatch screen, and I stepped inside to find my pack, an oil lamp and a plate of steaming food. It was the rice and tuna I had given the chief. I ate, then fell into a deep sleep.

THE JOHN FRUM STORY was a tree with many roots.

By the time the French and British set up their joint administration of the New Hebrides, Presbyterian missionaries had already established what amounted to a theocracy on Tanna. The Church subjected the island to Presbyterian law enforced by roving bands of zealous "police." Anyone suspected of drinking *kava,* singing or dancing could expect to be arrested and taken to "court." Christian converts shunned their unclothed cousins.

All that changed in 1940. That's when the British district agent, James Nicol, heard rumours that a mysterious stranger had been calling the island chiefs together for secret meetings. The stranger wore a broad-brimmed hat and a white sports jacket with silver buttons. No one ever saw his face in the shadows, but they remembered his high-pitched voice and how he berated them for following the white man's laws. He said the Tannese should turn their backs on the Presbyterian missionaries who had banned the things they took delight in. They should return to *kastom:* their extravagant dances, their rainmaking magic, their polygyny and their circumcision ceremonies. They should rid themselves of European money. They should guzzle *kava,* get back in touch with their ancestors. If the Tannese did all these things, the colonial police and the strict Presbyterian missionaries would miraculously disappear. And then the prophet would return on a big white ship, and that ship would be loaded with riches from America. The stranger's name was John Frum. Some said he took his name from John the Baptist. Others said he was John-with-a-Broom, and that his broom was for sweeping sickness, trouble and white men off the island.

Rumours flew. Some islanders said that John Frum was the king of America, or perhaps the son of God: like Jesus, only older. Others insisted thousands of his soldiers were inside the volcano, waiting for the right moment to charge out and chase the British and French away. Several chiefs claimed to be Frum himself.

The prophet's followers exploded into action in 1941. They slaughtered cattle and pigs and turned in their European currency in preparation for Frum's golden age. Hundreds gathered to swill *kava* and dance all night on the south end of the island. Then one Sunday in May, the Presbyterian ministers found their churches empty for the first time in decades.

Nicol had had enough. He called in reinforcements from Port Vila and arrested the John Frum leaders.

The movement might have died had Frum's prophecies not come true. In December 1941, the Japanese bombed Pearl Harbor. The American fleet reached the New Hebrides the following March. More than half a million soldiers passed through the islands during the war. The U.S. soldiers were spectacularly generous, handing out pots, pans, cigarettes and tinned meat. One black G.I., hearing of the Tannese struggle, reportedly gave them a flag to fly the above their village. (Some say it was red; others insist it was the Stars and Stripes.) He told them that America would always be there to protect them from their colonial masters. Now the Frummers were even more sure of their prophet's connection with America. They raised that flag at Sulphur Bay on February 15, 1957. They built a cross and painted it red, to match the crosses they had seen on U.S. Army ambulances. They carved wooden "rifles" and gathered U.S. Army surplus clothing. To honour the day of their redemption, the Frummers now don those fatigues, take up those rifles and perform marching drills around their Sulphur Bay parade ground on each February 15. This is what the anthropologists write.

But Tanna was hardly unique in the messiah department. In fact, Melanesia produced dozens of cargo cults in the last century. Across the archipelago, a generation of messiahs promised the arrival of shiploads and planeloads of untold riches, but only for those who obeyed their edicts. The striking feature about these cults was that they emerged independently on at least a dozen islands but still managed to come up with similar philosophies. All of them revolved around the manipulation of supernatural forces to bring about an age of prosperity and freedom. Most advocated giving up foreign goods and customs while at the same time promising the spontaneous arrival of consumer goods. Refrigerators, Spam, radios—they would all arrive, if the faithful just followed instructions. People built wharves, warehouses and even airstrips to facilitate the cargo magic. The cults that emerged before World War II relied on returning ancestors to bring wealth. But after the war, that changed: the magic cargo would come from America.

My favourite cargo movement emerged soon after the U.S. Army left Espiritu Santo at the end of World War II. It was dubbed the "Naked Cult" after its leaders told followers to cast off their clothes and, among other curiosities, to conduct all their sexual intercourse in public, "like dogs and fowls." Doing so would bring the Americans back and usher in a golden age of prosperity and everlasting life.

There were so many cults in Melanesia that Church leaders were compelled to create guidelines for the missionaries who battled them. A 1971 paper advised missionaries that cargo cults were not a "special Satanic attempt" to destroy their work. Christian pastors should be patient. Divert the cultists' attention with movies and sports events. Try to ignore the villagers' use of Christian crosses in pagan rituals.

Some anthropologists suggest that the cargo cult phenomenon was a response by primitive cultures to the seemingly supernatural levels of material wealth possessed by Europeans and Americans. The theory goes like this: The industrial products white men used were so shockingly different that islanders thought they must have come from the spirit realm. Guns, jeeps and tinned food were also seen as evidence of the white man's wealth and mastery over Melanesians. The possession of those things would bring to islanders a kind of material and spiritual emancipation. There was a secret to white men's wealth. Discover that secret, grab the cargo magic and the days of slavery would be over.

While most cargo cults fizzled, the John Frum movement lived on. Frummers have been elected to Vanuatu's national parliament and government ministers have attended the annual John Frum marches at Sulphur Bay. The movement's longevity suggests that it is about something more than cargo. One anthropologist wrote that the promises of cargo were really just window-dressing for a sophisticated attempt by pagans to halt the social disintegration that they felt Christianity was causing. Ralph Regenvanu, the director of Vanuatu's national cultural centre, told me much the same thing. John Frum was not a ghost. He was not crazy. He knew exactly what he was doing, and so did the chiefs who have invoked his name—and changed his story—for sixty years.

I AWOKE WELL AFTER dawn with the grey sponge of *kava* still hanging in my head and a hint of diarrhea stirring in my gut. Isag Wan was squatting in the dirt outside my hut, agitated. At his heel, two piglets fought over a banana peel. The chief had a watch, which he checked three times before losing patience and calling me out. He led me to a dirt plaza in the middle of the village, and then we stood at attention together. After an uncomfortable minute, the chief consulted his watch again and coughed loudly. It was eight o'clock. Women stopped their sweeping. Pigs ceased rooting. The village fell silent. Even the volcano seemed to stop rumbling for a few solemn moments. Then a whistle sounded, and on a hillock in front of us, the Stars and Stripes was hauled up a bamboo flagpole. The cult of John Frum was alive and well.

The chief led me to his "office," a broad hut decked with grass mats and filled with bric-a-brac. There were wooden clubs and woven baskets, an airbrushed poster of frolicking cats and lions, a picture of a white Jesus and a calendar with scenes from the coast of France. A carved wooden eagle stood on the table. Dominating it all was a crude painting of Yasur, with slogans painted across its slopes in a mix of Bislama and English. I remember one of them:

MANI HEM GUD LAIF

BUT MANI I MEKEM

MAN I STAP RAPEM BROTHA

MO SISTA BLONG HEM

Money is good life but money makes a man exist to rape his brother and sister. It didn't quite seem like a plea for cargo. Isag Wan cleared his throat, tossed his cigarette to a lad sitting on the floor and told me his version of Tannese history. The boy translated.

"Before there were cars and trucks, before white people came, there was darkness time on Tanna. We had magic stones to make our gardens grow: stones for yams, banana, taro, any kind of food. We had stones to make the ocean rough, to make sun and rain, to kill men. But then the Church came and preached, and they won almost all the people with their gospel. The Presbyterians made a law to stop us using our stones, to stop circumcision, to stop making food the right way. They stopped our dances. No more killing pigs. No more *kava*. No more swapping women for marriage.

"John Frum looked and he saw the Church destroying *kastom*. That's when he came to us—as a spirit. He showed himself to our grandfathers in 1937.

"He told the grandfathers, 'The white man has a light, the light of his Church, but he wants to use it to destroy your *kastom*. Go back to *kastom*, hold tight to it, because God created *kastom* for us to live by.' All the chiefs agreed, but when the missionaries and the government heard about this, they were plenty cross. They arrested the John Frum chiefs. They put an iron in a fire, and they forced them all to sit on it, one by one."

Except for the part about hot poker torture, Isag Wan's story paralleled written accounts from the early days.

"But what about John Frum?" I asked. "Are you still waiting for him to come back from America with his ship full of cargo?"

"John Frum speaks to me often."

"How? Has he returned?"

"No, he sends others to talk with me. Spirit men. They come through the volcano. There's a road underneath the fire, it goes all the way to 'Merica."

Bingo. I decided not to break his rhythm. "Have you been to America?"

"Yes I have."

"How did you get there? Through the volcano? Did John Frum take you?"

Isag Wan looked at me, eyes narrowing with irritation. Of course not, he said. A visitor to Tanna had paid for him to fly to America on a plane. "I have seen Atlanta, Dallas and Washington," said the chief. "I went to the White House and I spoke to Mr. Clinton's general secretary. He was happy to talk to me because he knew that Tanna has flown the U.S. flag for so many years. But 'Merica made me very sad. Too many trucks, too many poor people. Did you know that some men there have no land at all? I met them on the road. I gave them all the money I had in my pockets."

"I thought John Frum promised to make you all rich, like Americans."

"We will not follow 'Merica. 'Merica should follow us. Look," said Isag Wan, doodling in the sand with a stick. " 'Merica has lost the road. They think money is Jesus. 'Merica must remember the promise of John. Remember the true path."

I took a deep breath and closed my eyes. I could feel the previous night's *kava* pulsing behind my temples. "Tell me about this true path."

"The life way. Don't follow government. Don't follow Church. Don't follow money. Follow *kastom* and peace. That's what Jesus and John Frum say."

I nodded. But what was with all those references to Jesus? I remembered my night of ice cream with Jack and Kay Rudd back at the Joy Bible College. They had insisted that their friend John Rush had converted Isag Wan.

The chief had his own version of that story. "I remember John Rush. He came and told us John Frum was inside of him, but I never believed it. John Rush is only *wan man blong* Church. He and his friends keep trying to push us inside their churches. We don't need that. We need to stay together and follow John Frum."

"But you aren't staying together, are you? You've abandoned Sulphur Bay. You are fighting your old neighbours. You are fighting with this man—this prophet—Fred."

"Fred is not a prophet. He is an evil man. He tells people he has the spirit of John Frum, but it's a lie. I know where Fred's power comes from. He is using the power of the black sea snake to trick us all."

The whole Fred business had started two years before, said Isag Wan. "Fred made bad talk. He told the old men in Sulphur Bay to kill nineteen pigs and drink nineteen shells of *kava* in order to wash away their sins, but look what happened instead: he broke the lake and he washed away half the village. Fred promised to turn all the old men in Sulphur Bay into children again. But the old men are still old! Fred promised that if people followed him to the top of the mountain, Jesus would come and take them all to heaven. Jesus didn't come. He said he would stop the sun from setting, but look at the sky. Fred lies!" The chief paused to swipe at a dog that had poked its head through the door of his office. Embers flew from the end of his stick. "Worst of all, Fred told people to destroy the last of the *kastom* stones, and now he is trying to make everyone go back to the Church. That's why we had to leave Sulphur Bay. It belongs to the Church again. Namakara is the new home for John Frum."

I SPENT THE AFTERNOON lounging in the bathtub-warm waters of the creek, trying to make sense of the histories that were colliding on Tanna:

Jesus, John Frum, Fred . . . three prophets had danced their way into island mythology. Their stories were melting together. My mind reeled.

At dusk a drum sounded, and I followed it back to the plaza in the middle of the village. The John Frum Sabbath was beginning. Boys poked at a bonfire. The pilgrims from Port Resolution shuffled quietly across the dirt, carrying four guitars, a homemade banjo and a couple of bongo drums. Stanley was with them, still wearing his tequila T-shirt. The people settled onto palm mats. The women made a circle around the men. Then the band started to play, slowly at first, softly; then the women joined in and sang a song tinged with an autumnal sadness that made me homesick. The night sped on, and Stanley's band gave way to three others. The rhythm quickened until the chorus rose in great triumphant arcs, suggesting a time of flowers and love and smiles and cumulonimbus clouds touched with sunset gold. "Namakara! Namakara! Namakara!" The people chanted the name of the village over and over again to the stars.

Now more than a hundred figures had emerged from the shadows: men, women and children, all swaying in loose formation around the band. The women had glitter paint around their eyes and wore rainbow-painted grass skirts. Some of the men wore skirts too, over their rolled-up trousers. As the music rose towards a crescendo, those grass-skirted bums began to shake. Boys jumped and writhed. The air filled with whoops, chirps and rhythmic hissing. Stanley bobbed beside me, smiling broadly and touching my elbow: "Come on! Come on! Sssst! Sssst!"

I saw Isag Wan in his grass skirt and camouflage T-shirt, cigarette burning in the corner of his mouth, his frail frame shaking, his eyes rolling ecstatically. I was struck by the thought that there was really nothing at all strange going on in Namakara. Whatever its beginnings, the John Frum movement was no more audacious now than any Church. Indeed, Jesus and a rough idea of heaven had embedded themselves into Isag Wan's philosophy. It was almost beside the point that the chief claimed to receive instructions through the fiery gullet of the volcano. John Frum's message had evolved: the chief didn't pray for cargo any more or to divert the white man's wealth. His cargo was the spiritual riches the world would share when Churches and governments stopped fighting each other. Or something like that.

Isag Wan wasn't asking for anything radical from his people. He didn't claim to be a prophet. He wasn't the chosen one. Not like the mysterious Fred, who, depending on whom you asked, was either in direct communication with God or was working a terrible kind of magic on all who opposed him. I looked up above Namakara's huts and flagpoles, past the forested ridges to where flecks of magma arced through the night sky like sparks from a distant campfire. I knew I couldn't leave Tanna without making a pilgrimage to Fred's New Jerusalem, which waited somewhere among the darkened folds of the volcano.

4

THE PROPHET
RAISES HIS HANDS
TO THE SKY

Our Faith rests on a Revelation from above.
God has spoken to us, and we have heard His voice and have
been assured that it is the voice of God Himself.

HENRY MONTGOMERY, *Life's Journey*

THE CHIEF of Port Resolution lay on the dirt
floor of his hut holding his stomach. There
wasn't much to him. Flies gathered at the edge
of his eyes, which had sunk deeply into his skull. Skin hung from his face
like soggy paper. A doctor had told the chief that his liver had simply
given up trying to process all that *kava*, but the chief and everyone else in
Port Resolution knew that grog wasn't the problem.

"It's Fred," Stanley told me as we retreated from the hut. "He has
poisoned the chief with his magic."

Port Resolution, the jumping-off point for pilgrims headed for Fred's
mountain camp, lay on the south side of the volcano. It was a perfect
teardrop of glowing aquamarine nestled against a long sweep of black
sand. Palms hung languidly over the beach. Men threw fishnets from
outrigger canoes. Steam curled from vents on the forested ridges that led
to Yasur.

The bay had once served as a base for Melanesia's most famous missionary. The Reverend John G. Paton and his wife landed in 1858. His autobiography racily described the Tannese as voracious cannibals who "gloried in bloodshedding" and delighted in the taste of human flesh. Paton outlined how he duelled with pagan warriors and sorcerers; how they burned his house to the ground and stole all his possessions; how his wife, his child and a colleague all died within three years of their arrival; how he sat for ten days, gun in hand, guarding his dead wife's grave to prevent islanders from getting their hands on her putrefying remains. After one tribal battle, Paton recalled that the bodies of half a dozen men had been cooked at a boiling spring near the head of the bay. This presented a unique problem, as reported by the missionary's own cook: "At the boiling spring they have cooked and feasted upon the slain. They have washed the blood into the stream; they have bathed there till all the waters are red. I cannot get water to make your tea. What shall I do?"

(Anthropologists have since argued that Paton's and other missionaries' claims of widespread cannibalism were exaggerated. Enemies were eaten not because they tasted good but as a means of capturing their *mana* and honouring their own ancestors. A single corpse might be passed from village to village as a means of solidifying alliances. On Tanna, home to tens of thousands of people, there were never more than twenty-eight families with the right to consume human flesh.)

Paton fled on a passing ship in 1862. His story was so captivating he managed to wring £5000 from church audiences during a speaking tour of Australia. But most historians agree that Paton was as grand an embellisher as he was a survivor. And while God failed to punish the Tannese for their hostilities, Paton did not. Four years after his departure, he returned to Port Resolution on the warship HMS *Curaçoa*. The ship shelled the villages along the bay, then its men landed to smash canoes, burn houses and destroy crops. At least four natives were killed. Paton, who insisted he acted only as the ship's interpreter, nevertheless claimed that the attack did wonders for the mission.

Now, there were two hundred people and four churches in Port Resolution. The residents drifted back and forth between faiths like butterflies on flowers. There was a Seventh-day Adventist school, which meant that children born to pagan families learnt the Bible early on, then switched back to *kastom*, pigs and *kava* when they hit puberty. Church bells rang each morning, but Stanley's John Frum string band practised on the soccer pitch each afternoon. If a boy was Adventist he couldn't drink *kava*, but he was still expected to chew it for his father's nightly brew. The chief of Port Resolution was pagan, but his son, Wari, was Adventist. That caused a slight problem, since Wari was responsible for the village's shark stone, a magic rock which could be used to manipulate the habits of sharks and mackerel. He wouldn't show me the shark stone, but he told me how it worked.

"If you want to attract fish," said Wari, "you get some *kastom* leaves and rub them on the stone and leave it in a special *tabu* place."

"But you are Adventist. You can't eat fish without scales. You can't eat shark."

"True, but if I am the keeper of the shark stone, I'm not allowed to eat the shark anyway. The shark is *olsem* as my god. It's *tabu* for me. And besides, the ancestors didn't use the shark stone for fishing. They used it to make the sharks eat our enemies."

The villagers had built a kitchen and a clutch of rough bungalows on a bluff above the bay and erected a sign: Port Resolution Yacht Club. For years, yachties had been attracted by a friendly dugong (a chubby, cowlike marine mammal) that grazed on the grasses in the bay. The dugong was now dead, but the yacht club still had a commodore who told me he went to great lengths to take care of visiting yachties: for example, if the radio forecast a cyclone, it was his job to put special leaves in the ocean in order to calm the wind and waves.

Nobody wanted to help me track down Fred. No wonder. The prophet had eclipsed John Frum as the overriding concern on Tanna. Everyone had a Fred rumour to pass on. Some accused Fred of cursing people. Others said that Fred was a pervert. According to one story, he enjoyed sitting in a pit above which were placed two thin boards; women were forced to step across those boards so Fred could peer up their skirts. Then there was the bit about Fred throwing babies into the volcano.

Those were rumours. What seemed more alarming to me was the effect the prophet was having on human geography. Families from all over

Tanna had abandoned their gardens and their pigs in order to join Fred on the volcano. Farmland was going fallow. Pigs were disappearing. Things were falling apart. While Fred's followers waited for their ride to heaven, they pilfered the gardens of the villages at the base of their mountain. It was whispered that a handful of old folks and children had already died up at Fred's camp.

I finally convinced Stanley to take me to the prophet. At least I thought I convinced him. We walked together along the beach towards the mountain, Stanley dawdling all the way. When we reached the end of the beach and started up a faint trail, Stanley slowed to a shuffle. At the edge of the last coconut grove, he stopped.

"I can't go up there," he said.

"But why? I'm with you. Nothing will happen."

"I want to help you but I can't. If I see Fred, if I even look at him, I know I will get sick."

Stanley traced me a map in the dirt, and I continued on alone up a series of braided trails. I passed two abandoned villages. The forest changed. The benevolent jungle of Port Resolution gave way to a ragged and desperate landscape of stumps, cracked coconut palms and clinging brambles. I heard screams and hoots in the forest. As I climbed away from the bay, I began to encounter people. Children with machetes hacked branches from breadfruit trees. When they saw me they screamed, *"Waet man!"* They called back and forth in Bislama, which meant they didn't share a common tongue. Of course: Fred's followers came from all over Tanna, and there were at least six distinct languages on the island. I saw adults, too, all coming down from the mountain with empty baskets and water jugs. One old man grabbed me by the sleeve and pulled me close. "Go on," he hissed in my ear. "He is waiting for you."

I followed the trail through a great maze of vines and spiralling banyan roots, up through a series of cliffs and onto a ridge pockmarked with vents which steamed and oozed iron-red mud. From there, I could see over the forest and coconut plantations to the Pacific. Storms seemed to be coming from all directions. Shadows raced across the ocean. Then the rain swept across the mountain and hit just as I entered a village, making it seem especially squalid. Hundreds of grass huts jostled for space on a small plateau and spilled down a series of mud ravines. The huts were new, judging by the pale jade of their thatch, but they were not like the quaint bungalows I had seen elsewhere on Tanna. These were makeshift lean-tos and A-frames, all of them ill-proportioned and too low to stand in. Children shrieked and rolled in the muck. Sores glistened on their ankles and on their heads. There was a dirt parade ground too, with a bamboo pole planted dead centre. Dangling limply from it was the U.S. flag.

A man stepped forward.

"Fred?" I asked.

"No, I'm Alfred. Come with me."

I followed him towards a broad, open-air shelter. Trailing behind us was what appeared to be the village idiot: a quiet fellow with an abnormally large and slightly misshapen head. He made me nervous. He walked so close I could see the patches of hair missing between his dreadlocks and the tears that streamed constantly from his left eye. He had an untidy beard and wore a filthy ski parka which had once been green and pink. But it was the man's head that captivated me. It looked as though it had been fashioned from rubber and then squeezed at the temples, or melted, so that his forehead seemed on the verge of collapsing around his eyes. He had no eyebrows. Of course. Leprosy. This was Fred, the prophet.

We sat on a bench under the shelter. Rain dripped through the roof. I explained that I was here to help Fred spread his message around the world. Fred mumbled like a child in his own language and dabbed at his teary eye with a pair of torn bikini briefs. Alfred interpreted. This, he said, was the prophet's true story.

Fred was born in Sulphur Bay but had spent a decade working on a Taiwanese fishing boat. In his last year at sea, he began having visions. They came to him as lights from the sky, like stars, only they shot straight at him. Fred wasn't afraid when the lights came. He would just close his eyes and go to sleep. When he did, he heard the voice. It reassured him. It gave him clues about the future. Fred knew the voice was God talking to him. One day, the voice told him he should return to his own island to bring the people together in peace, so Fred came home to Sulphur Bay and began sharing his predictions with his neighbours.

In one vision, Fred saw the lake at the base of the volcano, Lake Siwi. He saw that the water in the lake was not good. The volcano was polluting it with ash. The voice advised Fred to pray to make the water run out of the lake. He did. It worked. And now, said Fred—through Alfred—the water in the creek at Sulphur Bay was much better for drinking. Fred gained credibility, at least with those whose homes hadn't been destroyed by the flooding.

Then Fred predicted the bombing of the World Trade Center in New York. When the prophecy came true, his followers paraded in Port Vila to show their sympathy for 'Merica. That's when an American gave Fred the flag which now flew above his village.

"Any other miracles?" I asked.

Fred gave a long, slurred reply. Alfred gave me the Reader's Digest version: "Before Fred came back, the volcano used to explode and kill many people. But Fred asked God to make it stop. It did. Oh, and the hurricanes. There will be no hurricanes on Tanna for five years."

I asked politely about Fred's alleged dark side. "Some people say you are working black magic here to trick people and make them sick."

Fred rolled his eyes back into his skull, then levelled them at me. *"Hem i no tru. Hem i rubbish toktok,"* he said. *"Disfala power, hem i power blong God."*

Black magic and prophecy are not covered by Vanuatu criminal law. That must have been why the police had tried to use the Canadian doctor to oust Fred. I told Fred what the doctor had told me: that he was not crazy. He nodded his appreciation.

"But what are you doing up here on the mountain?" I asked.

Fred returned to his mumbling.

"God told Fred to bring the people together in Unity," translated Alfred. "All the Churches, John Frum people and *kastom* people, must come together and follow one God. One people in Unity. So we sing John Frum songs on Wednesday beneath the flag. And on Sunday we go to the church."

The rest of the days, I thought, Fred's hungry followers steal food from surrounding villages.

"How long will you stay up here?"

"Fred had a vision about that, too," said Alfred. "He saw that twelve virgin boys would be circumcised. Only then will God tell us what we should do next."

"I thought all boys on Tanna were circumcised."

"Yes, but these boys would be circumcised by God." Alfred paused for effect. "And the miracle has already begun. The first boy has been cut. Nobody touched him. His parents simply found him circumcised one morning last week."

"Can I see it?"

"The boy?"

"Well, yes, but really, it's his fixed penis that counts."

"Of course not. But you come back tomorrow. Tomorrow we bring John Frum together with Jesus."

Alfred patted my shoulder encouragingly. Fred offered me his hand, which was as soft and cold as an oyster, then wandered off to gaze at the clouds. Fred might not have been crazy but he certainly didn't seem to have enough of a grip on reality to be in charge of this operation. Who was? And who was in charge of Fred? Before I left, Alfred made me promise to return the next day with my camera so the world would have proof of Unity.

THE NEXT MORNING Fred preached to a rapt crowd of four hundred up on the mountain. I couldn't understand any of it, other than the words "New Jerusalem," which he shouted over and over. Encouraged by Alfred, I climbed through the brambles at the edge of the clearing and took photos. That's when I learned there was no toilet in New Jerusalem.

Most of the congregation wore rags, but there were two men in white shirts and ties. They sat on a bench behind Fred, beaming and nodding with approval as he spoke. The younger one waved to me as I attempted to wipe the shit from my sandals. He motioned for me to come sit with him on the VIP bench.

"You must take many photos," he said, straightening his tie. "Fred is a very important man. Take many photos and send me copies of them. I want to present them to the Presbyterian Congress on Makira, to show them our work here."

The man's name was Pastor Maliwan Taruei. He was the grandson of the Presbyterian minister who had battled it out with the John Frummers back in the 1940s. Isag Wan's grandfather had driven his grandfather out of Sulphur Bay, then torn down his church. Now Maliwan Taruei had rebuilt it. The family feud was still on.

"Isag Wan is destroying this island with his idol worship," the pastor whispered to me as Fred preached. "But look at Fred, he is just like Moses. He led four thousand, four hundred sixty-six people up this hill, just like Moses led the Israelites out of Egypt to the promised land. And best of all, Fred invited the Presbyterian Church."

Wasn't it strange, I asked, for the Church to support a man who championed both God and *kastom* magic? It didn't fit with any version of Christianity I had ever heard of.

"Aha, you don't understand Tanna, do you? Our *kastom* stories are just like the Bible stories. Don't you know the real name of our volcano? It's not Yasur. It's Yahweh, the Hebrew name for God. The Bible tells us that one day the world will become paradise. But *kastom* tells us that one day Tanna will become a paradise, a new Jerusalem. Tanna people know we have two choices. We pray for both of them."

"But is your saviour Jesus or John Frum?"

"My friend, God will give us the answer, and it will be one of them. Either way, I assure you that the Church has returned to Sulphur Bay, and all these people will be there on Sunday."

The crowd had disappeared. Now they were back, filing onto the dirt plaza by the hundreds. They had changed out of their rags. The men came first, banana leaves tied around their heads and bare chests shining in the sun. Women followed, their faces painted yellow and orange like hornets. They wore feathers in their hair and grass skirts dyed with rainbow checkers. Wreaths of Christmas tinsel dangled from their necks. Their dance was not the dead-eyed shake of Kelsen's *nambas*-clad friends, nor was it the cheery campfire rumba I had joined in in Namakara. It was like a war dance. The men stamped the earth, grunting and exhaling simultaneously in great stormy whooshes. The women gathered around them in loose whorls, wailing and waving tree branches towards the Stars and Stripes. They charged the flag, jumped back again and raced in circles until the plaza became a maelstrom of dust and leaping bodies. The Presbyterian Congress, I thought, would be mortified.

The pastors shifted nervously on the grass mats where they now sat. The older one adjusted his glasses. He looked like the square kid in a room full of marijuana smoke. Maliwan reached for my hand, but I couldn't sit still. Shaking with excitement, I dashed across the clearing, climbed to the roof of a hut and pulled out my camera. There was Fred, sitting alone on a footstool, watching the dance with one eye and me with the other. He nodded when I pointed my camera at him. Maliwan shouted to the dancers, who quickened their pace. I raised the camera to my eye, and the frame was filled with dust, flashing colour and shining skin. The crowd had spread across the plaza: the frame couldn't contain them all. I stood up, straddling the gable of the hut, raised my arms above my head, motioned like Jesus on the mount. Closer together. Move closer together. The crowd responded.

"Closer!" I shouted when the dance ended. The crowd moved closer still. Adrenaline rushed through my veins.

"Raise your arms to the sky," I shouted when the dance ended. "Not Fred, just the rest of you!" They did as they were told, sweat-drenched men, dust-caked women, naked children, all four hundred of them; even the Presbyterian pastors stretched their arms in the air. It felt wonderful to see them obey. The dancers all looked up at me, knowing that they had done good work, knowing they were among the first to proclaim a message of peace and unity that would certainly sweep across Tanna and, with my help, around the world.

I gazed down at Fred, standing serenely among his followers. It would be easy to be a messiah here. You have your visions. You make your prophecies. You lead your people to the mountain. You tell them a new story. Then, if you are lucky, you are martyred like Jesus or you disappear like John Frum. If you are unlucky, you just go on living while your aura fades and you become ordinary again. But the key to success is your own faith. It must be rock solid. In other words, you either possess supernatural powers or you are nuts. There is no middle ground.

It was one thing to believe in yourself. But the faith of the people: where did it come from? The Tannese seemed to have the capacity to accept any prophet, any myth. They were more than just tolerant. They had sponges for souls. *Kastom* traditionalists sacrificed to the spirits and waited for John Frum. John Frummers waited for Jesus *and* John. Christians hedged their bets. Nobody was interested in discussing the contradictions.

The anthropologist Ben Burt had told me in London that what impressed him most about Melanesians was their capacity to hold onto apparently conflicting belief systems at the same time. It was not a sign of intellectual weakness, Burt had said. It required a sophisticated mind to perform such spiritual acrobatics.

The logic was somehow less mind-boggling on Tanna, where the landscape was as powerful, as crowded, as sharply schizophrenic as the island's apparent train wreck of faiths. The island was a confluence of primal signals. The vibrating jungle. The dusty stillness of the ash plain. The torrential rains. The fires of Yasur.

I slid back down the thatch roof, shook two hundred hands, then jogged to Port Resolution. I caught a lift on a Land Cruiser headed for Lenakel but jumped out when we reached the ash plain.

I stood for an hour there, at the foot of the volcano. The mountain didn't make a sound. In the last few years, tourists had begun to fly down to Tanna from Port Vila, drawn by the spectacle of Yasur's eruptions like moths to a giant flame. A handful had been struck and killed by flying rocks. Two weeks before my arrival, a woman had ventured onto the mountain and was hit by a rock which melted a hole in her leg. Kelsen had advised me that the bombs only flew north. Or was it east?

Almost without thinking I started up through the ash, slowly at first, pausing to gaze at the crest of the cinder cone with each tentative step. I sank up to my ankles in the rubble, sliding a step back for every two forward. Sand gathered between my toes. I cursed my sandals. I stumbled over bucket-sized pockmarks and metre-wide craters. They all cradled stones: some were as delicate and light as pumice, others looked like pieces of flesh ripped from a burnt corpse. Some were all bubble and froth, the texture of water frozen in mid-boil. Some were as big as bathtubs. Some had settled into the earth, as though they had been spit from the volcano decades before. Others were young: the sand around them had been heat-seared into a frosty white ring still undisturbed by rain. But hadn't it rained just that morning?

I was three quarters of the way up the mountain when it made the most terrifying sound. I could tell you it went boom, but that wouldn't be enough. Roared? Not enough. Thundered? Perhaps. It was the kind of sound that assures you that you are a fool, and that if you die, everyone will know you were a fool. A fool, a fool, I thought as the ground trembled and the sand trickled around my feet. I couldn't see past the crest of the cone. I remembered what Kelsen had told me. Don't run away when the mountain explodes. Don't turn your back. Face it, so that you can sidestep the bombs when they come at you. Ridiculous. The mountain shook again, hollering at me to turn back. I did think of turning back. But sometimes a journey takes on a momentum that won't listen to logic.

I carried on, pulling at the sand and ash, my knees grinding into the scree. My feet bled under the straps of my sandals. I suppose that was when I began to whimper. Despite myself, I begged the mountain not to rain its rocks down on me, not to send them flying out of the crater in those lazy arcs to fall gracefully onto my flesh. I didn't decide to beg: the words just came out in moans each time I exhaled. *Please don't kill me. If you spare me, I promise not to point my camera into your crater.* It was all I could think of to offer. I know it sounds absurd, begging to a mountain. I knew it at the time. Mountains cannot hear. But if you were there you would have done the same thing, even as you reminded yourself that the unthinking forces of gravity and physics and geology were never meant to be anthropomorphised.

I reached a cornice of fractured rock and peered over it into the crater, which was the size of a soccer stadium. There were three pits at the bottom. One glowed faintly orange. Another smoked like a bonfire of wet leaves and sucked at the late afternoon air like a steam engine. The third had no bottom. I gazed into that crater and I didn't see John Frum's armies or a fiery spirit or a devil. I didn't see the power of a heavenly God. Of course not.

I did not believe in spirits. I knew the rumbling, the explosions, the tremendous heaving power, all of it came from the earth. The mountain did not have feelings. It was not capable of listening. It would not respond to my prayers any more than it would to Fred's commands. I was certain about these things. And yet I did not pull out my camera from my bag. I reached instead into my pocket, pulled out a 500 vatu note and slipped it under a rock.

The sun was setting. I scrambled along the south edge of the crater until I reached a fence made from bamboo sticks. Someone had built a makeshift lookout on the lip of the precipice. This would be the pristine side of the volcano. I followed a trail that led down from the lookout towards a plateau a few hundred metres away. There was a truck there, and someone waving. As I waved back, the mountain boomed like a cannon, then boomed again behind me. I turned and froze. Magma sprayed into the purpling sky: great gobs of red-and-black mottled jelly spiralled, spun, broke apart in the heavens before finding their weight, losing momentum and falling back down towards the earth. The igneous rain exploded across the slope I had just crossed.

I stumbled numbly towards the truck. It contained four men, vulcanologists who had flown down from Vila for a night of fireworks. They were drinking instant coffee from tin cups. Those cups were being filled by a bearded fellow with a heavy brow. I should have known. Kelsen. He had lugged a kettle up from his village and lit a little fire at the edge of the plateau. Coffee was 100 vatu a shot.

"If you come back and stay at my hotel," Kelsen was saying to them. "I'll tell you the legend behind the volcano."

5

NINETY HOURS ON
THE MV BRISK

*We cannot show where primitive mentality stops and modern
mentality begins. In fact, when rationality has conquered
its rights, the mind sometimes needs to have recourse to myth . . . Might myth
have a function which should not be destroyed by rationality?*

MAURICE LEENHARDT,

Do Kamo: Person and Myth in the Melanesian World

THE PROTESTANT missionaries who descended
on the southern New Hebrides in the nineteenth century were as hostile towards Catholi-
cism as they were towards paganism. When the Presbyterian Reverend
John Geddie spotted white men wearing the telltale robes of Catholic
priests on the shore of Aneityum in 1848, he despaired: "In this we recognized at once the mark of the beast."

But competition among the Protestants themselves was nearly as
fierce. The austere Presbyterians and members of the populist London
Missionary Society had little time for the gilded finery and high-church
pomposity of the Anglican bishops and their Melanesian Mission. Bishops Selwyn and Patteson were graduates of Eton, Britain's most presti-
gious public school. They were of a different class from the members of
England's grass-roots mission societies, and both sides knew it. The

Anglicans felt that their competition—lowbrow firebrands who were forever waving their Bibles in the air and screaming warnings of eternal damnation—lacked the necessary intellect and temper for the task at hand.

"Well-meaning Englishmen who have been brought up in a somewhat narrow circle of thought and opinion are apt to make non-essentials into essentials, to the grievous hurt of the great cause," opined my great-grandfather—himself a Harrow boy—condescendingly.

The Anglicans thought themselves so different from their Protestant peers that one mission historian dubbed them "God's Gentlemen." They endeavoured to remain polite and unfailingly reasonable in the face of defiant heathenism, but they also adapted a tenuously tolerant stance towards *kastom.* Dancing, smoking, drinking *kava,* the payment of bride price, even membership in secret societies: none of these traditions was seen necessarily as a barrier to Christian salvation. Bishop Patteson told converts they should make up their own minds about them. As long as they pledged allegiance to the One True God, as long as their *kastom* didn't break the Ten Commandments, then islanders weren't necessarily *against* Christianity, even if they weren't altogether *for* it just yet. The Anglicans delighted in traditional dances and costumes. Some gained a fondness for *kava.* They prided themselves on their tolerance, and they pooh-poohed the Presbyterians, who had a habit of outlawing any practice that reminded them even faintly of paganism.

The Anglicans were determined to avoid the ungentlemanly squabbling that saw mission societies battling over various islands throughout the New Hebrides. After a few years of haggling, they agreed to leave the Loyalty Islands near New Caledonia to the London Missionary Society, and to let the Presbyterians and Roman Catholics fight over the southern islands of the New Hebrides—including Tanna and Efate. Selwyn and Patteson promised to concentrate on Espiritu Santo and points farther north.

For decades, the doctrine of "Christianity-with-civilization" had been an axiom for English missionaries around the world. The gospel was just one part of a curriculum that included aesthetic "improvements" such as the introduction of clothing, homes with separate bedrooms and encouragement to enter the market economy. But here in the South Seas, the Anglicans were concluding—at least on paper—that Melanesian social and cultural tradition could be one of the cornerstones of a strong Church.

R.H. Codrington (whose notes I had found in Oxford) went so far as to point out that *kastom* had already equipped Melanesians with a sense of right and wrong, a belief in life after death and a concept of something like a human soul. In other words, there was already some light in Melanesia before the missionaries arrived. *Kastom* had in fact provided the heathens with a good foundation for Christian teaching.

By the end of the century, many Anglicans had even dismissed the notion that "civilization" was a necessary companion to Christianity. They encouraged islanders not to adopt heavy clothing and not to become "imitation Europeans." While the Presbyterians were arresting Tannese dance troupes, the Anglicans were romancing *kastom*.

As for Tanna, I couldn't help feeling that it was the Presbyterians' 150-year crusade that had transformed the island into a psycho-spiritual Disneyland—that and the volcano's constant expressions of supernatural fury. The Presbyterians had allowed no middle ground, no compromise between *kastom* and Christianity, so the Tannese rebelled. There was never an official entente, even as the competing world views began to infect each other. The collision of the two systems buried the island's soul in an avalanche of discordant cosmology.

THE ANGLICAN ISLANDS would be different, I thought as I flew back to Port Vila. (Of course I flew: VanAir offered daily, air-conditioned flights between Tanna and the capital.) The spiritual realm of Anglican Melanesians would be infinitely less conflicted. God's Gentlemen would have eased their converts away from ghosts and magic while ever so politely applauding their quaint dances. Knowing this, I was not particularly keen to leave the cold beer and air conditioning of Port Vila for northern Vanuatu and Anglican territory.

That changed when I met Karen, a sales executive for one of Port Vila's posh hotels. She took me out for dinner so we could discuss her hotel's golf course.

Karen was a modern woman. She wore a smart blouse, navy skirt and perfume. She had shaved her legs. She was as thin and skittish as a model. We didn't talk about the golf course though, not after our first bottle of Chilean Merlot. Yes, Karen drank wine. In fact, she whispered, these days she even drank *kava*. She would sneak down to the *kava* bar near her house and down just enough of the bitter brew to cloud her mind and make her forget all that business about her husband. It had been a year since he had taken up with another woman, leaving Karen to fend for herself and their seven-year-old daughter.

"It's hard," she said as we sipped at our second bottle of red, "but I know if I trust in God, everything will work out. Now about the golf course . . ."

"This husband sounds like an unreliable man. Why would you want him back?"

"Because he never meant to leave me. He was tricked. The family of his new woman slipped him a magic potion. That potion made him forget me. It made him turn away from our daughter, too."

"How did you find out about this potion?" I asked, a little more engaged now.

"The new girl's parents confessed to me just last month. You see, now my husband and the girl are fighting. Her parents want to undo the love magic, but they can't. The potion was too strong. It was made by a sorcerer who lived under the volcano on Ambrym. Strong, strong, fire magic."

Karen poured herself more wine with her tiny hand and then took another gulp. "But don't you worry about me. My uncle is a sorcerer too. He is working in his village on Maewo to break the spell. I call him every week to give him updates."

It was common knowledge that the islands of Ambrym and Maewo, north of Efate, were sources of competing magic. The interior of Ambrym was dominated by a 20-kilometre-wide caldera of black ash and steaming volcanic vents. That's why it was called the island of fire magic. People everywhere were afraid of Ambrymese sorcerers, whose most infamous trick was to float into the homes of sleeping enemies, cut them open and pull out their guts, then replace them with leaves and sticks.

The victims showed no scarring, but they tended to cough up plenty of leaf mulch before their deaths, which usually occurred within a few days. In 1997, Prime Minister Fidel Soksok told the *Vanuatu Trading Post* that black magic and poison were the biggest obstacles to economic development in the country.

Karen assured me, however, that Maewo magic was much stronger than Ambrym magic. Maewo didn't have a volcano; it was a long spine of uplifted coral rock which squeezed torrential rains from every storm that came Vanuatu's way. Hundreds of fast-running streams tumbled down its flanks, and those streams gave Maewo magicians their power. Everybody knew, said Karen, that water magic could extinguish fire magic. It was only a matter of time before Karen's uncle from Maewo drew her man back.

Karen had a special bond with her uncle. When she was a little girl, he would cross the ocean from Maewo to visit her at her village on Pentecost. No, he didn't come by canoe, said Karen. He changed himself into an owl and he flew across the water. Mind you, he had to be careful never to fly over a church while in his owl body, because every church had a column of energy, like a ray of light, shooting up into the sky from its roof. If he flew over that ray, he would crash. So the uncle flew carefully but he flew often. When he reached Pentecost, he would sit in the breadfruit tree outside Karen's window.

"Um, Karen," I said. "You are Anglican and so is your uncle."

She squinted at me through reddened eyes. "Yes, of course. Very strong Anglican. We even chased the evangelical preachers out of our village when they came to talk to us. We told them, 'Leave our *kastom* alone. We are Anglican.' Oh yes, strong, strong Anglican. I go to church every Sunday."

"But *magic*, Karen. That's not allowed!"

"Why not? God made all the plants and herbs, so he must have made the magic in them as well. Magic is a lot like God, you know. You have to trust. You must have faith."

Karen had been educated in New Zealand. She was a modern woman. She had a business card, an e-mail address, and an uncle she insisted could fly. Perhaps Anglicans weren't so dull after all.

The next day I went looking for a boat headed north towards Espiritu Santo, the southern edge of Melanesia's Anglican heartland.

I FOUND THE MV *Brisk* at sunset, docked—or, rather, run up like a World War II troop transport—against a grassy wharf on Vila Bay. One look at her explained why the *Havanna* held such an exalted position among Melanesian cargo ships. The *Brisk* was more barge than ship; a shallow tub with all the crude geometry and elegance of a sheep dip. I couldn't imagine her navigating the house-high swells which we would surely hit on our four-day journey north to Espiritu Santo. But I no longer feared the sea. I had acquired a supply of motion-sickness pills.

We set sail after dusk. There were two dozen passengers on the open cargo deck. They built mounds of pallets and luggage on which they huddled like penguins on bergs. As we left the refuge of the harbour, I saw why. The *Brisk* rolled pleasantly enough in the swell, but waves spilled over her bow anyway. Gradually, the cargo deck filled with water until it was as deep as a wading pool. I climbed up to a makeshift roof of corrugated iron in front of the wheelhouse. A thin layer of cloud spread across the sky, like a veil thrown up to protect the moon from the sparkle and glare of the sea. A warm breeze ran over me. I dozed off to the murmurs of the crew, the rumbling of the engine, the whoosh of the waves and the rhythmic click and bang of the wheelhouse door, which opened and shut with each roll of the ship.

My dreams were peaceful at first. But then I drifted away from the *Brisk* and a forest grew up around me, and the knocking became the sound of tree branches jostling in the wind. I peered through the forest, through shadows that shifted across the moonlit earth, and there was the prophet Fred, sitting cross-legged, mumbling indecipherably and cradling a baby wrapped in gauze. A bloodstain appeared on the cloth and spread across it. I knew that Fred was performing another spontaneous circumcision. He raised his head and scowled at me. He had known all along I would betray him. The stain turned black and broke apart into a thousand tiny wings which rose from the cloth, swarming around me, droning in my ears, dancing around my eyes, landing on my neck. The mosquitoes prodded, poked, tested the surface with their invisible probosces, and then, one by one, they injected their poison into me. I was vaguely troubled by this, but it would take me weeks and a dozen islands to realize that such visions were part of the story I was chasing. My skin, though, began to itch even before I had awoken.

I dozed on the roof for three days as the *Brisk* bounced from island to island, threading together villages, mission stations and coconut plantations, running into dozens of sandy shores, dumping cement mixers, rice and rebar, collecting sack after sack of yam, taro and sweet potato. We headed north, following the protected lee sides of Efate and low-lying Epi. When we rounded the northern tip of Epi, we were broadsided by the southeast swell. The *Brisk* did not cut through the waves like the *Havanna*. It was lifted by them, carried up over their shivering crests and swept down again into canyon-like troughs. Those waves were unnaturally blue, the colour of transmission fluid. They lumbered. They were not violent. But they carried smaller waves which jostled, broke and exploded over the ship's bow until the cargo deck frothed and churned like a river in flood. We passed a volcanic cone which rose steeply into the clouds. That was Lopevi. We made three stops on Paama, a dark fin of black rock and jungle.

My skin itched. An angry rash had spread across my forearm. I wanted to leap into the ocean.

"You cannot swim at Paama," the ship's engineer told me. His name was Edwin. He was a rough man with cunning eyes and sores on his neck. "You will be eaten by the shark."

"They have sharks here?"

"Just one shark. A *kastom* shark. We call him a *nakaimo*. He is the spirit of a dead man, and he likes white flesh. He ate his first white man fifty years ago. I can swim here, but you can't. Ha!"

We crossed from Paama to Ambrym. Dark clouds hung over the island of fire magic, obscuring the rims of its great caldera. Codrington wrote that the heathens of Ambrym once buried their dead under the dirt floors of their homes. After the flesh had decayed, they unearthed the bones and hung them from the branches of trees. But a chief's corpse was too precious to leave outside. It held too much *mana*. It was placed in a canoe or a drum inside his house, where women and children could sleep close to it and remove the worms that inevitably crawled through the rotting flesh. After ten months, the skull, jawbone and a few of the departed chief's longer bones would be hung from the rafters. The rest would be buried at sea.

We slid through a gap in the reef that guarded Ambrym's west coast and stopped to pick up a couple of red-eyed men at a Catholic mission station. The passengers on deck stepped back—or rather, recoiled—to make room for the Ambrymese, who chuckled and cooed menacingly.

Another night. The *Brisk* chugged towards specks of light on the horizon which grew into shoreside bonfires as we approached. The fires, which had been lit by people who hoped to send or receive cargo, marked passages through unseen reefs.

I was not permitted to read or sleep. Men gathered round to eat my cookies and do what Melanesians like best, which is *storian* (story-on). Edwin, the engineer, was the bravest. He asked me if I liked island pussy. I sidestepped by asking him the first question most Melanesians usually ask strangers: "To which Church do you belong?" He was a Seventh-day Adventist. In other words, no *kava*, no alcohol, no promiscuity, no dirty talk, I said. Edwin admitted he broke all those rules. He was *wanfala backslider.*

There was another backslider on deck. Graeme was a handsome, neatly dressed man who cradled a young boy in his arms. He shook my hand and asked me what my business was. I told him I was following the route my great-grandfather had taken aboard the *Southern Cross*. His eyes narrowed.

"So that means your granddaddy stole my granddaddy, doesn't it?" Graeme asked in English.

"I suppose, um, yes."

"Yes, that is exactly what happened. I know the story. They took our granddaddies to New Zealand and taught them the *kastom* stories of Israel. Then our granddaddies came back to Pentecost and convinced everyone to join the Church. It was easy to do, because the teachers had knives and axes and tobacco, all the good things that foreigners had."

The crowd laughed jovially, but Graeme was earnest and breathless in his monologue. His eyes reflected the flame of an approaching fire. "Most people have forgotten that we once had our own god on Pentecost. Taka was his name. He helped us work magic to bring rain and food. Only a few people can do the magic now, but I am learning it. I go to the old *kastom* chiefs. I drink *kava* with them. We *storian*. They teach me."

"Teach you what? Magic? Show me," I said.

"I am just now learning magic. But I know how to make sweet mouth."

"Show me this sweet-mouth magic. I want to see it!"

The crowd exploded with shrieks of laughter.

"Sweet-mouth is magic for love," explained Graeme. "You rub a chicken feather on a special stone and then you say the name of the girl four times. After four days, she will come to you. She will follow you like a puppy."

"What about flying? Can you turn yourself into an owl or a flying fox?"

"No, I haven't learned that yet. But I will. And I will also learn how to swim under the ocean like a fish."

"So Graeme, you are not a Christian," I said.

"Oh yes, of course I am. All my family is Anglican."

GRAEME'S BRAND of fusional cosmology was hardly unique to Melanesia.

The Roman Catholic Church, in particular, has mastered the art of overlooking the lingering heathen habits of their flocks. As early as the seventeenth century, Catholic missionaries in the lower Congo Valley were compelled to turn a blind eye while their converts made offerings to their ancestors, particularly during the Christian holiday of All Souls' Day.

In Brazil, a generation of jungle prophets combined African ritual, Christianity and a powerful psychoactive tea to spawn at least three new proto-Christian Churches in the latter half of the twentieth century. The tea, known as *hoasca* in Brazil and *ayahuasca* elsewhere, was brewed from the bark of a rain-forest vine. It was once an essential tool of pre-Christian shamans, but it has now replaced wine as the new Churches' sacrament. Church leaders say tea drinkers experience direct contact with the divine, though it almost always induces vomiting and cataclysmic diarrhea.

A similar kind of psychosyncretism has occurred in the Southwest United States, where the Native American Church adopted peyote—a small, spineless cactus also considered a tool in pre-Christian shamanic ritual—as its own sacrament. The group still combines its hallucinogenic pre-Christian ritual with biblical teachings and has been credited with reducing alcoholism in Native American communities.

Spiritual syncretism naturally bothers fundamentalist Christians. If theirs is the one true religion, then to water it down and distort it must certainly be blasphemous. Of course, some of these theological hard-liners also happen to be the most likely to cling to a version of Christianity that has created an image of a tall, pale, decidedly un-Jewish Jesus.

Modern Anglican theologians have adopted a more nuanced stance. A black Christ? No problem. Rejigged pagan dances and grass skirts in church? Sure. Ancestor worship? Well . . .

There is a library devoted entirely to new versions of Christianity at Selly Oak Colleges, in a leafy suburb of Birmingham, England. After a day in that library, I met a Nigerian Anglican priest and theology student who told me that yes, of course, he and his parishioners still worshipped their ancestors.

"I thought all that stuff was against the rules," I said.

"Rules?" he chortled. "Look, when the missionaries first came to Africa, they saw us worshipping our forefathers and they called it idolatry. They condemned us for it. But we soon realized Jesus was an ancestor shared by all of us. That is the Christian message, isn't it? Jesus was human and he was also divine. So now we do not feel at all bad about worshipping our ancestors along with Jesus in church. I trust you won't belittle this. After all, you are the one who has followed the ghost of your ancestor to England. Your great-grandfather has spoken and now you are following him. Good for you. Listen to him."

Melanesians, however, took their syncretism to mind-numbing heights. A teacher at Fiji's University of the South Pacific told me that his housekeeper was a devout churchgoing woman who also believed in shark gods. The same teacher gave one of his students several months' extension on an assignment so that the boy could return to Vanuatu to battle a band of sorcerers in his hometown. An Australian woman working in Papua

New Guinea was told by a Melanesian colleague that he could solve her romantic troubles by having his brother turn into a crocodile that would eat her problem boyfriend. Christians, all of them. Educated people like Graeme and Karen and Stanley were weaving together competing belief systems. Which system was more powerful? It wasn't Christianity that was producing their daily miracles.

Were these people fools? Daydreamers? Liars? I was disoriented and strangely compelled by their stories, but I wanted more. The idea of magic was beginning to obsess me.

I closed my eyes. I made a self-conscious prayer to the stars, asking for this magic to show itself to me. I wasn't looking for biblical miracles. I wanted to feel the *mana* that once and perhaps still surrounded these islands, seethed through their forests, flowed through the hands of their sorcerers and made believers out of Melanesians, even as I was certain it had never existed, even as I chastised myself for imagining it was more than a fantasy.

As the constellations turned in the clear sky above me, the rash on my arm began to spread. Sores like tiny red stars appeared on my shoulder, my back and my abdomen. When the sun rose again, its light felt like knives stabbing through my eyelids. My bones ached, and I trembled at the thought that Graeme was wrong, that the secret power that had once lurked in these islands was fiction—or if it had existed at all, it was now dead, nothing more than a puff of nostalgia that comforted Graeme as he nodded off in the back row of his village church.

6

THE BOOK OF

ESPIRITU SANTO

The green and stagnant waters lick his feet,
And from their filmy, iridescent scum
Clouds of mosquitoes, gauzy in the heat,
Rise with His gifts: Death and Delirium

LAURENCE HOPE, "Malaria" in *India's Love Lyrics*

T DAWN on the fourth morning, the MV *Brisk* tied up at Luganville, on the southern end of Espiritu Santo. This was the end of the run. I did not intend to stay long. Luganville was supposed to be Vanuatu's preeminent port and a jumping-off point for the Banks and Torres Islands on the country's northern frontier, not to mention Maewo, the island of water magic. But the harbour was nearly empty. Luganville was also touted as a bustling commercial hub; however, when I stumbled off the *Brisk* I found a town not so much empty as anaesthetized. There were a hundred broken hedgerows, a hundred empty lots, a hundred rusting Quonset huts collapsing in the grass. There was a boarded-up cinema. There was an empty park with an empty bandstand, from which a loud-speaker blared country gospel songs to no one in particular. Luganville's lethargy was so thorough that nobody I met could be bothered to wrap their lips around the town's full name, let alone the full name of the island. Both were reduced to a tired grunt. Santo.

It hadn't always been this way. This shore had once seen unimaginable wealth. It had served a war. It had nurtured a revolution.

In June 1942, U.S. warships steamed into Santo's Segond Channel. It took the Americans five days to build their first airstrip. Then came two more bomber runways, a dozen wharves, a giant floating dock, hospitals, workshops, stores, factories, laboratories and barracks for a hundred thousand men, all of whom had plenty of money and spare time to spend on beer and women. Almost overnight, sleepy Santo became the primary staging area for the war against Japan. The locals were outnumbered twenty to one, and they were awed by the display of power and wealth.

The carnival ended as abruptly as it had begun. The Americans started packing their bags as soon as they had pushed the Japanese back across the Pacific. Problem was, their ships just couldn't carry all the bulldozers, trucks, engines, furniture and refrigerators they had brought to Luganville, but they couldn't just give them all away—if they did, the goods would certainly be dispersed across the South Pacific through the black market, and American manufacturers wouldn't be able to sell anything new in the region for years. The New Hebrides government bought a few buildings and bulldozers. The Americans dumped everything else into Segond Channel. By the end of 1945, heaps of junk covered the area of five football fields below the tide line.

Melanesians were used to seeing chiefs demonstrate their rank by staging great feasts at which they gave away years of accumulated wealth. But this was awe-inspiring. In an instant, all the wealth and excitement the Americans had conjured from the sea had disappeared again into the deep, like magic. It was the most audacious display of power the islanders had ever seen. Starry-eyed, they returned to their villages and the coconut plantations of their French employers, who exhibited little of the Americans' wealth or generosity and who had been quick to grab land that Melanesians had vacated during the war. Naturally, islanders fantasized about America's return. Naturally, they pined for the day that soldiers would land with more planes and jeeps and bulldozers, this time to free Melanesians from their colonial masters. The obsession with America grew, crested and got the better of Santo islanders just as they were about to achieve independence from British and French rule.

The movement, known as Nagriamel, began reasonably enough. Its founders wanted to take back the vast tracts of land to which Europeans had obtained title but never developed. In the late 1960s, the Nagriamel leader, Jimmy Stephens, led hundreds of people onto French-titled land in the bush near Luganville, where he set up a model town. But Nagriamel soon became mired in cargo mythology. Stephens's followers took to calling him Chief President Moses (he had, after all, led them into the proverbial wilderness and built a chapel for the Church of Christ). However, unlike the biblical Moses, Stephens kept a stable of concubines, one of whom, according to rumour, became pregnant by the Holy Spirit and bore a son called Jesus Christ, who disappeared shortly after birth. It was also widely believed that American battalions were massing in caves under the island, revving their jeep engines, waiting to roar out and help Stephens run the colonialists off Santo. Some followers began constructing roads so that American cargo might reach inland settlements.

In fact, Stephens did gain support from America. His source was the Phoenix Foundation, a group of Carson City, Nevada, real estate developers who had been trying for years to find a suitable place to build a capitalist mini-state. The foundation's leader, Michael Oliver, had built a cement platform on a reef near Tonga in 1972 and named it the Republic of Minerva. The King of Tonga sent out work crews to demolish the new tax-free country. Oliver was not deterred. The next year, he tried to cleave an island from the Bahamas before its independence from Britain, but he couldn't get his revolutionary army trained in time. Then, Oliver set his sights on Espiritu Santo. He tried to forge an alliance between Nagriamel and Santo's French planters. As unholy as the plan appeared, the planters actually preferred Stephens's potentially malleable anarchy to the rule of the Anglican-dominated Vanua'aku Party, which had won Vanuatu's first free elections in 1979.

Stephens and his followers staged their revolt shortly after the polls closed. Armed with bows and arrows, bankrolled by planters and mentored by the Phoenix Foundation, they blocked Santo's airport, ran the police off from their small station and proclaimed the new nation of Venerama. They even had a constitution, penned by a Phoenix Foundation lawyer. But the Nagriamel rebellion was short-lived. Upon Vanuatu's independence in 1980, the Vanua'aku government invited troops from Papua New Guinea to crush the rebellion. Stephens was jailed and Espiritu Santo's cargo dream died for good.

The French planters were long gone. Santo now felt like a South Pacific version of an abandoned prairie town. Its one paved avenue might have crumbled to dust and been blown away entirely if not for the trading posts that anchored it. Two dozen Chinese stores lined Santo's one paved avenue, each tended by a granny in pyjamas and each stocked with the same selection of corned beef, flip-flops, yellowing braziers and Bob Marley T-shirts. Wong Store. Shing Yau Store. Ah Yuen and Company. Every now and then a beat-up minibus sputtered down the middle of the avenue.

The Hotel Santo stood in the middle of all this sleepiness like a relic of misplaced post-war optimism. With its earthquake-proof buttresses and modernist aspirations, the hotel could have been lifted from the outskirts of 1955 Las Vegas. So could its owner, a terse and strangely elegant half-caste woman who was constantly disappearing to change her outfit. No one else in Santo could be bothered, but Mary Jane Dinh kept up appearances. She had white cotton jumpsuits for morning coffee, floral-print dresses for the afternoon and a series of exquisite silk gowns for cocktails. Her necklaces were just right. She wore gold earrings and Liz Taylor frog glasses. She sipped white wine before dinner with a posse of rumpled expatriates. Mary Jane had seen the French plantation owners run out of Santo and the Australians buy in. She had rebuffed Jimmy Stephens's flirtations after he was freed from jail. She told me she had run the hotel by herself for two decades.

Mary Jane also told me she knew malaria when she saw it. And she saw it in my face.

I was heartened by her diagnosis. By the time the *Brisk* had ground into shore at the edge of town, the rash that had begun as an artful smattering of stars on my arm had spread across my body. The stars were so numerous they had lost their form and blended into one another, and my skin was one vast welt. My body sizzled with fever. My head ached. I was dizzy. The sky had broken apart into fluorescent pixels, but the sun had fallen towards the earth and grown spines.

Santo had the only hospital in all of northern Vanuatu. I hoped that Mary Jane would take me there in her car, holding my hand, whispering reassurances all the way. She did not.

"There's no need for hysteria," she said, hustling me out to a cab. "Malaria's as common here as the flu."

The government supported a small army of nurses whose sole task was to gaze through microscopes at drops of blood, looking for the tiny, thread-like plasmodium parasites that female mosquitoes are so good at injecting into humans. One such nurse determined that five per cent of my red blood cells had been consumed by the parasite. If I were Melanesian, said my doctor, I would have built up a resistance to the disease, and I wouldn't have to worry about dying from the fever or the cranial swelling that the worst strains of malaria produced. But I was a white man, an autoimmune weakling. The doctor insisted that I stay at the hospital. I gazed around at the peeling walls, the spit-smeared cement, the twittering cockroaches, the torn fly screens, the noses dripping with phlegm, the flickering fluorescent lights. I thanked him, then collected my plastic bag full of pills and retreated to the Hotel Santo.

I found Mary Jane taking coffee on the veranda with her sunburned posse. They were Australian, so they were drinking beer. One was a cattle rancher. Another was a retired agriculturist who was very keen to discuss yam productivity. There was also a man with a walrus moustache. He owned a little Cessna which he flew north to all the airstrips in the Banks and Torres Islands. Wherever he went, the walrus man would unload his lawnmower and trim the grass. It was a very important job, said the man's wife, because the Ni-Vanuatu needed their airstrips. Few ships bothered to travel to the northern islands any more. Why would they? There was no cargo to carry, other than the odd bag of low-grade copra (the kiln-dried coconut flesh that once had fuelled the South Pacific economy).

I did not want to hear these things. Nukapu, my grail, lay only a couple of days' sail north of the Torres Islands. But it was becoming hard to care about the geography beyond the Hotel Santo. I just listened and swayed and let the sweat roll off the tip of my nose.

The lawnmower man looked at me quizzically and slapped his knee. "Mary Jane!" he barked through his moustache. "Lookitem! The boy can barely stand straight. Har! The malariar's got 'em. Get 'em a beer at once."

I shuffled off to my room, irritated by the amusement Mary Jane's posse took from my exotic and possibly deadly malaise—and yet feeling vaguely heroic for having caught it. Hadn't malaria crippled empires, murdered conquistadors and baffled healers for thousands of years? Hadn't it been blamed for killing half the people who ever walked the planet?

It was malaria, not poison arrows, that had finished off the Spaniard Mendaña on Santa Cruz. Ironically, the cure for malaria would eventually come from the explorer's departure point, Peru, though it wasn't until half a century after Mendaña's death that Andean Indians introduced the Spanish to the shrub whose bark eased tropical fevers. By the 1840s, exports of *quina quina* bark to Europe were worth £1 million. Without the bark, and later its active component, the alkaloid quinine, the British Empire would never had held onto its possessions in India or Africa. By the end of the century, the British Army was consuming 750 tons of the bark per year in India alone. No wonder tonic water laced with quinine—and gin, of course—emerged as the quintessential British drink.

In 1906, when writer Jack London arrived in Melanesia on his attempt to sail around the world, the crew of his 55-foot ketch were still arguing about the benefits of quinine pills, even as they were struck helpless by fever, chills and diarrhea. "Everybody had fever, everybody had dysentery, everybody had everything. Death was common," he wrote shortly before giving up his adventure. London had no fear of hyperbole, but he did take his quinine tablets.

I swallowed four tablets of chloroquine (quinine's synthetic descendant), turned on the ceiling fan and lay down on my bed. I had nothing to read but the King James Bible, which a cousin had pushed into my backpack ("So you can understand your great-grandfather," she had said).

It took an hour or so for the chloroquine to hit. When it did, it felt as though it was joining forces with the malaria rather than fighting it. It stole my sense of balance. It gave me cotton balls for fingertips and needles for nerve ends. It seeped into my brain like a yellowing fog, then wrapped itself tightly around my eyeballs until I could not focus on any-thing more than a couple of metres away. But I could still read.

The next four days passed in a series of grand hallucinations, inter-rupted only by the chattering of my teeth and the occasional lunge for the toilet. I turned pages with damp fingers. The Old Testament rose around me in a phantasmagoria of dream, delirium and liquid vision, all spinning through my skull to the rhythmic hiss and click of the ceiling fan.

I saw the god make two great lights, one to rule the day and a lesser one to rule the night. The god gathered a handful of dust and pressed that dust into a shape with arms and legs. Then the god breathed life into that shape and called it man. I drifted through the garden, saw the oily glint of the serpent's scales and the shamed flight of man and woman. I saw the flaming sword, spinning in all directions to keep them out. I saw the face of Mary Jane in the blinding light of my window, a vision from a Kennedy cocktail party, flickering like a Super-8 angel. Somewhere a loudspeaker crackled and echoed a call to prayer.

Genesis. Exodus. Reggae from a distant bar. Abraham's knife, raised above the delicate throat of his son.

I didn't eat. I floated above Sinai, where the god opened a hole in the earth to swallow those who doubted its word. The god spoke to men through ghosts and spirits. It came to Moses as a cloud and then a firestorm. It thundered in his ears: *I will send my terror in front of you.*

This was a god of war. It told its followers to kill everyone in their path, and when they were not strong or merciless enough to kill, the god used its invisible hand to dash enemy armies to pieces, or to place un-speakable sores on their genitals, or to incinerate them with bolts of fire. The killing flooded my room with a series of gory tableaux. The fan turned above my head, spinning the years away. There were rivers of blood. The ashes of the dead fluttered in the wind. It went on for cen-turies. And then, suddenly, forty-two generations after the reign of Abra-ham, in the first book of the New Testament, in the first verse of the Gospel according to St. Matthew, at dawn on the fourth morning of my convalescence, at the apex of my fever, the divine tide of violence stopped.

The miracles became humbler. There was the man-god, calming the sea. There he was, turning water into wine. There he was on the mountaintop. He spoke softly, but his voice was lifted and carried by the breeze. *Just love each other.* He said this over and over, and the idea somehow became its own miracle. It was as though the god of vengeance, favouritism and thunderbolts had fallen asleep.

Dawn came as a faint glow through the curtains of my room. Then the piercing glare of day. Then, always in the afternoon, a tapping on the roof and the smell of rain. Then darkness again, and more dreams shot through with miracles and dust and blood, and in those dreams I recognized the twinned god of my own family. A god who took sides, who helped them smite their enemies yet claimed to love and forgive even those he cast into the wilderness. God had two faces. My ancestors claimed to have been guided by the god of love, but from their stories I suspected they were fired by the god of war. Time and again they asked for their god's help in battle. They offered their god thanks for every victory their clan ever won and for the spoils they enjoyed in peace. My ancestors wove their certainty into their own myth, which was every bit as bloody as the Old Testament.

This is how they told it: They once worshipped the moon and the sun, and fire too. Their eyes were blue-grey and cold as the fjords of their Scandinavian homeland. A thousand years after the crucifixion of Jesus, the children of the Nordic warrior Gomeric wandered south to the coast of France, and there they were introduced to the god of war and love, whom they embraced.

They traded their heathen names for ones that better suited baptized Christians. The warrior-wanderer Biorn Dansk became Bernard Danus— Bernard the Dane—and he ruled over vast tracts of Normandy from a hilltop fortress. Bernard's clan honoured the god by taking care of churches and monasteries, and that is why they prospered in an era of assassination, treason, violence and plundering.

The Dane's great, great-grandson, Roger de Montgomery, sailed across the English Channel with William the Conqueror in 1066. William wanted the English throne, and he had the Roman Catholic Church on his side. Roger lent sixty ships to the enterprise. Once they reached England, Roger marched into the Battle of Hastings at William's right flank. At the height of the fighting, an English giant led a charge of one hundred men against the invading Normans. That English knight was as strong and swift as a stag. As he ran, he swung his great axe and slew himself a path of dead Normans with its foot-long blade. He drove that axe through the neck of a horse, dragging its rider to the ground. The Normans were shocked and awed, and ready to turn back, but Roger de Montgomery saved the day. He galloped up on his own horse and, without a thought for that great axe, drove his lance right through the English giant, knocking him down just as David had knocked down Goliath. Then he cried out: "Frenchmen, strike, the day is ours!" The English armies were humiliated, their king was sent to hell and the Normans planted their holy flag on the bloodied earth. And so it was that God delivered England to William the Conqueror and to my ancestors.

Roger was handed three counties. He was grateful to his god, even after discovering that, in his absence, his wife in Normandy had been beheaded in her bedchamber; even after learning that his first son had had both eyes poked out with a red-hot blade. Roger channelled the spoils of war to the Church. He built an abbey at Shrewsbury, to which he attached a Benedictine monastery. His grandsons honoured their god by pillaging their way towards the Holy Land on Louis VII's Second Crusade.

Six hundred years later, after Henry VIII had cleaved the Church of England from the Roman Church, Roger's descendants fought their way into Ireland, where Protestant armies were being handed huge estates for their loyalty to the crown and the Church of England. James Montgomery, an Anglican curate, fought the Irish Catholics with a Bible in one hand and a sword in the other. The Montgomerys built a grand estate on the Inishowen Peninsula, where, to this day, they collect rent from the Catholics.

When the British Empire spread to India, Montgomerys followed and brought their god with them. After the East India Company named him commissioner of Lahore in 1849, Robert Montgomery built himself a sprawling stone villa in the Punjab. His servants were Muslim and Hindu. So were his troops, and so were his enemies.

In 1857, Indian regiments of the East India Company's Bengal Army rebelled, killing hundreds of white soldiers and colonists, and capturing Delhi. British schoolbooks refer to the uprising as a mutiny. Indian schoolbooks call it the First War of Indian Independence. Some said it was triggered when the British furnished the soldiers with cartridges coated with grease made from the fat of cows (sacred to Hindus)—and of pigs (anathema to Muslims). In this, the Indian soldiers saw evidence that the British were trying to convert them to Christianity.

The rebellion spread rapidly through north-central India. Robert worried the winds of revolution would sweep west from Delhi towards his base in the Punjab. He didn't trust his Indian soldiers, so he ordered tens of thousands of them to the parade grounds in Lahore. Before the soldiers knew what was happening, Robert's white garrisons had surrounded them with cannons. The Indians were told to lay down their guns. They obeyed. Robert ordered his officers across the district to march disobedient regiments straight into the stockade—and, naturally, to blow to pieces any soldiers who refused. The Delhi rebels were chased down and hanged, the white garrisons were saved and the Punjab became the base for the Britain's reconquest of northern India.

Robert later explained his god's role in the conflict: "It was not policy, or soldiers, or officers that saved the Indian Empire to England, and saved England to India. The Lord our God, He it was who went before us and gave us the victory of our enemies, when they had well nigh overwhelmed us. To Him who holds all events in His own hand, and has so wondrously over-ruled all to our success, and to His own glory do I desire on behalf of myself and all whom I represent to express my devout and heartfelt thanks."

It was just like the Old Testament. My family's god was not detached from politics. The Lord stood for England and vice versa. Our version of this story does not mention the thousands upon thousands of Indians who died at the hands of the British and their allies.

Two years before the rebellion, Robert ushered his eight-year-old son, Henry, into the sitting room of their Indian villa. They knelt down together in the marbled shadows, and Robert prayed that God would take care of the boy. Then he sent him home to England. Henry attended an evangelical preparatory school which stressed the lessons of Revelations. The future Bishop of Tasmania was brought up on regular doses of undiluted hellfire. "On the whole such diet has done me immense good," he later mused, "for it has left behind in me an awful sense of the Holy Will of God. The thunders of Sinai should not be forgotten by any Christian."

If the Old Testament taught Henry about his god's power and the New Testament taught him about his god's love, then it was the Victorian era which taught him that the English were God's new chosen people. Henry was convinced that his race was ideally suited to saving the world—that is, teaching English manners, morals and spirituality with the same resolve with which England spread its commerce. And why wouldn't he think so? As far as Henry had seen, God clearly favoured the British Empire above all others, granting Queen Victoria dominion over lands, seas and peoples from Africa to the Americas to Australia.

"Englishmen would do well to remember that their wonderful supremacy throughout the world is due in great measure to the existence of races inferior to their own," he wrote. The point, which he made often, was that it was England's God-given duty to nurture the lesser races.

In 1901, Henry Montgomery was named secretary of the Society for the Propagation of the Gospel in Foreign Parts, which made him the most influential Anglican missionary in the world and a sort of foreign minister for the Archbishop of Canterbury. He fought for years to formally bond the Empire and its Church in one common evangelical mission. He once told a congregation in St. Paul's Cathedral that all over the world, dark faces looked gratefully towards the unselfish builders of the British Empire and that a special crown in heaven awaited the English missionaries who suffered hot, damp places in the service of their god.

The bishop passed on his faith to his children. But he must also have passed on his certainty that, even when it came to killing, God could be petitioned for favours. One of his sons entered the priesthood. Another became a war hero. In 1942, Field Marshal Bernard Montgomery led the Eighth Army into battle against Rommel in North Africa. After routing the Nazis at El Alamein—and effectively turning the tide of the Second World War—the field marshal issued a reminder to his troops: "Before the battle began I sent you a message in which I said: Let us pray that the Lord mighty in battle will give us the victory. He has done so and I know you will agree with me when I say that we must not forget to thank him for his great mercies."

This was the god of my ancestors, the myth that Henry Montgomery had carried across the ocean to deliver to a people who would consume it, make it their own, let it flood their dreams, change their magic and guide their lives. I did not yet understand that the struggle between the god of war and the god of love, which lived as vividly in the story of my family as it did in the Bible, was still being played out in Melanesia. I did not understand that my journey north would draw me into it, force me to take sides, wound me and change me. For the moment, I did not fight the miracles that swept through my own dreams as I rolled and sweated, certain in my doubt and yet surging with the fever of vision, the emboldening tingle of closeness to something unseen, the immeasurable longing, the anticipation of a diver before the leap.

On the fifth morning I awoke to dry sheets. My fever was gone.

7

THE WORD
AND ITS MEANING

Every day, every week, every month, every quarter, the most widely read
journals seem just now to vie with teach other in telling us that
the time for religion is past, that faith is a hallucination or an infantile disease,
that the gods have at last been found out and exploded.

MAX MULLER, *Lectures on the Origin and Growth of Religion*, 1878

OME PEOPLE use the word "myth" to describe stories they think are fanciful and false. That is not how I wish to use it, because I am learning how hard it can be to discern the frontiers between history, propaganda, dreams and the terrain of miracles. And besides, the power of a myth has more to do with its function than its historic origin.

Here is my definition. Myth: a story, often involving the expression of supernatural power, which explains its believers' relationship with the world.

What, then, is the difference between the Christian belief in an intervening god and the Melanesians' traditional belief in spirits, stones and sorcery? If you believe any of it, you may as well give all of it a chance: the fires of Sinai; the army-smiting staff of Moses; the rainmaking rocks of Tanna; the miracles of Jesus, John Frum and the prophet Fred; the angels descending, the sorcerers flying like bats into the steel grey night. If you say that the god-ancestor Qat is a mythical character, then you must also agree that Bernard the Dane is too, and so are John Frum, Jesus and John Coleridge Patteson, because regardless of their historic origins, they have been kept alive in stories in order to perform various mythic functions. They represent certain ideals. They inspire. They offer their believers clues about the nature of the universe. Et cetera.

The line between truth and fiction is entirely dependant on the observer's faith, as opposed to any empirical evidence he or she might have gathered or witnessed.

Even the Greeks, those titans of mythmaking and rhetoric, had a hell of a time making sense of the relationship between so-called rational truth and their traditional religious beliefs. Some Greek philosophers claimed that all those stories about neurotic gods and tragic heroes were allegories meant to illustrate aspects of a moral code. The Roman Emperor Julian regarded myths as divine truths whose mysteries were only apparent to the very wise (among whom Julian included himself, naturally). Others insisted myths were fabrications, introduced to bolster the authority of priests and rulers. The Greek philosopher Euhemerus argued that myths were all built on shreds of historical fact. They really were based on the lives of great men and women.

The Greeks' arguments have been recycled and embellished in the last century and a half. At about the time my great-grandfather was sailing through the South Pacific, his countrymen were digesting Sir James G. Frazer's *The Golden Bough,* in which the Cambridge anthropologist reduced magic, myths and religion to primitive and futile attempts to control the natural world. Charles Darwin's *The Origin of Species* had already shaken the foundations of Christian fundamentalism. Now Frazer was placing Christian texts under the same microscope as "primitive" religion and assuring readers that science and technology would inevitably extinguish the superstition inherent in all this mythology.

Myth has had a hard time since then. Most of the people who studied and wrote about myth during the twentieth century focussed on their function and structure, while generally accepting their factual falsity. (The Bible is a curious exception: Christian scholars and archaeologists continue to scour the ancient texts and the rubble of the Holy Land for proof of the historicity of the miraculous resurrection of Jesus.)

Myth had no greater enemy than Sigmund Freud. After reducing our dreams to mere manifestations of unconscious fears and delusions, the father of psychoanalysis projected his theories onto the divine. Myths, he argued, were all public dreams. Ghosts, heroes, magic, miracles and gods were nothing more than expressions of collective neuroses. They were baggage that needed to be shed in order to get to the truth of things.

The first argument against this theory came from Melanesia. Bronislaw Malinowski, the Polish anthropologist who spent the years of the First World War in the Trobriand Islands, was certain that for the communities he studied, myths were essential tools for expressing values and safeguarding morality. They may not have contained historical truths, but they were nonetheless a vital ingredient of civilization.

Freud's one-time protegé, Carl Jung, would later agree with Malinowski, but from a psychological rather than a sociological point of view. Jung argued that myths represented the wisdom the human species had gathered over the millennia. Myths contained essential truths which the "collective unconscious" had carried for generations and which science should never be allowed to displace. Thou shalt not kill. Honour thy father and thy mother. Do not marry your sister.

Jung's idea may explain why there is a common underlying structure to myths from various corners of the world. Creation stories are a good example. In Genesis, Yahweh shaped man from dust. In Banks Island *kastom* stories, the ancestor Qat carved man from a hunk of wood. A serpent in the Garden of Eden convinced Adam and Eve to taste the forbidden fruit. A snake did the same thing to the first man and woman in the legends of the Bassari in West Africa. The great flood is the most universal myth of them all: the Greeks and Romans told of a cataclysmic flood that transformed the world, but so did indigenous people on Canada's west coast. Qat made a deluge too. It spilled out from the volcano on Santa Maria and carried him away forever.

The American mythologist Joseph Campbell went a step further. He insisted the first mythmakers knew they were creating great allegories to help people understand the nature of their souls and their relationship

with the universe. The Garden of Eden was not a lush corner of Meso-
potamia so much as it was a description of the geography of the human
soul. It is the place of innocence that lies within all of us, the place we cannot return to because we have tasted the knowledge of good and evil.

Of course, all of these theories wound myths, because even as they
value them they defang them with their deconstruction. A myth without
believers is merely a fairy tale. It is a fiction, stripped of its sacredness. It is
mere entertainment.

After decades studying the tribes of southern Sudan, the pioneering
social anthropologist Edward Evan Evans-Pritchard returned to Oxford
in the 1960s and announced that non-believers would never come close to
understanding religion and myth as well as believers. Non-believers
tended to try to explain religion away as illusion, using sociological, psychological, existential or biological theories. (It's what most anthropologists had been doing for decades, despite the fact that, in the absence of
historical evidence, they had absolutely no way of knowing whether the
spiritual beings of primitive religions existed or not.) Believers, on the
other hand, explained religion in terms of how people conceived and related to their reality. Since believers of all kinds have an inward experience
of religion, they understand it better than non-believers. Thus, even a
missionary would make a better anthropologist among pagans than an
atheist. While the atheist might find allegories or codes for living, the believer experiences epiphanies, tendrils of some divine thread.

I was discovering this in Melanesia. As soon as you stand apart from
myths, divorce them from faith, pick apart their function and their origins, you become like an anthropologist, like Frazer peering through his
ancient texts. You may be fascinated and amused, but you will never see a
ghost, or magic, or the hand of God, because you have stepped outside
the realm of faith. People say that religious fanatics are blinded by their
faith. Evans-Pritchard asserted that there is something just as blinding in
rationalism.

The difference between myself and the people I had met in Vanuatu was not just that they held fast to their faith in magic and God. It
was not a clash between Christian and pagan—no, the Christians and
pagans stood together with my great-grandfather and against me in this

confrontation—but a meeting between believers and someone knocked free of the solid footing that myth may once have provided. It was a meeting of faith and lack of faith. Melanesians, like my great-grandfather, knew they were not alone in the world. They held their stories sacred. I did not. They were believers. I was not. I was sure they were all wrong about their magic. But the more time I spent among the believers, the further I ventured through the archipelago of miracles, the harder it was becoming to keep hold of my scepticism. With every saltwater crossing, with every cup of *kava*, every sweaty night, every fitful dream, I felt myself sinking into their ocean, letting myself imagine that men could make rain or transform themselves into owls, sharks and gods. You must accept mystery in order to reach for it.

8

MAEWO:

MAGIC AND FEAR

And, behold, the Lord passed by, and a great and strong wind rent
the mountains, and brake in pieces the rocks before the Lord;
but the Lord was not in the wind: and after the wind an earthquake;
but the Lord was not in the earthquake: And after the earthquake a fire; but the
Lord was not in the fire: and after the fire a still small voice.

1 Kings 19:11–12

YOU NEED to employ certain amount of guile if
you are going to convince people to show you
their magic. I learned that on Maewo, but not
until I had slighted, alienated or angered anyone who might have been
my conduit to the supernatural side of the island of water magic. I tried
appealing to their egos. I tried shaming them. I told them I could write a
story that would bring them American tourists. I begged. All mistakes. I
suppose I did not have my wits about me. The malarial haze hadn't quite
worn off the morning I left the Hotel Santo.

A passage north by boat was out of the question. It had been six
months since a cargo ship had made the rounds of the Banks and Torres
Islands, and it would likely be another six before another did. I had no
choice but to carry on by plane. VanAir sent a mail plane north from Espiritu Santo to each of the larger islands at least once each week, barring

storms. VanAir also flew east to Maewo, which had drawn me ever since Karen had told me about her sorcerer uncle. I decided to give the island of water magic a week to prove itself.

At Pekoa, the last of Santo's WWII airfields, I climbed inside a scuffed de Havilland Twin Otter along with a dozen other passengers, a clutch of grass mats and twenty sacks of rice. We bounced off the tarmac, and the plane's shadow danced away between the tidy rows of coconut palms, through a herd of cattle, over a dusty road and into a powder blue bay. We glided over a coral reef that stretched like a pink stain along the coast, over the rust-red skeletons of wrecked ships and over the open sea, which was rippling and empty and expectant.

My seatmate peered over my shoulder. His name was Alfred, and he happened to be a brother of the Right Reverend Hugh Blessing Boe, the Anglican Bishop of Vanuatu. Alfred was proud of his famous brother, but he was even prouder of his other brother, whose name was Dudley. Not only did Dudley own a truck—one of four on Maewo—but he was a *kleva*, a tremendously powerful *kastom* medicine man. When the previous prime minister of the Solomon Islands had heart trouble, it was Dudley who healed him. Dudley could make the ocean spill over the land, said Alfred. He could dump sea snakes into the coconut groves.

"Do they get along, Dudley and the bishop?"

"Yes, they do. Why do you ask?"

"Because of the magic, of course."

I had met Bishop Boe in Santo. He was a kind fellow, and smart too. I had asked him about the persistence of traditional magic in Vanuatu. The bishop told me (and I was sure he meant it as a criticism) that many Melanesians still used religion as a kind of technology. For example, if a man was sick, he would see a medical doctor, but he would also ask a priest to pray for him. If that didn't work, the man would turn to traditional magic or make a sacrifice to some kind of spirit. Sometimes he would pursue all three methods at the same time. Sometimes, said the bishop with a sigh, Melanesians had trouble separating what was God from what was not God.

Now, yelling above the drone of the propellers, Alfred told me what Bishop Boe had not. It was the bishop who had advised the prime minister of the Solomon Islands to see his brother the *kleva* about his heart trouble.

"Dudley's magic is not against the Church. It is a gift from God. It's his work. It's how he paid for his truck," explained Alfred.

Maewo had become a regular stop for the *Southern Cross* after the missionaries discovered a waterfall on its west coast where the ship could fill her tanks with fresh water. Henry Montgomery landed there in October 1892 to find a French cutter up on the rocks, its cargo long gone. Blood was smeared on the mainmast. The officers had been murdered by their Melanesian crew. Henry later reported the incident in Vila and, though the facts of the case were unknown, a French man-of-war was promptly dispatched to bomb the hell out of the nearest village.

After half an hour, Maewo appeared beneath us like the serrated back of a surfacing crocodile. The pilot banked the Twin Otter into a steep, descending arc. We landed on an airstrip whose grass was as tall and robust as prairie wheat. Dudley was waiting for us. He was no withered mystic. In fact, he seemed altogether plain for a witch doctor. He had the capable appearance of a roofing contractor or a mailman. He must have been about forty. He chain-smoked Peter Jacksons under a drooping moustache.

Alfred and I climbed into the box of Dudley's Mitsubishi. Dudley drove. We followed a cart track south along Maewo's leeward coast. The landscape reminded me of the greenhouse at the Royal Botanical Gardens at Kew, only more lush, more surreal: patches of big-leaf taro, flowers and manioc exploded between great battlements of uplifted coral stone. Green parrots flecked with crimson flapped back and forth between palms and glistening breadfruit trees. White orchids sprang from tree branches. Piglets rooted in pens fenced with heaps of moss-covered rock. Smoke curled from makeshift sheds where men stoked fires in rusty steel drums and tossed bags full of coconut shells on the racks above. It was copra-harvesting time. The air was sweet with the scent of drying coconut.

Clear water flowed everywhere: it rushed down fissures in the grey rock, bubbled along irrigation channels, cascaded artfully from stalactite-laden cliffs, over the road, down, down to the sea. We forded thirty streams in an hour.

"Water, water," said Alfred. "All the people are scared of man-Maewo because of our water magic. This island is *full-up* poison. But no magic can hurt me, because I bathe in *tabu* water every day. If you were a jealous man and you tried to kill me with a spell, it would fail. Your poison will bounce back and kill you instead. Would you like protection from evil? A charm? Dudley can make you one."

Yes, of course I wanted a charm. I wanted love magic. I wanted to see rain pour from a cloudless sky. I wanted to see Dudley turn himself into an owl. Anything.

Maewo seemed idyllic and a wealthy place, especially compared to Tanna. There were cement-block houses with tin roofs. At first I didn't notice the fences, the wire mesh that wrapped the yards of Maewo's most prosperous families. I ignored the sullen faces and the suspicious glares directed at Dudley's truck.

We stopped beside a huge open-air church. Dudley didn't cut the engine. He barely stopped long enough to say good-bye. This was Betarara, site of the island's only rest house.

"The chief," said Alfred, as a filthy-looking man approached. "*Yumi* can meet tomorrow after church."

I jumped out, and then they were gone. Strange.

The chief scratched his belly through a rip in his shirt and smiled at me anxiously. I handed him a letter of introduction I had obtained from the National Tourism Office. The letter advised readers that I had come to promote tourism and that they should help me. The chief peered at it, furrowed his thick brows and studiously ignored the young man who panted and squirmed behind him. The boy rolled his eyes, giggled, leaped in the air with a yelp, then dashed away squealing.

"My son," said the chief shyly. I turned away so that someone could turn my letter right-side up without completely embarrassing him.

The rest house inhabited a corner of the village church hall. It had all the ambiance of a medium-security prison. It was protected by a tall wire-mesh fence, which baffled me, because people on the islands did not steal.

I cooked myself a dinner of instant noodles and ketchup. Under the weak light of an oil lamp, I thumbed through R.H. Codrington's *The Melanesians,* and in particular his transcriptions of stories that boys from Maewo and Pentecost had told him about their ancestor spirit Tagaro.

Tagaro was superhuman. He had the power to create things, and he wanted the things he created to be good for the world. His companion,

Suqe-matua, wanted only badness and suffering. When Tagaro created a new fruit, he or Suqe-matua would throw it up in the air. If Tagaro caught the fruit, it would be good to eat. What he missed became worthless. Tagaro made the sea. He also invented magic and handed down the songs and charms that went with it. The world was once like the Garden of Eden, but that changed when a man stole Tagaro's pig. Tagaro was so angry, he cut a canoe for himself and paddled away, taking all the best things in the world with him.

I lay awake in the dark, listening to the tortured groans and howls of the chief's son somewhere in the distance. And closer. The crunch of footsteps on gravel, then a sound that made me shiver: a barely perceptible rasping, like tiny fingernails or claws scratching against wire mesh.

ALFRED DID NOT COME to meet me the next morning, so I walked south until I reached his village, which was really more of a family compound. There were several cement-block houses around a broad lawn.

Alfred and Dudley had a sister. Faith Mary was a broad woman with a stern brow and a booming voice. She wore an Anglican Mothers' Union T-shirt and was constantly digging through the dusty leather purse she carried around her neck. When I arrived, she spread banana leaves on the lawn and served baked taro root and coconut crab on it. Alfred and Dudley and a dozen others gathered round to eat. Faith Mary told me that Maewo was a very modern place. Look at Alfred and Dudley, she said. They cooked and washed the dishes if she told them to. Alfred laughed. Dudley exhaled a plume of cigarette smoke and gazed at the sky. Faith Mary smiled and pushed more food towards me. Then she narrowed her eyes.

"Now," she said, "tell me what you want from us."

"Well, I know that people everywhere are afraid of Maewo because of the magic here," I said as soberly as possible. "I want to see that magic. Not crazy stories. Not conjuring tricks. Proof."

"You know why the people are afraid of Maewo? For the same reason we are all afraid: death! You make a Maewo man angry and he will kill you with poison, right now!" she said, slapping the earth. "And Dudley is the strongest magic man of all. Tell him what you can do, Dudley."

Dudley was not so enthusiastic. *"Mi mekem kastom meresin."*

"Tell him what kind of medicine, Dudley!"

"Wanfala drink blong curem cancer."

"And . . ."

"Wanfala drink blong bringim daon blad presa."

"Tell him Dudley, tell him more." Faith Mary clearly wore the pants in this family.

Dudley sighed and made an attempt at English. "*Oke,* suppose you *garem wan nogud spirit* living inside you. I take a white cloth *blong yu* and I sleep on it. Now I travel inside your body to look at that *nogud spirit,* then figure out how to make it leave you. *Oke?* Now suppose you *ded* from some mystery problem. I put a stone on the grave *blong yu* to make you rise up and tell me what *killim yu i ded. Oke?* Now suppose you knew you were going to die and you wanted to make sure your wife didn't go marry *narafalla man,* I give you a special drink that would *killim hem i ded* five days after you."

"But Dudley doesn't do the bad magic, only the good magic," interrupted Faith Mary.

"So what is your most popular, um, medicine?" I asked.

"Well, suppose you want some girl to love you, I could make a leaf for you to eat at night. Then you would get up early *tumas long moning,* and say the name of the girl just as the sun hits you. By and by you will *stap* inside her dreams. She will come find you."

"Ah, sweet mouth," I said. "That's the one I want."

Dudley looked away. Alfred fidgeted. Faith Mary cleared her throat. It was against the rules for the men to share their *kastom* with me, she told me. The provincial council had decided that white men couldn't be trusted.

"When a white man sees magic, he learns it and he kills it. We know you white people have got *savve.* For example, a few years ago an Australian came here. He threw a piece of tin can on the ground and it turned into a snake. Then he told us that white man's magic was stronger than ours."

Faith Mary said she liked me. She said I should not be staying in Betarara, because the people there would certainly poison me if they got the chance. I should come and stay in Navenevene, where Dudley could protect me. Dudley showed no particular enthusiasm for the idea, and I had already paid for a week's stay at the rest house, so I thanked her and left.

Dudley caught up to me a short way down the road. He rolled down the window of the Mitsubishi and sheepishly offered me a ride.

"I've got legs, I can walk," I said.

"*Hem i tru.* But you might step over *wanfala* black magic on the road, *wanfala* leaf that would do terrible things *long penis blong yu.*"

The gravel felt suddenly hot beneath my sandals. "My penis?"

"Now and again people here get cross with each other. They leave poison lying *albaot.* The worst is the poison that makes your penis shrivel up *olsem ia,*" he said, holding his thumb and forefinger together, "and swim up inside your body. I cure people of *disfala* curse all the time."

No wonder people on Maewo protected themselves with wire fences. I got in the truck. Church was out, and everyone in every village along the way saw me riding with my good friend the witch doctor. At the time I didn't think that was such a bad thing. Dudley dropped me off at Betarara and promised to meet me the next day.

MOST COMMUNITIES in Vanuatu have a *kastom* chief, a man who holds no political power but whose job it is to ensure that the old ways are kept alive. Geoffrey Uli was Maewo's *kastom* chief. He lived in a shack near Betarara. I figured his mandate would include helping me.

Uli managed to evade me for four days. I finally caught him in his yard one afternoon just before *kava* time. He was an old man. With his shirt off, his skin looked as though it had been shrink-wrapped to his bony frame. His eyes were bird-like, sharp and cunning. They darted back and forth across his garden as though looking for an escape. Eventually they settled on me.

Uli told me that people on Maewo already had God before the missionaries came. Their *kastom* stories were the same as the ones in the Bible. Only a few names had been changed. Maewo's own version of Eve was created not from Adam's rib, but from his collarbone. There was a great flood, and a Noah figure with a big canoe. As Uli told me these things, his wife, who was sitting in the dirt, howled with laughter.

"That *rubbish* woman had me baptized when we got married," he said. "Now I must pray twice a day. First I do *kastom* prayers, then I pray to the church God."

Uli wouldn't say exactly to whom his *kastom* prayers were directed. Not to Tagaro, anyway. But he did make this point: the old gods never had a problem with magic, so why should the new one?

"But isn't the Christian God opposed to *kastom* magic?" I asked.

"The Anglican missionaries never told us our *kastom* was *rubbish*. It was their students, boys from Maewo, who smashed the *tabu* stones. They went into the *nakamal* and spoiled the *kava* grinders and the drinking shells, too. They thought that this would get them into heaven. Now we know better. We have our *kava* back. And there is plenty of *kastom* magic left on Maewo."

"I don't believe it. I don't believe you people still have the power," I said, hoping to shame him into a demonstration.

"Sir, you are wrong," said Uli. " We have rocks that can make rain, wind and sun."

I looked at the sky. There was rain, wind and sun every day on Maewo. "How about thunder?"

"The thunder man lives far, far away in the bush. You'll never find him."

"There must be something, some way to prove . . ."

Uli's wife spoke up from the shadows. *"Sipos hem wantem looklook long kastom magic, hemi mas findem tufala ston blong etkwek,"* she suggested.

Uli shot her an irritated look. She ignored Uli's glare and turned to me. She lifted both hands as if shaking an imaginary rock. Then she trembled and fell over on her side. I got it.

"Yes, yes, earthquake stones. Wonderful," I said. "When can we go see them?"

"I cannot help you," said Uli.

"Why not?"

"Because I have no time. Sir, I have been keeping an eye on you. I know you have been on this island for four days already. If you had come to see me first, I could have helped you. But I know what you have been doing. You went off with Dudley, didn't you? You have not paid me respect. You have spoiled your luck."

I tried to explain that he was wrong, that Dudley had been avoiding me for days. But there was no point in arguing. Uli had told me just enough to make it clear that he was the real *kastom* expert. He hustled his wife back towards their shack, leaving me to gaze east towards the serrated crest of the island and ponder the location of the stones that made the ground shake.

I MET FAITH MARY on the road one day.

"Dudley is avoiding me," I said.

"You have chosen the Betarara people and Geoffrey Uli. We won't interfere," she said with a shrug. "We can't protect you any more."

My fever returned. I spent most of my days in bed. The citizens of Betarara, pleased—or perhaps relieved—that Dudley had spurned me, took me on as their cause. They brought me crackers. They boiled water for tea and instant noodles. They sat and watched me for hours.

First, there were the chief and his wife, who mumbled to me soothingly. One night, a handsome young catechist dropped by to read me excerpts from the New Testament. Then came the lady with magic hands. She leaned over me, her immense breasts inflating the expanse of her island dress. She prodded my belly, grunted knowingly then kneaded my internal organs for an hour, whispering, *"God, plis mekem alraet disfala boy."*

The people at Betarara told me stories, and all their stories were infused with magic and fear. Like the one about the pelicans that had recently appeared on a beach near the airport. Pelicans were not native to the island. Everyone was terrified of them. "They haven't attacked us yet but they are huge. We are quite sure that white men brought them," said one woman. But there was hope. A boy had brought one of the pelicans down with his slingshot. His family cooked and ate the bird. Now there were only four.

The villagers told me about suspicious foreigners. Once, a white yachtsman came ashore near the village and dug for an hour in the sand. When he sailed away, the village children discovered that he had buried crocodile eggs. Such an evil man! Once, a Russian ship had anchored just off the west coast. One of its crew came ashore and dumped a copra snake out of a canvas bag. The snake slithered up a tree, and now everyone was afraid to go into the palm groves. That wasn't the worst of it: the Russian sailor had been asking very strange questions about cats. People were sure he had let a tiger loose on Maewo.

The villagers told me about curses. The strongest kinds of poison on Maewo were not sprinkled on your food or left on the road for you to step on. They were administered to you *after the fact*. In other words, a sorcerer could use your footprint or a banana peel you might have discarded to make you sick. The best way to stay healthy on Maewo was to bury your dinner scraps and sweep away your footprints. It was especially important not to make enemies, since many sorcerers kept their talents secret. Never forget to lock my door at night, they said. The people of Betarara were scared of things they could see and things they could not see.

Each night, after the villagers went home and I had extinguished my oil lamp, the noises would start again outside my window. Scratching on wire. Rustling. Clucking. Whooshing. I locked my door and did my best to contemplate the rationalist tradition.

Then came a white man. Wes was Texan, barely out of high school. The Peace Corps had sent him out to teach English. He had the trusting eyes of a puppy. Wes explained to me why the chief of Betarara's son spent his time howling and barking like a dog. The boy had once been considered quite clever and had been sent to the Anglican high school over on Santo. That's when he had fallen in love. The boy's passion went unrequited, so he turned to *kastom* magic for help. He tried using a variation of sweet mouth on his beloved, but the magic somehow boomeranged. He had been crazy ever since. No prayer or exorcism could save him.

It was Wes who helped me find the earthquake stones. It was no secret, he said, that the stones resided in Kwatcawol village, which clung to the crest of the forested ridge that ran the length of Maewo. I was still too weak to make the trek on foot, but a track had recently been bulldozed up the mountain from Betarara. Wes's adopted brother had a truck.

We left at sunset, following the red scar of the new road up through the jungle. The evening's first fireflies twittered like green sparks. Flying foxes dropped out of the banyan trees to chase them up and down the road.

We pulled into a field in the middle of the village. A crowd formed around the truck. I stood up in the box and explained my mission. There was a whispered debate. Wes interpreted. He told me my timing was per-

fect. The custodian of the earthquake stones had never permitted outsiders to see them. But the old man had died a year before my arrival, and
his seven sons, all Christians, were not quite sure how they should handle
their pagan legacy. Voices were raised. Heads were shaken. Finally, one
man's eyes lit up: perhaps the visitor could offer a gift. Ah yes, a gift. It
was not so much a bribe or an admission fee as a tribute to Melanesian
kastom. Traditional relationships in Melanesia were always based on symbolic exchange. A murderer could be let off the hook with the right exchange of pigs.

I handed over my usual currency—a bag of rice and a can of corned
beef—and we all filed sombrely towards the sturdiest hut in the village. It
had been built in the traditional style: one great room under beams of
black tree fern trunks, with palm leaves hanging so low to the ground they
were spattered with mud. The roof beams were reinforced every few centimetres with smaller poles. This was the Melanesian version of the earthquake-proof bunker.

Inside, it was dark, crowded and confused. Then someone lit an oil
lamp, revealing what looked like two bundles of garbage hanging on the
wall at the back of the hut. The earthquake stones. I moved closer. Hands
reached out from the shadows towards me, not touching me, but straining
and ready.

The stones may have been the size of potatoes, or they may have been
bigger. I couldn't actually see them. They had each been wrapped in strips
of dirty canvas, then bound in chicken wire and suspended from a cross-
beam by lengths of hemp rope. It hardly seemed dignified.

The new guardians of the stones appeared to be a husband-and-wife
team: he was bare-chested, tattooed and scowling suspiciously; she was
plump and beaming warmly in the glow of her oil lamp. At first nobody
said anything. Then an old man stepped out of the shadows. He wore a
towel wrapped around his head like a turban. His pupils were opaque
with wind-scars. He pushed his face into mine. I will translate his monologue into English:

"Ages ago, in the time of the ancestors, the people found three stones
in the forest," he said—or rather, shouted through the silence. He cupped
his leathery hands together as though he were holding a great weight.

"The stones were all hanging in mid-air, and they were shaking. One man touched them and they stopped moving. He played with those stones. He put one of them on the ground—that caused the ground to shake in another village. Oh yes, that man saw how powerful the stones were. He played so much and caused so many tremors that one of the stones rolled into the ocean and was lost forever. Since then we have been very careful with the other stones."

"Can I touch them?"

The old man made a gurgling sound, as though he were choking. The guardian exhaled through his nostrils like a bull, but his wife steadied him with a glance, then nodded her head at me encouragingly. I reached for the bigger of the two bundles, lifted it, turned it in my hand, peered through the chicken wire. It was like an industrial-strength cocoon.

I felt a hand on my elbow. Foreigners could not be trusted. It was true. I was desperate to test the stones' magic.

"Can I untie it? Just touch it to the ground to see if the stone still works?"

"No! Of course not," croaked the old man, now breathing hoarsely. "If you did that, you would cause a terrible earthquake."

"But if we did it quickly, you know, a quick touch to the floor, perhaps we could make the ground shake for only a few seconds. Wouldn't that be fun to see?"

"*Yu no savve!* The last person to try anything like that was this boy's grandfather," said the old man, pointing at the bare-chested guardian. "He made Maewo shake for eight days. Eight days! It was one awful something. But at least the *olfala* knew how to make the tremors stop, he had a special leaf. But he never passed on his secrets. The knowledge is dead in the ground. That's why we have to take such great care of these stones. They are very sensitive. When a big wind comes, someone has to stay here to hold the stones tight, even if the house collapses around him. And if a rat or a pig was to find its way inside this house, watch out! The ground would shake, because the stones don't like those animals. We have to be careful!"

Finally, the bare-chested guardian took a deep breath and said in a commanding baritone, "*Yumi go long drink kava nao.*"

"Um," I said.

"Nao ia," he said, and he stepped towards me. *"Yumi go raet nao."*

I was heartbroken. I looked to Wes for support. But he had already turned for the door.

"Kava," Wes was murmuring to the men who clung to him like a teddy bear. *"Mi likem kava."*

LATE THAT NIGHT, after three shells of muddy *kava* and a dizzy ride home, I lay awake in bed listening, for the last time, to the distant cries of the chief's son. I listened to the rain on my tin roof, drumming and dripping me towards sleep. And then I heard the rasping, the same staccato click and metallic hum I had heard every night on Maewo, and I knew that something was tapping at the wire-mesh fence outside my room. I rolled quietly out of bed and crept to the window, holding my breath. The rain had stopped. The yard was empty. The sky was starless and muddy. A shadow teetered on the curled edge of the mesh fence. Before I could focus, there was a sudden, explosive beating of wings, and the creature flapped down onto my porch. I could just make out a great plume of tail feathers and the glint of tiny eyes. A rooster. I exhaled. I suppose I should have felt relief. I didn't.

"Go on, out!" I shouted.

The rooster didn't take flight. It simply cocked its head and glared at me with cunning, familiar eyes. I hung a towel over my window and locked my door. When I did fall asleep, I dreamed of the *kastom* chief, Geoffrey Uli. I saw him in a clearing in the forest, standing with a knife in one hand and a stone cup in the other. There were black feathers tied to his arms. At his feet lay a pig with its legs bound together. I saw Uli bend down. I saw his knife slice through the beast's throat, saw the blood run in bright red streams into the stone cup, overflow and trickle over Uli's talon-like hands. I saw his eyes narrow with pleasure and secret knowledge, and I recalled what he had told me: I have been watching you.

It may be true that people all over Vanuatu were scared of man-Maewo. But here on the island of water magic, people were fearful of absolutely everything. They trembled at the thought of unseen curses and charms, at the terrible power of two small cobblestones. They suspected treachery from visitors, from their neighbours and from the natural world. All that magic had made them vulnerable. It always had. My great-grandfather had described an encounter between a white missionary and a murderer on nearby Ambae. The missionary only had to fix a disapproving gaze sternly on the man to send him scurrying for safety. The murderer returned to his home village, declared, "The man looked at me!" and promptly collapsed. He died, I suppose, of shock, or fear, or some life-sucking disorder he felt the white man had directed at him. My great-grandfather was intrigued, not so much by Melanesian magic as by Melanesian fragility. "Like peaches ripened in the hot sun, the slightest shock seems to upset their balance and cause death," he wrote.

Bad intent, hostility alone, could be lethal. I couldn't shake the idea that the rooster that had been prowling my yard each night for a week had something to do with my recurring fever and with Geoffrey Uli. Yes, this would be a silly hypothesis if proposed from an easy chair in an apartment in London or Toronto or Los Angeles. But when you are breathing the air of sorcery and fear, it is difficult not to fall in with the local view about these things. If myth is the form we give to our idea of the universe, of God, then it must also occasionally be the vessel into which we pour our fears. I returned to Santo empty-handed but strangely relieved.

9

THE CURSE OF GAUA

One day, long ago, a man was fishing on a reef, and he saw something
out in the sea. It appeared to be an island, but it moved. He ran
to the beach shouting, "An island is coming here," and quickly the people gathered
on the beach to watch a sailing ship approach and anchor on the reef.
The inhabitants of the island came ashore, and our island world ceased to be.

CASPAR LUANA, *Buka! A Retrospective*

MY FAILURE at Maewo filled me with a sense of urgency. I wanted to get closer to the old stories. I wanted to push north. When the Twin Otter landed back at Pekoa, I did not head for the bar at the Hotel Santo. I left my pack on the tarmac and watched the plane refuel. The mail run would zigzag through the Banks and Torres Islands, touching down on every shore with room for an airstrip between Santo and Vanuatu's northern frontier. Its first stop would be Santa Maria, where Qat, the most enigmatic of Banks Islands ancestor spirits, had left the world forever.

Let me tell you about Qat.

Like Jesus, Qat had no earthly father, but he was not a god or even the son of a god. He was a *vui,* a spirit with extraordinary powers. His mother was not a woman but a stone which had cracked apart to bring him into the world. He was not the world's creator, but he did make people, pigs, rocks and trees to amuse himself. Qat didn't make the sun, but he did bring night to his islands. It happened like this: Qat had eleven brothers who complained that the world was too bright, so Qat loaded a pig into his canoe and paddled all the way to the foot of the sky, where he traded his pig for a piece of night. When Qat returned home, night followed him, and for the first time the sun slipped down the sky towards the west. Qat's brothers were terrified of the dark, but he taught them to close their eyes and sleep. When night had lasted long enough, Qat took a sharp stone, a piece of red obsidian, and cut open the darkness to reveal the dawn.

Qat was born on Vanua Lava, but later he floated to Santa Maria to live under the volcano Garat with his companion, Marawa the spider. Once, Qat spent six days carving bits of wood into the shapes of men and women. He danced for his dolls and they stirred. He beat his drum and they moved some more. He kept on dancing and drumming until he had coaxed them all to life. Qat was pleased, because he had made humans. Marawa tried to imitate Qat, but the spider was so startled when he saw his own dolls stir that he buried them in the dirt. After six days Marawa scraped the earth away to find his dolls rotten and stinking. Marawa had made death.

The island of Santa Maria is shaped like a doughnut with a wide crater at its centre. When Qat grew tired of the world, he carved himself a huge canoe from a tree. He loaded his wife, his brothers and every living thing, even the smallest ants, into the canoe, and built a roof over them. Then came the greatest rainstorm the world had ever known. Water filled the crater and flowed over its rim. Qat's canoe ripped a channel through the edge of the caldera, tore a ditch all the way to the sea then floated away beyond the horizon.

Uncountable generations later, a giant canoe eased up to the eastern shore of Santa Maria. Islanders knew the vessel was not of the world, because nobody in the world—which ended just past Espiritu Santo in the south and the Torres Islands in the north—could build a vessel so big. A creature left the canoe and swam to shore. Most of the old folks suspected that the creature was Qat, finally returned to the world. In fact, it was Bishop John Coleridge Patteson, and his message was heartbreaking: Qat would never return, because Qat was a lie. Patteson did not tell the people—he didn't yet know—that his arrival heralded a series of plagues that would devastate the island.

The mythical Lake Letas remains in Santa Maria's caldera, wrapped around the base of the steaming volcano. A cascade now pours from the notch in the caldera's eastern edge where Qat made his run for the sea. I saw these things from the greasy window of the Twin Otter as we drifted out of the clouds towards a patch of grass at Gaua, the name given to Santa Maria's east coast.

The most striking thing about the island was not its volcano but its ruins. The coastal lowlands were covered with them: hundreds and hundreds of stone platforms, broken walls, chest-high foundations, all built from stones fitted tightly and without mortar in the style of Peru's Inca palaces, though more modest in proportion. The ruins appeared in gardens, under mounds of grass among the coconut groves and bound by knots of banyan root. They collected moss in the shadows of the forest and on the mountainsides, and suggested that once, long ago, there had been something of a metropolis on the Gaua coast.

That was certainly the impression gained by the island's first European visitor. The Spaniard Quirós—who gave Santa Maria its name—noted in 1606 that the island was populated by "innumerable natives" of three different colours: yellow, black and off-white. Other early visitors estimated the island's population in the tens of thousands.

But now there were few people on the Gaua coast. They lived in a scattering of small hamlets, their houses rustic affairs with no tin roofs or stonework or milled timber to speak of. I followed the only road—two ruts zigzagging through the rubble—but I never saw a car or truck on it, and I rarely saw people. What had become of the metropolis and all its citizens?

R.H. Codrington blamed a turn-of-the-century population decline on the blackbirders. Tens of thousands of Melanesians had been taken to work on the sugar plantations of Queensland and Fiji in the nineteenth century, but most of them returned home after a few years. Henry Montgomery blamed the fighting nature of the islanders. He wrote that war was as regular and systematic on Santa Maria as cricket tournaments: in fact, combatants would convene on marked grounds at arranged times, when young men from neighbouring villages would arrive with bows and arrows, and ask to join in. The sport resulted in a cycle of murder and vengeance which Henry insisted only got worse when labourers returned from Queensland with rifles.

Still, such blood sport rarely ended with more than a single death and could not account for the almost complete decimation of Santa Maria and almost every other island in Melanesia. Each year, fewer and fewer canoes came out to meet traders and missionaries. A resident missionary at Wango was shown the sites of forty-six once prosperous villages, of which only three remained. In the nineteenth century, the population of Erromango, north of Tanna, fell from more than three thousand to less than four hundred. Some historians estimated that the population of the New Hebrides was reduced by 90 per cent in the late nineteenth century. What was killing the islanders?

After a visit to a village on Vanua Lava in 1861, Bishop Patteson complained that local men were avoiding him and that some had remarked rudely about the "unusual sickness" connected with his new teaching. Patteson found Mota in good health in August 1863; two weeks later, he returned to find the island in the grip of a terrible scourge of dysentery and influenza. Fifty people had already died from it. After seeing four of every ten baptized Melanesians die in the decade straddling the turn of the century, the third Bishop of Melanesia, Cecil Wilson, wrote that all that could be done for this "dying race" was to try to ensure its members went to their graves as Christians.

It would take the missionaries decades to realize—or admit—the part they played in the Melanesian apocalypse. The Reverend W.J. Durrad was horrified to realize it was his own arrival on remote Tikopia that sparked an epidemic of pneumonia that killed dozens. The incident convinced Durrad that the *Southern Cross*, oozing with New Zealand–bred germs, was the chief agent of disease. The ship's legacy of death lasted well into the twentieth century. "A fortnight after its visit everyone is ill," he wrote in 1917. As late as 1931, a stopover on Malaita unleashed an epidemic that killed eleven hundred islanders. Even when Europeans acknowledged the role they played in spreading disease, they put the catastrophe down to a lack of stamina among Melanesians. As Durrad put it, "There is a fatalism in their outlook which reacts upon their physical organism." When they fell sick, Melanesians tended to give up and wait to die rather than fight their illness. It was the same with sorcery: anyone who so much as believed he was the victim of black magic died within hours or days.

The people I met on Santa Maria disagreed completely with this analysis. It was not a slow dirge of pneumonia, dysentery and influenza that had decimated the island. *Kastom* magic was to blame, and it was God who eventually came to the rescue. Santa Marians told me that their home was once like Maewo: a place held hostage by sorcerers so treacherous and lethal that those who weren't poisoned or murdered finally just got in their canoes and fled.

"Once we had twenty thousand people on this island," the paramount chief of Gaua, Paul Wudgor, told me as we gnawed boiled fish in his hut. "But then came a time of terrible magic. Sorcerers cursed people using their garbage, their *poo-poo*, whatever they could find. People had to throw their dinner scraps into the sea to make sure sorcerers didn't use them to cast evil spells on them. Bad men used secret leaves to kill our *pikinini* even before they were born. They used smoke from fires to curse people. Hundreds of people died this way."

By the 1960s, said the chief, there were only seven women left on the Gaua side of the island. Finally, the Church took action. Esuva Din, an Anglican district priest from Vanua Lava, sailed south to confront the evil with an act of boldness and Old Testament audacity. He harnessed the Holy Spirit to create a boomerang curse: all black magic would now bounce back and kill anyone who tried to use it. Within days, dozens of known sorcerers had dropped dead. One sorcerer confronted the district priest and said, "I don't believe it's true; I don't believe you really have the power to curse anyone who uses black magic." Esuva Din did not like to be challenged. He said, "*Rubbish* man, just you wait and see." The sorcerer keeled over and died the next day.

Everyone I spoke to agreed that Esuva Din's curse had saved the island. During the 1970s and '80s, hundreds of families arrived from nearby islands to till new life into Santa Maria's ancient gardens. The population had rebounded to almost forty-two hundred people. Still, the Gaua coast felt eerily empty, like so many of those places—the highlands of Peru, the Thai plains of Ayuttaya, the Turkish Aegean—whose time has passed and where foreigners pay to see the rubble of once great cities. But there weren't any tourists here. Nor were there ghosts. Who would the ancient souls of Gaua have haunted? Most of their own descendants were dead, and the rubble of their ancient city was suffocating under a thickening blanket of vines. I walked the ruins and the empty forests, bought the last can of tuna from a village canteen, sat out a rainstorm and then lay down in the tall grass and waited for the mail plane to deliver me from the silence.

10

THE BOY WHO
KILLED THE STORY
OF VANUA LAVA

Warning: It is not wise to be dismissive of religion, particularly
Christianity, if you are a nonbeliever. Islanders are
likely to dislike you strongly if you are hostile to Christianity.

Lonely Planet: Solomon Islands

WHEN I WAS young, I learned that paradise was an island. There were mountains on it, and they were shaped like sandcastles melted by the rain. There were pink marshmallow clouds around those peaks, but not over the beaches or the kaleidoscope of reefs that sheltered the lagoons from the surf. You approached paradise by plane and drifted between those peaks and circled over its estuaries and you saw the palm shadows cast over sand. When you landed, you were greeted by a man who said, "Welcome to Fantasy Island," and you knew that paradise would be whatever you willed it to be.

Vanua Lava was twenty minutes by Twin Otter north from Gaua. The volcanoes, the beaches, the shining estuary, I did glide above them all, and I was carried into the lushness of a vivid green airfield, and then I was welcomed not into a fantasy but into the arms of the Church.

Vanua Lava and its tiny neighbour, Mota, were the epicentre for the explosion of Anglicanism that reverberated across Melanesia in the nineteenth century. These islands produced the first converts and the first indigenous priests. My great-grandfather had waxed poetic about the new age he and his contemporaries had brought: the "settled Christian life," the prayer gatherings (twice daily!) and the congregations whose members were more gracious and humble than in any English country parish. The bishop had indeed found his Fantasy Island.

Sola, the village adjoining the airstrip, was still ruled by the Church of Melanesia, which was the new name given to the Anglican Church in Vanuatu and the Solomon Islands.

Hierarchy spoke through geography: the provincial government office stood in the shadows of the ridge that overlooked the village. The ridge had the twisting shape of a snake. Locals believed it had once been inhabited by the spirit of an evil serpent. Not any more. The Anglicans had claimed it, cleansed it and built a residence for the Bishop of the Diocese of Banks and Torres on its crest. The snake's head had been pierced with a tall white cross.

The bishop's secretary was waiting at the airstrip with a truck, the only truck in town. I jumped in the back and was deposited shortly at a seaside rest house owned by an Anglican priest. We prayed before lunch, then again before dinner and then again at breakfast.

"Tomorrow is Sunday," the priest's wife told me. "You'll go to church."

Before my journey, several South Pacific scholars had advised me that if I wanted to get anything done in Melanesia, if I wanted doors opened, if I wanted to achieve any kind of intimacy with the place, I would have to strike up a friendship with the Church. The Church had trucks, boats, influence and many friends. So I did attend Sunday Eucharist in Sola, and I did not complain when the vicar rambled on for close to three hours, laying out the version of Jesus' walk on water I had heard back in Sunday school, ruminating on the Word, mumbling the same incantations that would be repeated before thousands of altars across the former empire during the course of the day. And I prayed along with the people: "For Thine is the kingdom, the power and the glory, for ever and ever . . ."

All that prayer. I was beginning to resent my great-grandfather, and not only because I would have preferred to be reading or swimming or slingshot hunting for flying fox with the local kids rather than praying. This is the sort of resentment shared by many Western travellers, especially those who consider themselves adventurous, when we discover that missionaries got to Paradise and transformed it long before we packed our bags. It is similar to the anxiety we feel when we discover a McDonald's among the palms. Melanesia, like all those warm places dreamed of during our long northern winter, is supposed to be exotic and primitive, not familiar. It is supposed to be otherly.

But Paradise is and always has been an invention. The cultural critic Edward Said argued that the Victorians ignored the real world in favour of an Oriental fantasy—a collection of exotic places filled with quaint but inferior races—in order to justify their colonial aspirations in the East. His theory could well apply to the Melanesian Mission: Henry Montgomery made no secret of his fatherly affection for his hotheaded and childlike "little Melanesians." So many dark-skinned people in need of guidance and improvement. We modern travellers claim to be different. We insist we don't want to change Paradise. But we are frequently bothered by the version of it we encounter.

The American writer Paul Theroux, for example, expressed constant disappointment in his South Pacific travelogue, *The Happy Isles of Oceania*. He didn't find the exotic world of bare-breasted beauties that had been immortalized by the French painter Paul Gauguin. Gone were the cannibals, the grass skirts and the brave outrigger voyagers of South Seas legend. Theroux was irritated to find churches on every populated island and maddened by the ringing bells which reminded him that Sundays were more sacred in the Pacific than at home in New England. He fled to increasingly remoter shores, but the only islands uninfected by Western influence were, in fact, uninhabited.

I knew how Theroux felt. I had read my *Treasure Island*. I had studied the accounts of swashbucklers like Peter Dillon, the Irishman who claimed to have repelled a cannibal army from a mountaintop in Fiji while the torsos and limbs of his companions were cooking in the valley below. I had seen Mel Gibson bewitched by an Oceanic love spell in *The Bounty*.

I had gaped at Bronislaw Malinowski's snapshots of Trobriand Island primitives, unaware that missionaries had arrived there decades before him. Despite everything that my great-grandfather had written about his mission's triumphs, I suppose I still hoped to find the same things all Westerners expected from the South Pacific: a remote shore unspoiled by European religion and commerce. I wanted it to be more authentic, more savage, more like the South Pacific other travellers had invented.

The romantic primitivist is bound for disappointment in Oceania. The spear-shaking headhunters, the Man Fridays, the Bali Hai girls—if they ever existed—were long gone even before Gauguin and company began to package them for northern audiences. Now, not even a photo opportunity at Port Vila's Cannibal House can fill the void. No island has escaped the whorl of cultural convergence that began nearly two centuries ago. But my time here in the Anglican heartland would help me see that my hunt for primitive authenticity had in fact blinded me to the psyche-delic collision of evangelism, *kastom* and globalization taking place on the islands. History had not ended with the baptism of Melanesia. Its other-ness lay not in some romantic stereotype but in the hybridization of myths, magic and spirit, in the eight-legged, Day-Glo love child pro-duced by the union of Church and *kastom*.

THE FIRST HINT of the mutating soul of Vanua Lava lay in its myths. Yes, the birthplace of Qat was still marked by a cracked stone on a Vanua Lava hillside, but the Christian stories had overtaken those of Qat and spread right through the archipelago. Mission epics were engraved in the landscape, starting with the bay that curled north from Sola. Once called Nawono, the bay had been renamed Port Patteson for the martyred bishop. There was a headstone in the bush near the north end to remind islanders of the heroism of the missionaries who had come to save them. The grave belonged to a teenaged boy whose life had both defined and been cut short by the clash of European and Pacific cultures.

Fisher Young was a half-caste, the great-grandson of one of the infa-mous *Bounty* mutineers and his Tahitian bride. The descendants of the *Bounty* mutineers had migrated to Norfolk Island, between New Zealand and New Caledonia, in 1856, shortly before Bishop Patteson moved the base for his Melanesian Mission to the same lonely shore. Fisher Young was drawn to the bishop. When he was seventeen, Young and another Norfolk lad, Edwin Nobbs, sailed north with Patteson aboard the *Southern Cross*. They wanted to help him spread the word of God to the heathen islands.

The day of their death began like so many others from Patteson's career. The bishop swam to shore on Santa Cruz, accompanied by the whaleboat from which Young, Nobbs and four other crew members watched and waited nervously. Three hundred Melanesians stood on the shore, all brandishing bows and arrows in a show of rising agitation. Patteson did not run. He tucked his Bible back into his top hat and retreated to the whaleboat. A giant raised a seven-foot bow and aimed at the bishop. Patteson gave him a steady look and a smile, and the giant lowered his bow, but the rest of them would not be calmed. The Cruzians charged into the water. Some tried to overturn the boat. Many others stood in the shallows, lifted their bows and began to shoot at the bishop. Patteson used the boat's wooden rudder as a shield, but his oarsmen were pierced like pincushions. One took a bone-tipped arrow in the chest, another through a cheek. Young was struck in the wrist but kept rowing until he returned his bishop safely to the *Southern Cross*. As the ship sailed south, Patteson removed the arrow and nursed Young's wounds, but he knew the lad was doomed. Patteson later wrote to a cousin: "On the fourth day that dear lad Fisher said to me, 'I can't think what makes my jaw so stiff.' Then I knew that all hope was gone of his being spared."

Young succumbed to lockjaw and his body grew as stiff as a rod of iron. The bishop nursed him night and day. One evening Young woke from a trance and looked directly into the bishop's eyes, and asked, "They never stop singing there, do they?" Patteson knew the boy's thoughts were already with the angels, whom he would meet before dawn. Edwin Nobbs, who had received only a superficial wound, died of tetanus a few days later. People said the bishop was never the same after that. It was as though he knew of the fate that awaited him on Nukapu.

The cook from the rest house offered to help me find Fisher Young's grave. Wilma was a gruff twenty-one-year-old with a black star tattooed between her eyebrows and a tiny yellow flower tucked into her frizzy hair. She was belligerent and flirtatious. She had been born on Ureparapara, which was a half-submerged volcanic crater just north of Vanua Lava. I told her my great-grandfather had sailed into that crater. Wilma scowled. No one will take you there this year, she said. *"Solwota big tumas. Mifala stap fraet."*

Rough seas? The indefatigable Captain William Bligh had survived those same waters in an open rowboat. After being ejected by the *Bounty* mutineers off Tonga, Bligh had drifted right past Ureparapara on a journey that took him and eighteen loyal crew members across 4,000 miles of ocean, all the way to Dutch Timor. Forget the lustful Fletcher Christian— someone should make a movie about Bligh.

We walked for an hour along the red sand beach, chasing the coconuts that rolled in with the breaking waves. We skirted a mangrove swamp and reached a river mouth. I began to ford it, but Wilma grabbed me by the shirt and pulled me back. She searched along the shore for stones, which she lobbed into the river theatrically. She yelled and shouted and slapped the water with her palms. *"For krokodael blong bisop,"* she said.

This was the second Christian myth of Vanua Lava. There had always been two crocodiles in the Selva River. Bishop Patteson had brought them from the Solomon Islands. When he set them free more than a century ago, he had made them promise never to eat humans.

"Have the crocodiles kept their promise?" I asked.

"Well, they have attacked some men, but they have never eaten them. They always let go. That was their promise to the bishop."

So it was the dead bishop, not Qat, whose soul now saturated the landscape.

Wilma led me into the current, eyes wide with daring and fear as we waded chest-deep through the churning grey water. We were not devoured.

We followed the beach to its north end, where we met a gnome-like man carrying a bow and arrow. He showed us Fisher Young's gravestone, then he fed us bananas and spongy grapefruit. We were on holy ground, the man said. It was here that Sarawia had pushed his canoe into the bay and paddled out to his destiny in 1887.

This was the third and greatest Christian myth of Vanua Lava. Sarawia was a boy whose curiosity led him to a world stranger than anything he could imagine, a world that would give him a new name and transform him into a hero as widely feted as any mythic ancestor. When he was an old man, Sarawia wrote down his story so it would not be forgotten. It went something like this.

The ship appeared on Nawono Bay one evening like a floating village. There were creatures with shocking white faces on board. Everyone who saw them was certain they had come from the rim of the sky, because they wore red clothes. Surely the creatures had coloured themselves using a liquid borrowed from the sun.

In the morning, Sarawia paddled out to inspect the vessel. Two of the creatures were dressed in black robes. They beckoned for him to come closer, but he stayed in his canoe, remembering his father's warning that the spirits would kill and eat him if he was not careful. But Sarawia was even more curious than fearful, and he wanted the fish hooks and biscuits that they held out to him. One man called so gently that Sarawia could not resist taking his hand and climbing on board. He saw the leather-shod feet of his hosts and was horrified: "I said to myself that these men were made partly of clam-shell, and my bones quaked." But Bishop George Selwyn and his young protegé, John Coleridge Patteson, did not hurt Sarawia. They sat him down and asked the names of people and things on Vanua Lava, and when Sarawia told them, Selwyn scratched symbols into what Sarawia later discovered was called a book.

The *Southern Cross* returned to Nawono the following year, and this time Selwyn begged Sarawia to leave with him. Sarawia was still unsure if his hosts were men or spirits, and he was unsure about the dangers that lay ahead, but like Ulysses, Sinbad and Skywalker, his mind was set on fortune and adventure. "I wanted to go myself to the real source of things, and get for myself an axe and a knife, and fish hooks and calico, and plenty of other such things. I thought they were just there to be picked up, and I wanted to get plenty for myself," he recalled.

Sarawia journeyed far beyond the edge of the world. They sailed for weeks, until the *Southern Cross* reached Lifu, an island near New Caledonia where Patteson had established a Christian school. Sarawia stayed there for four months until Selwyn returned on the *Southern Cross* to carry him home to Vanua Lava. Then the bishop presented Sarawia with a very large axe, and his family was proud. After the *Southern Cross* sailed away, Sarawia joined in a few battles against other villages.

The next year, Sarawia and twenty other boys travelled with Selwyn to his school near Auckland. One day, Patteson asked Sarawia which spirit had made the sky, the sun, the moon, the stars, the world and its people. Sarawia answered that of course it was Qat. No, said Patteson. It was God alone who had made everything. Sarawia did not think much of the bishop's idea: "I said to myself that this was just another spirit whom the white people think about, whereas we think about Qat."

After Patteson was consecrated Bishop of Melanesia, Sarawia sailed with him to Espiritu Santo, Gaua, Ambae and Ambrym. He sat in the rowboat and watched fearfully each time Patteson swam to shore to sit amongst bands of strangers armed with bows, arrows, spears and clubs. The strangers usually wouldn't start shooting until Patteson had finished handing out his presents and was swimming back to his boat. Sarawia was impressed by the bishop's courage. Patteson taught him to read. Sarawia studied the Bible, which impressed him even more. The stories were like nothing he had ever imagined, and if they were true, Patteson's God was certainly more awesome than Qat or any other *vui*. Even though Sarawia was now quite sure that he was a bad boy and not worthy of anything holy, Patteson baptised him and named him George, after Bishop Selwyn.

After four years, Sarawia was convinced. He concluded that all the people of the Banks Islands were prisoners of Satan, and he prayed for them. He returned to Vanua Lava and told people that Qat was not a true spirit but a lying one, that there was only one God who had created all things in heaven and in earth, and it was He alone who loved them, pitied them and looked after them.

That is how George Sarawia told his own story.

Sarawia was ordained Melanesia's first native priest in 1873, and he set up a model Christian village on Mota, transforming the tiny island into a Christian stronghold. He was a living legend by the time Henry Montgomery landed to conduct a mass confirmation service on Mota twenty years later. My great-grandfather declared that "Dear George" had shepherded the entire island, more than seven hundred people, to their Christian destiny. Men were no longer afraid to walk from village to village for fear of attack by humans or spirits, as they had been when Patteson first had arrived.

What my great-grandfather did not write, and what is now rarely said about Mota's first native priest, was this: his white mentors did not consider Sarawia to be bright ("He is not the cleverest of our scholars," Patteson noted) nor a particularly inspired leader. And this: Sarawia's great evangelizing influence came not from his office as a priest but from his stature in an ancient—and oft-banned—society that competed directly with the Church for the attention of islanders. And that society was far from benign. According to some, its members' use of black magic and poison led to a near-apocalypse on Mota long after my great-grandfather and Sarawia were dead.

Wilma and I walked back towards Sola, crossing the crocodile river as clouds boiled up over the peaks. A light rain swept along the beach. The sky turned shades of pink and gold, and so did the tongues of foam that licked the brick-red sand, and the whitecaps that danced in the riptide between us, and the silhouette of Mota, floating like a Chinese straw hat on the horizon.

Qat was dead. He would never return. It was Patteson and his followers who were immortal, whose stories were alive, growing, being wrapped in strands of mysticism. If you wanted to understand Banks Islanders, I thought, you did not go looking for Qat. You asked the Anglican Church for a ride across the waves to the holy island of Mota, where the Church had supposedly taken the sting out of *kastom*, where the well of faith had overflowed to spread across the archipelago. You went to Mota, and you did not expect to find a shred of the Old World or of the paradise you had once let yourself imagine.

11

DEATH AND

MARRIAGE ON MOTA

*It seems to be a fact that the nearer the home of your race is
to the Equator the easier it is for your race to see the unseen: and the
further from the Equator the harder it becomes. In other
words, no tropical races have any difficulty believing in God.*

HENRY MONTGOMERY, *Visions*

THE FIRST MISSIONARIES on the Banks Islands
were perplexed by the strange societies to which
the men all seemed to belong. The societies
weren't quite religious. But they weren't quite *not* religious either.

Take the *suqe,* the most influential of all Banks Island institutions. On
the surface, it seemed to be nothing more than a social club. Men gained
status by sacrificing pigs, giving feasts and paying long strands of shell
money to high-ranking members. Each village had a clubhouse decorated
with pig jawbones or fish skeletons and lined with cooking ovens, all
arranged according to rank. The *suqe* ranking was no trifle: R.H. Codrington was told that a low-ranking man who made the mistake of fool-
ing with a higher-ranking man's oven could be trampled to death for his
breach of etiquette. But the missionaries saw nothing overtly sacrilegious
about the *suqe* at first.

The *tamate* was harder to accept. It was a secret society whose members met deep in the forest to learn "mysteries" from *tamate*—the ghosts of dead men. The meeting place, or *salagoro*, was *tabu*, and strictly off limits to women and uninitiated men. The missionaries heard terrible noises coming from Mota's *salagoro* at night. Sometimes "ghosts" clad in leaf overcoats and masks would emerge to rampage through nearby villages, beating anyone they could catch. But sometimes *tamate* members would march out of the forest in the full light of day, wearing bark hats bristling with red and white quills, and they would dance. This beguiled and softened the Anglicans, who had a weakness for pageantry that seemed to extend beyond the bells and incense of their high-church liturgies, and who in their spare time taught some converts Gilbert and Sullivan show tunes. Codrington was delighted by the *tamate's* finery, the masks that looked to him similar to "the cowls of Italian becchini," the dancers who posed with their leaf fronds, much like the paintings he had seen of Christ the Martyr holding his palm.

On one occasion, Codrington heard the blood-curdling cry of Mota's great *tamate* ring out across the island. All business ground to a halt: the island was now in occupation by the *tamate* and its members. The great *tamate* was angry, apparently, because a man had disobeyed Bishop Patteson's teaching by pointing his bow and arrow at another man. The *tamate* "occupation" continued until the offender paid a pig to the society. This could hardly be a bad thing, noted Codrington, who concluded that the *tamate* and *suqe* societies were forces for social stability and a means of regulating political authority. He was sure that by 1881 the natives had divorced their societies from any association with ghosts and spirits. Patteson found both of the societies "distasteful," but still he advised Christian converts to make up their own minds about whether or not they should join and whether or not the rituals broke God's rules. They did make up their own minds: for decades, *suqe* and *tamate* rituals were simply delayed until the missionaries had sailed back to Norfolk Island.

Not until 1900, when a white missionary was stationed permanently on Mota, was the truth about the societies revealed. H.V. Adams reported that George Sarawia's church school was sparsely attended, while the *tamate* and the *suqe* were as strong as ever—and shockingly religious in their rituals. Worse, Adams discovered that Sarawia's stature and influence on Mota came not from his being an Anglican priest but from his standing in the *suqe*, in which he had ascended to the grade of head man. People listened to George Sarawia because he had followed more rituals, knew more secrets and obviously held more *mana* than most anyone on the island. One native deacon lamented on his deathbed that the *suqe* had become the Church's biggest enemy. In order to gain rank in the *suqe*, he noted, a man needed wealth. And in order to be wealthy, he had to resort to sacrifices to the old pagan spirits. "Rain, wind, sunshine, health and sickness were all bought from those who had power over these things," the Reverend Robert Pantutun confessed tearfully, then died.

In 1910, Bishop Cecil Wilson pronounced that the *suqe* was *nalinan Satan*—an utterly vile thing—and its members would be excommunicated if they persisted. George Sarawia was safe by then: he had been dead for nine years. Although the age of *suqe* and *tamate* was officially over on Mota, both lived on.

THE ANGLICAN DIOCESE of Banks and Torres owned a 5-metre wooden skiff, which felt vaguely seaworthy until it was loaded with ten passengers and the fixings for a week of feasts on Mota. We chugged out from Sola on a slack tide, following a series of ragged bluffs along the southern edge of the bay. It was calm there. Sunlight reflected off the water, illuminating the weathered face of our skipper, Alfred, and his teenaged son who stood proudly with him at the tiller. Alfred's wife, Jocelyn, crouched glumly in the boat's tiny cabin with an armful of squirming children. I was not exactly sure why these people were heading for Mota. I had heard something about a wedding, but nobody on the boat seemed particularly festive, except for one man, whose face was stretched into a permanent grin. He was not part of the family.

Alfred had an unruly beard and glassy, mournful eyes. He steered towards Kwakea, a palm-covered swath of sand just off the coast of Vanua Lava, and ran the skiff right up onto the beach. A bullock—or rather, the carcass of a bullock—was waiting for us on shore. The animal had been skinned and cut in half. Its shoulder muscles shone in the sun. Blood dripped from its buttocks as we wrestled the hind section into the boat.

We took the beast's head, too. There was still a half-chewed wad of grass between its teeth, and its eyes were fixed in a terrified stare.

The journey to Mota was not like my journey aboard the *Brisk*. It was not dreamy. When you are in a small boat, you do not cut through the ocean swell. You ride each wave as you would a great wrinkled beast. The wave rises above you, threatens to break over you, lifts you onto its broad back so you can see down into the blackness of the approaching trough, even as the next swell is bulging, shape-shifting, lumbering towards you. And then you fall.

I was coming to dislike the sea immensely. I held fast to the gunwale as we left the shelter of Kwakea. The bullock glared at me. The grinning man cupped his hand around my ear and told me why Alfred had such sad eyes. It was on a crossing just like this that the last diocesan skiff had taken a rogue wave over the bow. The boat sank within seconds, leaving Alfred in the swell with his six-year-old daughter clinging to his neck. He tried to swim for Mota, but the island just kept getting smaller and smaller, so he tried to swim west towards Sola, but the current was too strong. Alfred and his child drifted north through the morning and the afternoon. As the sun disappeared behind the mountains of Vanua Lava, Alfred treaded water and surveyed the explosions of surf along the reef that separated them from the beach at Port Patteson. His daughter grew weak. Alfred lost strength too. He held the girl as long as he could. A few hundred metres from shore, her fingers slipped from his neck and she sank into the blue shadows.

From a distance, Mota resembled a great nipple poking from the ocean. Closer, the island looked more like a shark's fin served on a thick platter. The fin was a dormant volcano. The platter was a 3-kilometre-wide plateau of uplifted coral rock, cut short on all sides by black cliffs, down which spilled vines with purple flowers, trailing all the way into the surging ocean. There were no beaches, only shelves of wave-beaten coral hanging over the edge of the electric blue abyss.

Alfred drew up against a submerged shelf on Mota's leeward side. We waded ashore, carrying the bleeding bullock on our shoulders, and then ascended the side of a deep, mosquito-filled ravine. The cracked rock was imprinted with the shapes of seashells. Alfred's village, Mariu, sat in a grassy clearing on the edge of the plateau. There were dozens of the usual thatch huts. Next to them was a church with cement foundations and the only tin roof for kilometres around. I pitched my tent under a grapefruit tree behind the church.

That evening the men lit a great bonfire in a pit outside Alfred's house. An ancient woman heaped rocks on the fire and tended it into the night. Through the mesh wall of my tent, I could see her bent frame as she stirred the embers and poked at the glowing stones long after the flames had ceased licking them, long after the rest of the village had gone to sleep. She ignored the animal-like hoots, the choruses of grunts and squawks, that echoed through the forest.

I WAS AWOKEN EARLY the next morning by the sound of the church bell, which was not a bell at all but an old propane tank against which someone banged a steel bar. Then the wailing began. It came from the direction of the firepit. It was the voice of a woman. It began like a song, rising softly in the cool morning air, but it grew more insistent and less melodic. The crying broadened until finally it was one, long, repeated chorus of anguish. I slipped on my sandals and crept around the edge of the church. There was the firepit steaming in the cool morning air. There was the old woman furiously sweeping around the pit with a straw broom. There was Alfred gazing silently into the embers. And there was his wife, Jocelyn, who had not said a word since we left Sola. She was on her knees, rocking back and forth, clenching her fists so tightly I could see the whites of her knuckles. Tears were streaming down her face, and she was howling her agony to the dirt, the fire and the empty sky.

Later, I asked Alfred to take me to George Sarawia's grave. Instead, in a clearing just outside the village, he showed me his daughter's grave. I was confused.

"I thought your little girl drowned. I thought the sea took her body," I said.

It had, he said. This was another daughter, a teenager, who had died exactly a year ago. Cancer got this one. Tomorrow, Alfred would give a feast marking the anniversary of her death. Alfred and Jocelyn would share out their bullock, let the second girl go as they had the first. Alfred would shave for the first time in a year and Jocelyn would stop crying until the next tragedy befell them.

THE OLD WOMAN who had been tending the fire was waiting with her broom at my tent. I had been told she was a *romoterr,* the last of the Mota big women. She was also Alfred's mother. Her name was Lengas Wotli-maru. Her face was as furrowed as a walnut. She had black flowers, or perhaps they were stars, tattooed on each of her cheeks. The tattoos were proof that she had been a high-ranking woman in the time of the *suqe,* she told me. Her father had killed many pigs and paid many lengths of shell money in order to give Lengas her high status.

"So the *suqe* honoured women as well as men," I said.

"Yes, but it doesn't matter any more, because the *suqe* is dead," she said in Bislama.

"Right, because the Church killed it a century ago," I said.

Lengas chuckled. The Church certainly did not kill the *suqe,* she said. In fact, the *suqe* had grown stronger and stronger during most of the twentieth century, through the patronage of a powerful Anglican priest who just happened to be Lengas's late husband, Mama Lindsay Wotli-maru (*mama* is Motese for "father"). Not that there weren't problems. In the 1940s, *suqe* members had grown increasingly competitive. Their jealousy led to fighting and a renaissance of black magic. Sorcerers used all the usual tricks: poisonings, curses, miscarriage-inducing leaves. By 1949, Mota's population had fallen to a hundred. The island was as devastated as Santa Maria had been, and everyone knew that sorcery was to blame. That's when Mama Lindsay summoned every man, woman and child on the island to his village and ordered them, one by one, to put their hand on the cross and swear that they would abandon the use of poison and magic. Those who lied or resisted would face the immediate wrath of God. It worked, said Lengas. A handful of sorcerers died. Everyone else was so scared of the *mama's* curse that they forsook all *kastom* magic. Even beneficial spells were abandoned. Now the population of Mota had climbed back up to nearly eight hundred, but nobody had any idea how to induce the spirits to bring sun, rain or bigger yams.

"But why did the *suqe* have to die along with black magic?"

"Because these days our men work for paper money, white man's money. To go *up-up* in the *suqe* you must have shell money." Lengas pulled a plastic bag from her skirt and drew out a long string of red-brown discs from it. They were dirty and chipped. It looked like the kind of necklace you would buy from a beach vendor in Cancun.

"Shell money. It takes days and days to make these beads, put holes in them, make them smooth. Mmmm," Lengas said, cooing and stroking her beads. Then her eyes narrowed. She scowled and waved her arm towards the village, where the men were preparing the day's first round of *kava*. "Look at these men. They got no *savve*. They would like to have rank, to go *up-up* in the *suqe*, but they can't without shell money, and they don't know how to make it any more. This is the last of ours," she said, shaking her string of beads. A few tiny discs broke free and fell into the dirt.

"Why don't you teach them how to make it?"

"Mi no savve!" she howled. "This is men's business. Only a man can make shell money. And the shell carvers are altogether dead now. When I die, the *suqe* will die with me."

THE VILLAGE WOMEN fussed at the firepit all afternoon. They wrapped taro, cassava and root puddings in banana leaves, then buried them beneath the hot rocks which they covered in more damp leaves. The men sat around in the grass and prepared *kava*. They didn't get their sons to chew the root as was the *kastom* on Tanna. Instead, they stuck pieces of it inside a short length of plastic drainpipe, plugged one end, then pounded the *kava* to pulp using a wooden rod as a piston. Next, in plastic buckets filled with water, they massaged the pulp through cloth towels until the drug seeped into the water.

"You'll be drinking a bit of *kava* today," I said to Alfred.

"A lot of *kava*," he murmured.

"And tomorrow," said another man.

"And the next day, too, for the wedding," said another, whom I recognized as the rector who had given the previous Sunday's church service in Sola. He was as soft and furry as a koala, and he grinned like a teenager who had just raided his parents' liquor cabinet.

The death feast proceeded like a Sunday barbecue back home. The women did the work. The men got drunk and melted into the grass. We ate root vegetables and bullock stew. Alfred's brother showed me a copy of the Motese dictionary that Codrington had written. He said that two things made islanders proud. One was Mota's history as an Anglican stronghold. The other was dancing: the Motese still had the best *tamate* dancers in all of the Banks Islands. The *tamate* had never died, Alfred's brother said. In fact, half the village men were deep in the forest as we spoke, practising their dances at their *salagoro*. I asked if I could I go watch. Of course not, he said. The ghosts would not permit it. The *salagoro* was sacred.

"But you wait," he said. "You'll hear the *tamate* coming." He rubbed his eyes and lay back on his mat. The *kava* had done its work.

THERE WAS A WOMAN on the far side of Mota whose job it was to re-member the old stories. I went to see her, following the red dirt track that circled the island. At each village, I asked for the chief, in order to request permission to pass through his territory. At each, I was offered a plate of *laplap*, and a crowd would gather to watch me lick the pudding and co-conut milk from my fingers. At each, after I shook hundreds of hands, a hush would descend, and the question would come. Always the same question.

"Is he dead?" the chiefs asked.

"Is who dead?"

"Bin Laden. Is he dead?"

People on Mota had radios. They felt close to the great dramas of the world. They had heard about aircraft crashing into very tall buildings.

"I'm sure he's dead," I tried to reassure one chief.

"Well, that is not what they say on the radio," he replied. "They say that the Bible predicted the rise of bin Laden. And they say that when bin Laden dies, the world will end. The Apocalypse will be upon us. So please do not tell me he is dead."

I found the storyteller. She was a vast, fleshy queen ant who seemed to be sinking into the earth by her little cooking fire. Her name was Hansen Ronung. Her cheeks were tattooed with a grid of black spots. In a low drone, she sang me a story of Qat, then told me the words. It was like one of the stories Codrington had recorded in *The Melanesians,* except for one detail: once, when Qat's brothers had stolen his wife and his canoe, Qat made himself very small so that he could ride the ocean inside a hollow bamboo stick. In this way he caught up to his brothers. One of them, the cunning one, said, "Qat is near, I can smell him," but the rest did not believe him. Finally, another brother saw Qat's bamboo boat in the water and picked it up. Qat used a secret weapon to repel the brother, said Hansen. Oh yes, she said, Qat had let out one *wan bigfala* fart. The smell was so bad that Qat's brother dropped the bamboo stick before he could peer inside it, and Qat escaped. This detail may have offended Codrington's Victorian aesthetic; there was no mention of flatulence in his version.

I asked Hansen where she had learned the old stories. Some, she said, came from her father. But others, she had learned from a Norwegian anthropologist who had visited Mota six years previously. Since none of those stories contained naughty bits, I suspected that the Norwegian had a copy of Codrington's *The Melanesians* and that he had reunited the old myths with their one-time home.

THE NORWEGIAN ANTHROPOLOGIST's name was Thorgeir Storesund Kolshus. Mota's *kastom* chief lent me a scuffed copy of the thesis Kolshus had written for the University of Oslo. I took it to bed with me. In it, the anthropologist, who lived on Mota in 1996 and 1997, argued that Christianity had not sterilized traditional religion on the island: it had remystified it. The *suqe* had crumbled, but the *tamate* and the ghosts they celebrated were stronger, more respected and more feared than when the missionaries first arrived. After a year on the island, Kolshus had been partially initiated into a *tamate* group and taught the steps of a simpler dance. He was shocked to learn that the dance hats the Motese constructed in their secret glades were treated with far more reverence than the goblet used to serve the blood of Christ on Sundays. The hats were more than decoration: they were the abodes of the powerful, living *tamate* spirits. Kolshus was told that to disrespect or mishandle a *tamate* hat would be to anger the spirit and thus to invite sickness or death. When Kolshus was finally permitted to dance in public, he caused a panic by nearly allowing the hat to slip from his head. If that hat had touched the ground, the entire village would have had to be evacuated until the *tamate* energy had been contained and removed.

Thus the *tamate* had borrowed a bit of Christian sacredness. Meanwhile, the Church had taken on the Melanesian concept of *mana*. Priests on Mota had the power to work miracles, bring rain, even inflict sickness as punishment for wickedness (though, when pressed, they always named God as the source of the power). That's why Mama Lindsay's anti-magic curse had worked so well.

But how did the islanders reconcile these two conflicting world views? Kolshus insisted that the Motese had split their souls in two: there was the one they were born with, and there was the one they received when baptised. When a Motese died, his first soul, the soul of the world, became a spirit and roamed the island as a *tamate*, while the second soul, the soul of heaven, rose out of the grave after three days and flew up to meet God in Heaven.

Was Thorgeir Kolshus an expert on Motese culture? The islanders evidently thought so. Before Alfred and his brothers drank *kava*, one of them always said a little prayer and spilled a drop of it on the ground. But the men admitted it wasn't their fathers who had taught them that prayer. It was Kolshus. He, in turn, had clearly learned it from anthropologist W.H.R. Rivers's 1914 book, *The History of Melanesian Society*.

I dozed off, not sure if the faint howls and echoes I heard were coming from the forest beyond the church or the ether of my dreams, which carried me away from the tin-roofed church, through the forest, to the place where mysteries were revealed. Two souls.

IN THE MORNING, we gathered in the church for the Christian half of the marriage ceremony. First came an excruciatingly long sermon, in which the priest rambled on in English for a good two hours. There was chanting and much waving of incense. It was as formal and anaesthetizing as the high-church mass at St. Margaret's Westminster. I sat beside the gentle rector from Sola, who gazed dreamily into the rafters and yawned periodically. He still had *kava* in his veins. I realized with some irritation that we were among the few who actually had arrived early enough to catch the entire service. Most dribbled in just in time to kneel down and accept the body and blood of Christ. It seemed unfair.

There were two brides and two grooms. One bride was barefoot, the other wore a new pair of cross-trainers. They both wore white dresses. Their hair was combed out afro-style, and powdered white. The grooms wore hibiscus flowers behind their ears.

Later, both couples sat outside the church in a row of plastic chairs. One by one, we came forward to shake their hands and place gifts of rice and sugar at their feet. Then the brides began to wail. They pulled down their veils to cover the tears that streamed down their faces. The two grooms stared at their knees dejectedly.

"Why are they crying?" I asked the rector.

"Because for the first time in their lives, they will leave their families and go to a faraway village."

"But it's only an hour's walk to the other side of the island."

A string band struck up behind the wedding party: three guitars and a washtub bass. The musicians thunk-thunked and jangled away maniacally, and they sang:

> "Kava! Kava! Mi likem kava,
> Kava, oh kava hem i numbawan."

Now the grooms began to cry too.

Just as the scene began to feel unbearable, the brides and grooms stood up and went their separate ways. The crowd dispersed, the village grew quiet, and I was certain the wedding was finished. I was wrong. Mota's other soul was about to speak.

The rector from Sola led me through the forest to the neighbouring village, where members of one groom's family were gathering. There was a strange, apprehensive energy about the crowd: they reminded me of troops preparing for war. Old men argued. Young men paced back and forth, fidgeted, yelped. Girls tied red flowers in their hair. And then they all began to march, solemnly at first. There were more than a hundred people, all led by a dignified old man wearing a *lavalava* and a starched white shirt. He carried an unopened yam shoot—a sign of peace, according to the rector. The others carried bags of rice, sugar and root vegetables. One yam was so big it had been strung from a pole so two men could carry it. Men hauled buckets full of *kava*. As the marchers made their way through the forest towards Mariu, they began to whoop and howl. The string band appeared out of nowhere to lead the procession, which now bounced and shook with the joy of a giant conga line. As we entered Mariu, the guitarists strummed faster and the crowd broke into a sprint. They ran to the lawn at the centre of the village. They kept running as they were joined by Alfred and his neighbours, now all dashing together around and around in a wide circle, skipping, jumping, leaping, shouting, laughing ecstatically, heaving their yams and their sloshing buckets of *kava* high in the air until they had run themselves breathless and the circle closed in on itself.

Then the *kastom* wedding ceremony began. Banana leaves were spread on the grass. The father of one groom made a great show of arranging the bride price. First, he produced a thin string of shell money that had seen better days. Then there was a pile of cash: a stunning 42,000 vatu—about $340. The bride's father made his own pile of gifts, without money. There was a moment of uncomfortable silence, then whispers. A man in a Brazil soccer jersey stepped forward, shook his fist in the air and started yelling at the father of the groom. Something was very wrong. It wasn't about the money, explained the rector. Someone hadn't done their homework, someone had botched part of the ritual. The whole thing hadn't gone according to *kastom*.

"Shhh!" someone hissed at the critic. Three or four more men joined in. "Shhh! Shhh!"

The groom's father pointed his finger at the critic and yelled at him. The bride and groom stared at the dirt while the old men angrily debated the fine points of bride price etiquette. Lengas had told me this was just the kind of confusion that happened all the time now that the *suqe* wasn't around to reinforce *kastom*. Men didn't know their traditions. They didn't follow the rules.

"Shhh!" hissed the crowd. The string band started up again, young men joined in the *kava* song, and the critic was eventually drowned out. Meat was shared. *Kava* flowed. I sat with the rector from Sola, who was in his cups again. I tried to bait him with a story from the Norwegian anthropologist's thesis. Kolshus had written that ghosts were so strong, so present on Mota, that they could be cajoled into playing games with humans. The most popular spirit game was called *ravve-tamate*, or pull-the-ghost. The object was to go out into the forest and engage in a tug-of-war with the spirit of a dead man. What could be more heretical?

"Oh, I know about *ravve-tamate*," said the rector, pausing to wipe the *kava* scum from his beard. "When I first came to Mota from the Solomon Islands, they told me about it. I just laughed at them. I said, 'I am a leader of the Church, so of course I do not believe in your ghosts.' Well, one night they showed me their game. They filled a basket with the favourite food of some dead fellow. Taro, I think it was. They tied the basket to the end of a long pole, and we went out into the forest. There were a dozen of us, men and boys. Everyone started to shout at that *devil*.* They were cheeky with him. They teased him and they called him weak. And I tell you, I heard him answer back."

The rector paused, peered into the forest, cocked his head as though listening for something and continued: "We followed the voice while one man shouted out: 'Hey *devil*, if you think you are so strong why don't you prove it? Why don't you try to pull this food from us?' We were all holding onto the pole when something grabbed the basket and tugged it. It was strong, I tell you. It dragged us through the forest."

"Weren't you afraid?"

"Oh yes! The *devil* was very rough. It dragged us through the rocks and the bushes. I was bruised! I was bleeding! But the strange thing was, I never felt the pain of my wounds."

I didn't know what to say. The rector was not at all troubled by his demonic flirtation. He was enthralled by it. I sat and thought about the two souls of Mota, the Church and the *salagoro*. I remembered that morning's church service and the crowd that had trickled in just in time to take Holy Communion. Kolshus had written that the Motese took communion as often as they could. They were swallowing the body and the blood of Christ not only as a way of remembering their Messiah's sacrifice but as

---

* In Bislama, the word *devil* means "ghost."

an act of pragmatism. He was sure the Motese believed that the bread and wine of Holy Communion made them strong, not just spiritually but physically. It was a way of soaking up the *mana* of Jesus.

A storm was building in the late afternoon sky. The wind was up. I glanced around the crowd, looking for Alfred, who should have been readying the skiff for our trip back to Sola. His face, when I found it, always seemed to be obscured by the base of an upturned *kava* cup.

The rector peered into the forest again, grasped my shoulder. "They are coming," he said. "Stand back!"

Then I heard a familiar sound, a faint owl-like hooting. It echoed through the forest. It was the sound I had heard every night on Mota, the sound I was certain was a product of imagination or dreams, only now it was louder and undoubtedly real. *Whoop. Whoosh. Coo.* Then silence. Children ran squealing from the garden at the edge of the village. Shadows ducked among the glistening leaves. The brush stirred, gained legs and arms. The *devils* leapt out into the open. There were half a dozen of them. Their heads were crowned with brambles, bamboo branches and feathers, like oversized birds' nests, from which sprouted the tentacle-like bodies of snakes: Medusa meets *Apocalypse Now*. Their eyes were completely obscured by leaves. They wore leather thongs around their genitals. Their legs and arms and gaunt buttocks were smeared with charcoal mud and bands of chalk paste. They crouched and shuffled with bowed knees. They leapt through the air. They peered into the doorways of houses and shook long white sticks at the villagers.

Alfred's brothers grabbed wooden poles and began to pound on a plywood drum in front of the church. Everyone else drew back and watched from the fringes of the clearing. Parents held children close. The dancers drew around the drummers, lurching, ducking, craning their necks like snakes. This was the dance of the *mai,* the poisonous black-and-white banded sea snake, the rector said. He grunted and cackled with pleasure. The dancers had been practising in the *salagoro* all week—hadn't I heard their shouts at night?—and this was their gift to me. I was too busy fumbling with my camera to answer. I got on my hands and knees and began to crawl towards the melee. I wanted to fill the frame of my memory. The crowd stirred behind me. I looked back to see the rector gesturing at me frantically to stop.

"You must not approach the dancers," he said when I had retreated to his side. "The ground is hot. If you stop too close you will break it, and it will take days, weeks, to fix the ground. We will all have to leave the village."

It was clear that violating the dancer's space would be more than a breach of etiquette. This dance was more than a dance. But nobody could explain the source of its power, or its apparently volatile nature, or if it had anything to do with the *tamate* at all. The ground had been wound up like a spring by the energy of the dancers, and it needed to be unwound carefully. That was all the explanation I could get.

I was struck by the geography of the spectacle. The snakes strutted and ducked below the eaves of the church, ignoring the house of God completely. I remembered the chorus of screams I had heard each night since my arrival. The *salagoro* and the church were almost neighbours. The *tamate* members had heard the early morning clang of the church bell from their secret clearing in the forest just as clearly as I had heard their howls. The church and the *salagoro* shared congregations, they knocked against each other, and now the serpent was dancing in God's garden, and there was no competition, no conflict at all, because neither acknowledged the other. The island really did have two souls.

The snake dancers retreated into the woods. The wind picked up. The sky darkened. The storm was upon us. Alfred threw back one last cup of *kava* and shuffled liquidly down the ravine towards the ocean. I followed. The swell had risen even here on the leeward side of the island. The sea shivered and heaved, then surged across the rock shelf that served as our dock. Two of Alfred's children refused to climb aboard the skiff, which bounced dangerously off the rocks. Alfred did not force them. He just smiled dejectedly and left the boys with their uncles, standing knee-deep in the storm surge. He bade them a soft good-bye, gunned the outboard motor and steered us into the endless grey cordillera of swell. Alfred had plenty of fuel for the journey back to Vanua Lava: at his feet was a two-litre jug of *kava*.

12

THE SECRET OF

WEST VANUA LAVA

*How colonial of me, I later thought: I want
into their lives, but only as a voyeur.*

DEBORAH ELLISTON,
The Dynamics of Difficult Conversations: Talking Sex in Tahiti

MELANESIAN HISTORY has long belonged to
foreigners. It was white men who first wrote
down the islanders' stories even as they sought
to erase the *kastom* that went with them. Through sermons and schoolbooks, the words of those early missionaries, traders and colonial administrators lived on to shape collective memory. Now, Melanesians casually
refer to the time before contact as *taem blong darkness,* reducing thousands
of years of trading, agriculture, fishing and storytelling to a shadow world
of fear, violence and suffering. Whether this memory is accurate or not,
its foundations lie in the scribblings of foreigners.

On Mota, I found that European accounts of the island's *kastom*
always carried the most weight. Thus Hansen Ronung, whose job it was
to sing her way through Motese history, could be corrected and humbled
with a few anecdotes from Codrington's *The Melanesians,* and when
Motese argued about modern culture and rituals, their disputes were
now arbitrated by whoever was holding the tattered copy of Thorgeir

Kolshus's University of Oslo thesis. Simply because they were written down, the Norwegian's own theories were concrete compared to the shifting sands of oral tradition. Alfred's brother had told me that he thought Kolshus's big idea, the one about the Motese having two souls, was just plain wrong. But his words faded amid a haze of *kava*, conversation and guitar strumming; and they will continue to fade with every year, as conversations do. But Kolshus's version of *kastom* will live on, unchanged.

When Codrington published *The Melanesians* in 1891, it was hailed as the first thorough study of "primitive" culture. Ever since, anthropologists have flocked to the South Pacific looking for remnants of a primitive Other that they might romance, penetrate and ride towards scholarly recognition. These foreigners and their books have frequently been lauded as presevers of truth and traditional culture in modern Melanesia. Some communities are thrilled to be the subject of research. It brings them status and attention. But anthropologists, like the missionaries and traders before them—not to mention travel writers—don't necessarily get their stories right. The godmother of modern anthropology, Margaret Mead, proved that much. In *Coming of Age in Samoa: A Psychological Study of Primitive Youth for Western Civilization,* Mead presented "evidence" that cultural—rather than biological—factors were the most important determiners of human behaviour: testimony from a trio of Polynesian girls who claimed that they were not subject to any of the sexual taboos and shame faced by American teens. The girls led her to believe that they were both carefree and promiscuous. Mead, eager to prove her theories, ate the stories up. The book propelled her to fame when it was released in 1928, but half a century later, one informant confessed that she and her friends had been so embarrassed by Mead's interrogation that they had simply fibbed to her. The truth was—and still is—that sexuality is not a matter taken lightly anywhere in the South Pacific.

I wanted to meet an anthropologist who had managed to pierce the thick skin of the Melanesian Other. A month before leaving Canada, I had learned about a German scholar who had been living at Vureas Bay, on the west side of Vanua Lava, for nearly a year, researching a thesis for the Australian National University. She received my e-mail message at the post office in Port Vila during one of her quarterly visits. Just drop by, she had replied. Easy.

I had a map which showed a perfect red line wandering all the way west across Vanua Lava to Vureas Bay. Everyone in Sola insisted the red line was a road. But when Melanesians say "road," they aren't thinking about a highway or even a cart track. They mean there is a way. They mean that yes, once upon a time, perhaps someone walked in that direction.

I filled my pack with bags of rice, corned beef and Webster's Cream Cookies, then followed a gravel road over the snake ridge and down onto a plain bristling with rows of coconut palms. The road became two furrows in the tall grass. The wind hissed through the tops of the palms but did not stir the soupy air beneath them. My shadow shrank beneath me. Flies landed to sip from beads of sweat on my neck. At midday, the copra plantations gave way to jungle and merciful shade, but then the road disappeared, swallowed by a mound of boulders and an extravagance of shining leaves and knotted vines. Bewildered, I marched back along the track, looking for the turn I had missed. I poked around the roots of a giant banyan. Nothing. I drank the last of my water. The road had obviously intended to go west, so I went west. I clambered through the boulders and realized that the moss and lichen had been worn from some of them. I followed the route of bare rock until it became a trail. It led over a mountain, through a mosquito bog and down along a great bay, where the sea rose into house-high curls that slammed onto the crags below me. I saw no one.

The trail faded, reappeared, then was joined by others in the afternoon. Like a river, it strengthened and gained certainty with each new tributary. I stopped by a creek and opened my bag of cookies. I listened to my breathing and the roar of the distant surf. The solitude was a gift but it did not last. Melanesians do not believe in solitude. They will rescue you from it when they can.

It was mid-afternoon when the red-eyed man emerged from the forest. He carried a broad machete and used it to cut open a coconut for me to drink. He told me that yes, he knew my German scholar, Miss Sabine. She was a good woman, he said, but her story was a sad one: *"Hem i no gat famili. Ino gat husban. No gat brotha. No gat pikinini. I sad tumas."*

The man insisted that I needed his help to reach Vureas Bay. The problem, he said, was the big water. He took my pack and marched off, pleased with himself. I followed, irritated. Cattle stood beneath the palms. The heat had made them so lethargic we had to push them from our path. We descended into a black rock canyon and forded a river, hopping across a series of submerged boulders. The clear water tugged at my shins. "Men have been swept away here," said the man. "Yesterday the big water was so high you could not cross it. You should pray for God to keep the sun shining, or you will not be able to leave Vureas Bay for a long time."

As if on cue, the sun disappeared behind a mound of billowing cumulonimbus.

We splashed through water gardens bursting with big-leafed taro, all irrigated by dozens of narrow earthen canals. We hit the suburbs of Vetuboso just before dark. There were no roads. There was no power. But there were hundreds of huts scattered through the forest, all strung together by a network of trails slicked by centuries of bare footsteps. In the middle of the town, beneath the eaves of her own thatch bungalow, was my anthropologist.

Sabine Hess was a sparrow compared to her meaty neighbours. She seemed harrowed, thirsty. When she saw me she ran a hand through her blond hair, which she had trimmed into a precise bob, and sighed deeply. She seemed exasperated, or perhaps relieved. She embraced me like an old friend. The neighbours were scandalized, but I understood. I carried the aura of chocolate, books, rock videos, conversations in cafés, bad language: things that were as familiar in Heidelberg as they were in Houston or my own hometown, yet absolutely foreign to Vanua Lava.

Sabine introduced me to the village's *kastom* chief, Eli Field. He wore no shirt or shoes, but he did have a silver watch on his wrist. He had the chest of a bull and the sparkling eyes of a storyteller.

"*Bi yumi dringim wanfala kava tonaet!*" Eli said, crushing my hand inside a callused paw.

"*Kava, hem i numbawan,*" I replied.

Sabine rolled her eyes and led me inside to her kitchen. A thin dog rubbed his haunch across the dirt floor.

"One more month," she sighed. "Just one more month, then I will escape."

Sabine set a kettle on her fire and made me a cup of weak tea. She said she had come to Vureas Bay because the locals had asked for her. Nobody had completed an ethnography here since Codrington.

"All their old knowledge is scattered, it's disappearing. The chiefs thought that if I wrote it down, at least they would have a picture of the *kastom* they still possess. But . . ." she waved a thin arm dejectedly towards her door.

"Yes?" I said.

"But it has been difficult. Officially, these people want their knowledge preserved, but in reality they are incredibly possessive of it. These are jealous people."

A crowd gathered around Sabine's hut. Heads poked through the window, which was not a window but a rough gap in a wall of woven pandanus leaves. Men and boys strained to hear us. Sabine smiled weakly. "And there are other problems. It's hard to be a single woman living alone here. To the men, I'm a temptation. To the women, I'm a threat. I do have informants, but as soon as I establish a rapport with them, their wives get jealous. They gossip. Some men aren't even permitted to come drink tea with me. And then there are the creepers . . ."

I laughed. I had heard about creepers. Men and women on the islands were forbidden almost any physical contact until they got married. Men who couldn't control their libidos would literally creep through their villages at night, tapping softly at the windows of supposedly available women. It was regarded as a sport by some, but I imagined a creeper's approach would be terrifying for a foreigner sleeping alone. Unless she was unusually bold.

There were a generator and a television in Vetuboso. Someone had returned from Port Vila with porn videos. From them, the men had learned that white women were insatiable and eager to break all kinds of sexual *tabus,* especially the one forbidding oral sex. As a result, there was constant knocking at Sabine's window. The creepers didn't scare her, she said, but what a bloody bother they could be. The trick was to yell as loudly as possible, yell until the creepers were shamed into flight.

You would do that if you wanted them to go away, I thought. But what if you didn't? What if you were lonely? What if you were curious? What then?

Since Victorian times, anthropologists have claimed to follow a simple rule, which, though unwritten, is as powerful as any Melanesian *tabu*. One researcher put it simply for me: don't fuck with the natives.

Study the Other. Insinuate yourself into its life. Befriend it. Do its dances. Eat its food. Learn its secrets. Become intimate with it. Love it, even. But never cross the line. Anthropologists are less articulate when they try to explain why they should keep their distance, but the sex taboo is about more than scholarly high-mindedness.

Bronislaw Malinowski won fame in 1929 by revealing the amorous secrets of Melanesians in *The Sexual Life of Savages*. However, it wasn't until the posthumous publication of his field diaries that Malinowski's own erotic fantasies about his Trobriand Island hosts were revealed. After observing one local woman, Malinowski panted: "I watched the muscles of her back, her figure, her legs, and the beauty of the body so hidden to us whites, fascinated me . . . I was sorry I was not a savage and could not possess this pretty girl." Why could Malinowski not claim his exotic prize? Post-colonial critics say it was because sexual intimacy would have broken down the last barrier between the anthropologist and his Other. The sex taboo reinforced Malinowski's superior status; as long as he remained pure, he was not part of the Melanesian system but above it. Malinowski was the one with the right to ask questions, and, unlike his "savages," he would not be expected to give up his own secrets.

Plenty of Malinowski's intellectual descendants have broken the sex taboo, but few are keen to publicize their adventures. That kind of story could have you lumped in with three hundred years of sexual exploiters or worse: as one field worker told me in Port Vila, it could reveal you as weak. Either way, it could ruin your reputation. The community of anthropologists is hierarchical. To rise to the top, you must guard your power and your secrets. Now there's a community that needs studying.

I wanted to warn Sabine not to tell me her own secrets, but I did not.

AFTER DARK, SABINE LED me to the compound Eli had built for his family in the forest far from the village. Eli had decided that I should stay in a hut he had built behind his own. It was cluttered with dusty audiotapes and stacks of *National Geographic* magazines, the effects of a French linguist who had come to make a dictionary of the local dialect. Before the linguist, there had been a coconut biologist. Eli's hospitality was turning Vetuboso into a hotbed of doctoral research.

We arrived just in time for *kava*. Eli's eldest son pushed chunks of the root into a cast-iron meat grinder on the porch. His bright eyes and bare torso shone in the silver light of Sabine's headlamp. Cali was eighteen. He had a wife and a baby. He wore an ear stud with a tiny pink star on the tip of it.

Eli held up an oil lantern and began his lament.

His great-grandfather had been the most powerful *kastom* chief in Vureas Bay. Then the *Southern Cross* arrived. The missionaries converted Eli's grandfather and his father too. The missionaries built a school and started a coconut plantation. Everyone wanted to learn the language of the powerful foreigners, so the mission school was always full. The children learned English and, along with it, the new religion. Esuva Din— the district priest who had cursed the sorcerers of Gaua—arrived in Vureas Bay to stamp out *kastom*. Ten sorcerers died within a week. Magic stones were smashed. The *suqe* and its secrets were lost.

That's when Eli Field was born. He grew up hearing the old folks whisper about *kastom* and about the power and secrets the Church had banned. In 1988, he went to Australia, walked into a cathedral and was struck by the idea that his family was following someone else's religion. He had had enough of it. "I had looked at the world and I knew there wasn't only one true religion. I knew about the Buddhists, the Muslims, the Hindus. The world had always been *full-up* with religion. I decided that my *kastom* was the religion of my country, and I wanted to start living by it again. Christians say our grandfathers lived in darkness before the missionaries brought them the light of Christ. Don't tell me my *kastom* is darkness!"

The more excited Eli grew, the more he fell into speaking Bislama. It was hard to keep up, especially after my second shell of *kava*. I caught this much: Eli had planted *kastom* herbs among the ruins and built himself a house in the old mission schoolyard. He had started a culture club and invited the elders to come and share their knowledge. He had stopped attending Sunday services. The church elders declared him a heathen and a backslider.

The *kava* was strong. The night was dark. I was sitting on a high wooden bench when Eli lifted a plastic cup of *kava* in the air. Cali gestured for me to get down, squat on the floor. *"Taem kastom chief i drink, yu mas stap daon nomo,"* he whispered. Eli gulped his drink, stepped outside, spat into the wind and barked an elaborate incantation. It was an exaggerated imitation of the rituals that had felt so true on Tanna.

"What about magic?" I asked Eli. "I suppose that has been lost for years."

Sabine let out an annoyed sigh. I had forgotten she was with us. This definitely wasn't Tanna, or a woman of any colour would not have been permitted near a *kava* session.

"It has not been lost," said Eli, "Some old fellows hid their magic stones from Esuva Din, and now we are learning how to use them again."

"What about you? Can you do it, Eli?"

"Sabine knows I can. I have proved it. One time, Catriana, the last researcher, made me *cross tumas.* She spent two weeks interviewing me, making demands, asking me to *walkabaot* with her here and there. Then, to show me her appreciation, she gave me a box of matches. A box of matches! I said no worries. I did not complain. But when she went to the airport at Sola, I sent my boy to give her a message. I told him to tell Catriana that she had better find somewhere to stay in Sola because she would be stuck there for two weeks. Then I made it rain. *Hem nao!* I made it rain so hard that the airstrip flooded and the big water swelled. Didn't I, Sabine?"

"Well, it did *happen* to rain and Catriana *happened* to be stuck, but ..."

"Look," I interrupted. "On every island, people tell me they can use *kastom* magic, but nobody ever proves it. I'm tired of magic *toktok.* I want magic action."

"*Disfala* rain magic takes time. The rainmaker has to make sacrifices. No sex. No talking. He has to fast for three, four days."

"Fine. I'll stay five days, until Wednesday."

"Is that a challenge?" said Sabine.

"You bet it is."

"You careful," Eli said with a mischievous smile. "If we bring rain, you won't be able to cross the big water."

"Well then, hold off on the rain until Wednesday afternoon."

There was more said that evening, but I had taken a third cup. Shortly after my last spit, I lost Eli's voice in a congealed soup of mumbled thoughts, shards of flickering lamplight and distant dog howls. I remember the silver-blue glare of Sabine's headlamp, shooting across the yard. Swirling nausea. A fight with a mosquito net. A damp mattress. Rain seeping through the rafters.

THE NEXT MORNING, I was back in the village, sitting in Sabine's kitchen, when a few members of Eli's culture club arrived. Sabine stepped back and tended to her cooking fire. One man had the hungry eyes of a creeper. He sat down and told me that the club was working to start up the *suqe* again. It would be difficult, he said, giving up all those pigs, spending all those months in meditative seclusion.

"If the *suqe* is so hard, why bother reviving it?" I asked.

"For power!" he said. "Our grandfathers, they went to the *salagoro* and prayed, and they would *walkabaot* down into the ground, deep, deep, until they reached a place under the bottom of the ocean. There they met the sea snake, and he gave them secret knowledge so they could become wealthy." There was more. Something about eating a *tabu* fire in order to kill some distant and unsuspecting person. His ideas were a muddled fusion of *suqe, tamate* and *The Lord of the Rings*.

"So when will you start killing pigs again?"

"This will take a few years. We have to convince enough men to join us. Right now, most Christian men are afraid of this kind of *kastom*. They call it *devil* worship. So we have secret meetings each week to gather the old knowledge and rebuild *kastom*."

"How many have joined you?"

"Um, hum, six, I think." His voice trailed off. He scratched his beard and stared over my shoulder. I followed his gaze across the room. Sabine was bending over her fire.

VETUBOSO SAT ON A forested plateau above Vureas Bay. That afternoon, Sabine led me down a footpath to the sea. The mountains were girdled with low cloud. The breeze was warm and sticky. Waves curled along a black sand beach. Sabine swam fully clothed—it was *tabu* for a woman's thighs to be seen in public.

My conversation with Eli's culture gang had made Sabine grumpy. "You know, I have never heard those stories," she said. "The *salagoro,* the *suqe,* the snake spirits—the men won't tell me about any of that stuff."

Once, said Sabine, an informant had told her a *tabu* story, a particularly erotic one involving the god of taro and his tree-sized penis. When Eli got wind of the informant's indiscretion, he was furious. He said it was not a story to be shared with women or outsiders. He became even more angry after Sabine defended the old man and told her he would have nothing more to do with her. It took weeks for Eli to warm up.

"But why would Eli block you? You are here to help him save the *kastom.*"

Sabine wiped the sea water from her eyes and swam closer. "You have to understand that women here are seen as a threat to male power. I don't mean politically; men honestly believe that women can drain their energy. That's why, when men practise their dances, they steer clear of women. When the men go fishing, women are banned from walking on the beach. Some fish will simply refuse to be caught when women are around. Men even abstain from having sex with their wives for fear of losing this kind of energy."

Sabine had come to Vetuboso to write about people's sense of self. Who do you think you are? she asked them. Why are you that way? All she had gotten were superficial answers. *"Mi no savve,"* people would tell her. *I can't say. I don't know. It's just our way.* And the more time she spent in the village, the more an invisible grid of *kastom* rules and relationships closed in around her. The moment Sabine arrived in Vetuboso, she had become Eli's adoptive daughter and a member of Eli's wife's tribe. Her maternal cousins—of which, according to the mathematics of extrapolated kinship, she now had dozens and dozens—became like brothers and sisters. Half the village's unmarried men had suddenly become potential marriage partners.

The system landed her in a minefield of manners in a landscape filled with uncles, aunts, brothers, sisters, friends and enemies by default, all people who were bound by *kastom* to speak to her in specific ways or to not speak to her at all. Sabine was forbidden to utter the name of her "sister-in-law," Cali's wife. She couldn't even use words that sounded like that name. Sabine couldn't tease or joke with Eli or any of her maternal uncles. She had scribbled diagrams to remind herself whom she could talk to.

This, she said, was the real story of Vetuboso. The rules were everything. If a man took the wrong person—for example, an unmarried woman—to his garden, the gossip would start immediately. Then the elders would levy a fine. Or worse: they would send a party to trample all the man's garden, and perhaps those of his family as well. But it was the gossip that hurt the most. Trust me, Sabine said with the gravity of one who knew from experience: you do not want to break the rules in Vureas Bay. She had given up trying to extract *kastom* secrets—the *suqe* and *salagoro* mysteries would have to survive without her help—and she had focussed her research on the intricate web of rules she had to follow. She had dug deeper and deeper into the muck of the village's rules of etiquette, manners and kinship associations. The rules, she told me, were everything here. You write what you know.

I learned this in Vureas Bay: the rules were catching up to Sabine, tightening around her, suffocating her. I liked Sabine. We agreed on things, on the subjectivity of morality, for example, a concept that was a world away from the code that had to be followed in Vetuboso. Sabine had a secret of her own, I knew that much. She had broken a rule. The backsliders let it slip between belts of *kava*. The creepers whispered it at night, when they circled like sharks in the shadows of her garden. We know what you have done, they hissed. We know who you are. Open your door again.

I know now that Sabine's secret has been passed from fire to fire and village to village across Vanua Lava. It has climbed on the mail plane and bounced down to Vila. It has flown around the world. It has arrived like a scandalous guest at university cocktail parties where cold-handed academics snigger and debate the rules of engagement but cannot begin to imagine the lonely nights, the knocked-on doors, the jealousies, the dimmed lanterns of Vanua Lava. The secret will not be revealed in Sabine's thesis, nor is it recorded here. We are the storytellers of Melanesia, and we have decided that this is not the history we wish to preserve.

We own this story and we will transform it, just as the missionaries did with the myth of Nukapu. And our version will live on long after the gossip has been carried away like smoke from a dying fire.

ELI SPENT HIS DAYS away from the compound. Cali explained that he was doing Very Important Things Related to Culture. Eli was hard to catch, which seemed to be a trend among people I had challenged to prove their magic. I caught him after dark on my fourth night. He wouldn't talk until I had downed a cup of *kava* with him.

"Sabine came here to help you, but you and your friends won't share *kastom* stories with her," I said.

Eli scratched his belly and smirked. "She can always ask the women for their stories."

"But women don't know about men's *kastom*, do they? They don't know about the *suqe* or the *salagoro*. How is Sabine supposed to make a full report?"

Eli threw back another cup of *kava*, went to the door and spat into the night. He lowered his voice and spoke solemnly in English. "Let me tell you what makes a Ni-Vanuatu different than a white man. You people share out all of your knowledge, but you don't like to share your money. Your thinking is backwards. Here in Vanuatu, we are not too rich, and still we will share everything we have with you. If you want our food, we will cook for you. If you want our money, we will give it to you. We are generous with these things. But knowledge, that is our power, and there are some things only men should know. If you take the secrets that belong to us men, if you write them down or show them to women, you take our power away. And then we would have nothing. Sabine was angry when I first explained this to her. She cried for weeks. But this is our *kastom* and she must accept it."

"But the men have told me all kinds of secrets, and I am writing them down," I said.

"Mmm, but we will never tell you the most important things."

"Fine. It's not your secrets I'm after anyway. What I really want is to see that your *kastom*, your magic, still has power. Didn't you promise to bring a big rainstorm on Wednesday?"

"Hmm, well, *yumi garem wanfala problem*. It has rained so much this year, our mangoes are rotting on the trees. It would be irresponsible for me to make rain right now."

The truth was that it had been drizzling constantly since I arrived in Vetuboso. A rainstorm wouldn't have been much of a miracle.

"Okay then, how about sun?" I suggested. "Let's have some sun for Wednesday."

Eli shifted uncomfortably on his bench. His voice lost its authoritative tone. *"I gat wan narafala problem."*

"What? What now?"

"I have been trying to help you. I have. But the men who keep the *kastom* stones are scared. Today, I went to see the man *blong* shark stone, to see if he could bring you a shark in the bay. He refused. I told him that you would write a *bigfala* story about him . . ."

"To prove that your *kastom* lives," I said.

"But he was afraid *tumas*. He said if he played with the stone, the *tasiu* would kill him."

The *tasiu*, said Eli, was a tremendously powerful man of God. He lived with his apprentices on a hill near Vureas Bay. He had a magic walking stick. Wherever Eli had tried to promote *kastom*, the *tasiu* had smashed it. Even as we spoke, the *tasiu* was hunting down *kastom* stones, exorcising their spirits, wiping away their power. The *tasiu* also confronted the owners of those stones: he told them they must wrap their hands around his magic walking stick and confess their crimes or face a terrible punishment from God.

"I tell you," said Eli, "it is not easy being a *kastom* chief these days."

In fact, it was much harder than he admitted. It was common knowledge that black magic was being practised in Vetuboso. In the most recent case, a boy had been struck with a mysterious illness which caused his leg to swell up like a giant sea slug. Before the boy died, a *kastom* doctor had told his parents that their son was the victim of a curse. "Look in the dirt under your house," the doctor had told them. They did, and found several sinister-looking parcels—lumps of ash wrapped in coconut bark—under the boy's sleeping platform. The *tasiu* had come down from his hill to investigate. He declared that the parcels were evil charms. He dabbed holy oil on the suspected sorcerers to lubricate their confessions. One of them insisted that it was Eli Field who had paid for the curse. The accusations could easily have been lies planted by Eli's anti-*kastom* enemies—and the *tasiu* did not believe them—but rumours were as effective a weapon in Vanuatu as black magic, and these rumours were enough for village leaders to take away Eli's title of *kastom* chief for several months.

I had heard the word *tasiu* before. It is Motese for "brother," and it is reserved for members of an indigenous Anglican order called the Melanesian Brotherhood. I had been hearing stories about the brotherhood for weeks. Some said the brothers were a kind of spiritual SWAT team, dispatched by the Church to douse the fires of backsliderism and paganism.

I sent a message up the mountain and waited to hear from the *tasiu*.

MEANWHILE, THE DRIZZLE continued and my clothes began to rot. One afternoon an acquaintance of Eli's named Ben produced a magician. We all met outside Sabine's kitchen. The magician had the long, stubborn face of a mule. He handed Ben his wooden staff. Ben and I kneeled in the dirt and grasped the narrow end of the staff, hand over hand. The object was to keep the heavy end of the staff pointed upright. It would be difficult, said the magician, because soon a spirit would come to tug at it. It would be like a miniature version of Mota's *ravve-tamate* game.

"Why can't Chuck and I play the game together?" asked Sabine.

"Because you don't know the special prayer," barked Ben dismissively, then under his breath, added, "woman."

"*Yufala mas sarem eye nomo,*" said the magician, closing his own eyes to demonstrate his request. "*Sipos yu opem olgeta eye blong yu, devil hem i runaway nao.*"

By now a dozen people, including Eli, had gathered to watch. I closed my eyes, and Ben made a short incantation to harass the soul of some dead man. The stick swayed slightly. I strained to hold it still. Ben's fists flexed against mine. He was clearly trying to push the staff from side to side. I felt tempted to do the same, to make the staff bob and bounce and swing—what a show we could have produced—but I didn't. I held firm and the staff did little more than tremble. Ben gave up after a few minutes. "Open your eyes," he said.

"I don't know what went wrong," said Eli. Sabine just stood at her door with her arms folded and a half smile on her face, like a mother whose teenager had once again come home drunk.

The magician was not deterred. He led us into the forest for round two. We pushed through bamboo thickets and groves of sharp-leaved shrubs where black spiders clung to huge, sagging webs. The ground had been ravaged by rooting pigs. Birds screamed. Mosquitoes rose up from the muck. The magician hacked a clearing with his machete. He built a fence of pandanus leaves and gestured for Sabine, Eli and I to stay behind it.

The magician picked a coconut off the ground, cut a hole in it and turned it over so that we could see the milk pour out. Then he cut open a second coconut and turned it over. No milk this time. But Ben, who was kneeling a couple of metres away, had turned his face up and was gulping enthusiastically at the air. His mouth swelled like a fish, and his Adam's apple bobbed up and down. The idea was that he was drinking an invisible stream of coconut milk that the magician had mysteriously transported across the clearing into his mouth.

"Bigfala sapraes, no?" asked the magician after repeating the trick a few times.

I could feel Sabine's eyes burning into me disdainfully.

"Yu lookim power blong devil. Yu bilif, no?" he said hopefully.

"Well," I said, glancing back and forth between Sabine and the magician, "it would have been easy for you to have come out here and empty three of those coconuts early this morning, wouldn't it?" I felt a sudden pang of guilt, or maybe something closer to pity, for the magician. "Oh hell, sure I believe. *Hem tru—yu garem bigfala savve.*"

Sabine was not impressed with the magic show, or, for that matter, with me. Back in her kitchen, she spooned the last of her peanut butter onto a crust of bread and handed it to me. "What a performance! What a miracle! Now you have seen your *kastom* magic. Have you had enough yet?"

I gnawed on my bread glumly. "You've spent a year with these people," I said. "You have heard them talk about magic and spirits. Instead of acknowledging these things, you ignore them. Aren't you at least curious about what drives these beliefs?"

"What drives them? Fear. Jealousy. Superstition. We have all those things at home in Germany. I am not interested in fantasy. I am writing about what I see. You, on the other hand, are romanticizing these people. Look around. Look at this remarkable community, the complex society they have built. I don't understand why this isn't enough for you. Why the world isn't enough for you. Why you are so obsessed with magic when you have all the wonder of humanity around you."

What could I say? The magician's cheap tricks had thrown a humiliating light on my quest.

I am a slow thinker. It took me days to formulate my defence. If I had been quicker on my feet, I would have told Sabine this:

Modern anthropologists parachute into communities, dig around for people's secrets and myths, listen wide-eyed and stone-faced, as though they believe, pretending all the while to be neutral in matters of spirituality—or worse, converts to the local way of thinking—when, in reality, they, like all of us, hold very strong convictions about the nature of the universe. They may analyse the origins and usefulness of their study communities' beliefs, but they don't hold them to the same standard of critique to which they subject those of their own society.

It's a patronizing approach. Thorgeir Kolshus was so convincing that the men of Mota welcomed him into the *salagoro*. They taught him how to dance. They even let him leap around with that sacred and dangerous *tamate* hat on his head. But when Kolshus defended his thesis at the University of Oslo, did he insist that his dance hat actually contained a ghost? Not likely, unless he wanted to end his academic career. Field anthropology is a business of deception generally performed by unbelievers. At least the missionaries were honest about their convictions. (And, to her credit, Sabine was honest about her disdain for magic and the boasts of Vanua Lava's rainmakers.)

It had not been my intention to develop a taste for magic. I thought I could remain aloof in my travels, record the stories I heard, chart the legacy of the missionaries, while pretending indifference like an anthropologist or a journalist. But there was something about these islands and their inhabitants that lured me to test the waters of their faith. Perhaps it was because the well was so deep. Belief in supernatural forces had always been strong on the islands, whether that meant the power of stones, spirits, ghosts or God. Melanesians had always seen evidence of that power. But their European visitors saw the power too.

Nothing made the battle between good and evil seem more alive to my great-grandfather than the Melanesians' continued use of magic to inflict death or disease. He insisted that the charms were real: after all, their victims were frequently unaware they had been targeted. The charms worked like the curses doled out by southern Africa's Zulu wizards. They were "utterly inexplicable on any other theory than that of diabolical possession, or the co-operation of evil spirits," he wrote. "I see no cause to disbelieve, in fact, it seems to me reasonable, that Satan, in whose bond they are as heathen, should be able to bestow a hurtful power upon some of them."

But the light was as palpable as the darkness for Henry Montgomery. When new converts reported seeing a glow emanating from the altars of churches at night, he did not belittle their claims. He rejoiced that the natives' powerful faith had allowed them to see a representation of God on earth.

The islanders I met still share this certainty. The world is more than an accident. The cosmos is not empty. Humans are not alone. There are no half-believers in Melanesia. People may have chosen the Christian God over their spirits, or vice versa, but no one except the hapless foreigner doubts that both exist. They are two sides of the same coin. Faith is an all-or-nothing deal. In a way, this point of view makes sense to me. If one cosmology is a conduit to the world of miracles, then couldn't they all be?

Here is the thought I was too shy to admit to Sabine: despite everything I was sure I knew about superstition, fiction and science, I was allowing a small part of myself to imagine that the believers might, in some strange and tiny way, be right. Naturally, I envied them. Naturally, I craved a taste of the mystery that thickened the tropical air. But I wanted proof.

If the islands could produce magic, if some shred of Oceanic faith was grounded in something I could touch and feel, then it followed that the Christian myth that had sustained my family for generations might contain more than a metaphor. It was a bit of a stretch to imagine that God had helped my ancestors slaughter their enemies, but proof of magic would suggest they might have been on the right track when they knew, as Melanesians knew, that the world was more than a collection of serendipitously bonded atoms and spinning electrons; more than a series of accidents, collisions, explosions and diffusions bubbling endlessly in an insignificant corner of an otherwise empty cosmos.

13

MY FIRST TASIU

The day of the Lord cometh as a thief in the night
and when men shall say, Peace, and all things are safe, then shall
sudden destruction come upon them, as sorrow cometh
upon a woman travailing with child, and they shall not escape.

A Penitential Service to Be Used on the First Day of Lent,

The Book of Common Prayer of the Church of Ireland

SABINE WAS NOT the one to take me closer to the soul of Melanesia's magic. She had given up on secrets and mysteries. As for Eli, cultural revival had made him enemies in the Church and placed him on the bad side of the *tasiu*. His struggle to save *kastom* seemed doomed. The coconut trick was the last straw. If supernatural power was being exerted in Vureas Bay, Eli and his friends were not the ones directing it. Everyone knew the real power was coming from the hill above the village, where the *tasiu* lived with his apprentices. The latest news of the *tasiu*? He had issued a curse that resulted in the death of a Seventh-day Adventist rival. Spectacular!

The reply from the *tasiu* arrived on the lips of a long-legged runner: he was expecting me. The rain had been dumping for two days—incidentally, ever since Eli had rescinded his promise to open the skies. The big water was rising. At the risk of being stranded in Vureas Bay, I went to meet the *tasiu*. Ben, the magic coconut milk drinker, insisted on guiding me. Hymns were echoing from Vetuboso's church when we set off. It was George Sarawia Memorial Day. The service went on most of the morning. Ben was terrified the priest might spot him from the open-air chapel, so we slunk around the edge of the village, dashing from hut to hut like commandos.

"*Yu wanfala backslider!*" I hissed at Ben conspiratorially.

He nodded in agreement, then lowered his voice: "You must never talk this way around the *tasiu*."

We followed a mud track into the forest, up along a low ridge, through a dozen small clearings planted with young banana trees and trailing vines. The earth was the colour of boiled yam. Ben whispered to me as we walked. He said I should not run away even if I became frightened. Higher, the wind pulled at the forest. The trees creaked and shuddered.

A terrible scream rose from the forest. Two boys leapt out of the bush onto the trail in front of me. They wore loincloths and had smeared mud over their faces and thighs. They carried spears, which they pointed at me. I turned back. Two more approached from behind. Ben winked at me. Fine. I would not run away. The boys grunted and yelled until their adolescent voices broke. They jumped up and down threateningly, and slapped me gently with lengths of vine rope, which they then wrapped around my wrists. I put on a grimace and allowed them to poke me, prod me and pull me through the forest.

There was a bluff on the top of the ridge. It was bare, as though a forest fire had ripped across it. We trudged through a patchwork of broken tree limbs and seared rubble until we reached a white cross and a chapel overlooking the desolation. The *tasiu* met us at the chapel door. He was a magnificent-looking man with the physique and rough face of a rugby forward and the deep-set eyes of a mystic. He wore a black T-shirt and black shorts secured by a black-and-white striped sash. A copper medallion hung from a coral necklace. He said nothing but waved me into the chapel.

My faux-savages led me to a bench. The *tasiu* stood with his novices in a line near the altar, and they began to sing. It was like the opening number of a kindergarten variety show.

"You have travelled far from home across the sea. Welcome, welcome, we welcome you," the boys sang in English while flakes of crusted mud fell from their cheeks. It was sweet and heartbreakingly sincere.

Over coconut milk and cream cookies, the *tasiu* explained to me that the ambush was a traditional welcome for European visitors, so that we would know what captured labourers felt during the days of the black-birders.

"Thank you, I think," I said. I was their first foreign visitor in months.

The *tasiu* told me his name was Ken Brown. He was twenty-nine years old. When he was half that age, emissaries of the Melanesian Brotherhood had come to his village near Vureas Bay. Ken was captivated by the stories the brothers told him about their adventures in heathen places. He followed them back to their base on the island of Ambae, where he trained, prayed and emerged after three years as a full-fledged member of the Melanesian Brotherhood.

"But what do you do here in Vureas Bay?" I asked. His English was sparse, so we spoke in Bislama. Ben helped with translation. The conversation went something like this:

"Many things. We negotiate to stop land disputes. We help married couples work out their problems. We make rebaptisms for backsliders . . ."

"Magic?"

"Oh yes, we take care of that. We also organize a youth choir . . ."

"But the magic," I said. "What do you do about it?"

"Well, if there is a *rubbish* spirit hurting people, we stop it. For example, did you see the black stone down on the beach at Vureas Bay? That *devil* stone was making people sick, so we took some holy oil and made a small service, and we banged that stone with our sticks to drive the *devil* out of it, in the name of the Big Man."

"I'm sorry, who?"

"The Big Man, our Lord in Heaven."

Ben interrupted. Tasiu Ken was like the policemen of Vureas Bay, he said. If you stole something and hid it, he could find it just by praying. And if you were a bad man, if you worked black magic on someone, he could curse you.

"*Yu mas looklook woking stik blong mi,*" said Ken. He left for a moment and returned with his walking stick. It was black. A carved snake wound its way up the shaft. The snake's eyes shone with inlaid abalone. Exodus: God turned Moses' staff into a serpent to prove his power to the Egyptians. Ken had carved this stick himself. It had been blessed by the Bishop of Banks and Torres. It was the first of dozens of snake staffs I would see before my journey was done.

"I heard that people are scared of your walking stick," I said.

"He is one powerful something," said Ken, running a muscular hand over the carved wood. "For example, suppose I go to a heathen village and want to show people the power of God. I always bring my staff. I throw it up high and it hangs in the air. After the people see that, they know they must follow the Big Man."

"I can't even imagine it."

"*Hem ia nao!* It does take a big, long prayer to make the stick fly. We pray and fast for two weeks before visiting the heathens. That helps us work closely with the Big Man."

I wanted to ask him about the man he had cursed, but it seemed a rude question after all his hospitality, all those cream cookies. I didn't quite know how to bring it up. In the end, I didn't need to.

"You killed a man who defied you, didn't you, *tasiu*?" said Ben. "Tell him about Jim Bribol."

Ken lowered his head and spoke quietly. The trouble had started back in 1997, during a time of denominational turmoil. While he was away visiting Ambae, the Seventh-day Adventists had gained a foothold down in Vetuboso. Even Eli Field's brother had joined the new Church. But the Adventists weren't content with stealing Anglican sheep; they accused the *tasiu* of being a false prophet.

The *tasiu* challenged the entire Adventist congregation to meet him in their church, where he would prove he was no false prophet. The Adventist pastor was the only one brave enough to show up. Ken put his staff down and challenged the pastor to an unusual duel. He suggested they point their Bibles at each other and see which one of them was still standing after three days. The pastor refused to face him.

Ken had been due to return to Ambae after the standoff, but things got ugly before he left. He had a cousin, Jim Bribol, who had switched Churches. One day, Jim decided that his wife's King James Bible was a symbol of Anglican hegemony, so he burned it. That was Jim Bribol's first mistake. He would have survived if that was all he had done. But then he announced to the village that he was going to march up the mountain and break the *tasiu*'s walking stick in half. Ken sent his cousin a message: I will leave, and then you will die.

A few days later, Jim Bribol went wading in the sea. A strange fish—a swordfish, perhaps—swam up to him and cut his shin. The wound became infected. Bribol fell desperately ill. His family rushed him to the hospital in Santo. The doctors couldn't temper his fever, nor could they stop his flesh from rotting. They called in a *kleva*, a *kastom* medicine man, who told the family that no medicine could save Bribol because he had been cursed. Bribol's family sent a message to Ambae by teleradio, begging for the *tasiu*'s forgiveness.

"And you didn't help him?" I said.

"No," said Ken, solemnly.

"You just let him die. How could you?"

"Listen: we have our *kastom* and we must stick to it. We have one Church and one God. We were all born Anglican and we must stay that way. If Jim Bribol lived, people would forget the power of the true God."

Ben and I retreated from the mountain in silence. The oaks had ceased their creaking. Mist drifted up from the sea. Drizzle fell like sadness.

THE SOUTHEASTERN trade winds had eased for the first time in weeks, but the rain continued to fall through the night. The trails around Vetuboso were as gummy as *laplap*. My sandals were useless. I left for Sola in bare feet, letting the purée of mud, cowshit and rotten mango squeeze through my toes. In lieu of a sun-producing miracle, Eli sent his son, Cali, to help me across the big water. The river had swollen. The water was waist-deep and flowing swiftly. Cali held my hand tightly as we crossed. I felt like a grandmother. I carried on alone through the warm drizzle. I couldn't stop thinking of the fish that Tasiu Ken had sent to cut Jim Bribol, of Bribol's rotting leg, of the *tasiu*'s refusal to help the dying man. Had the *tasiu* used that coincidental death to reinforce his own mythical status, or was he guilty of some admittedly awesome, but extremely un-Christlike, behaviour?

I was surprised at midday by Tasiu Ken himself, who emerged from a trailside shack halfway to Sola, rubbing his eyes. Ken wasn't wearing his uniform; he wore baggy surf shorts and a tank top and looked like a surf bum. He had crossed the river the night before, hoping to intercept me. He wanted to carry my pack to Sola. There was no dissuading him.

We walked through the afternoon. The rain ceased, steam rose from the grass and the overcast sky radiated white heat. The *tasiu* was silent.

The path became a road again. We crossed the plain of palms and climbed the hill above Sola. Ken stopped on the crest of it and set my pack on the ground. He said he couldn't be seen in Sola without his uniform; he was turning back to Vureas Bay. I wasn't ready to part.

"Are you still glad you cursed that man?" I asked. "Did you do the right thing?"

A thousand tiny beads of sweat had broken out on Ken's forehead. He looked to the sky, kicked the gravel on the road. Here, without his local audience, he was less keen to take the credit. "Maybe I made the curse," he said slowly, "but I didn't kill Jim Bribol. No, I asked the Big Man to decide on his fate. I made prayer for hours. I said, 'God, it is for you to choose. You make Jim live or you *killim hem i ded.*' So it was truly the Big Man who ended the life of Jim Bribol."

"So your God is an angry God."

"He is a god *blong* love. But yes, he is also a god *blong* vengeance. The unrepentant will be punished."

Later, I would learn that the Bishop of Banks and Torres had given Ken a firm talking-to about that Jim Bribol episode. It just wasn't the kind of work a *tasiu* should be doing.

Ken Brown may not have been typical of the Melanesian Brotherhood, but the mystical aura that surrounded him certainly was. Farther north, amid the anarchy of civil war, the brotherhood had claimed a place in the modern mythology of the Solomon Islands. They had entered the very real battle between the forces of darkness and light. They had become the cultural heroes of their nation, keepers of the flame of supernatural intervention, and a bridge between Melanesian *mana* and the god that the missionaries had delivered to the islands.

The *tasiu* would become my friends and my guides. They would draw me into their myth. And they would change my mind about everything.

14

GUADALCANAL,

THE UNHAPPY ISLE

In the last days perilous times shall come. For men shall
be lovers of their own selves, covetous, boasters,
proud, blasphemers, disobedient to parents, unthankful, unholy.
Without natural affection, truce-breakers, false accusers,
incontinent, fierce, despisers of those that are good.

2 Timothy 3:1–3

I MET THE deputy mayor of Honiara, the capital of the Solomon Islands, in a plane high above the ocean, somewhere between Fiji and Guadalcanal. I had the window seat. He leaned into my shoulder, peered out into the blue and exhaled into my face. Rotting carrots. Grass mulch. Compost. The deputy mayor did not wish me a pleasant stay in the Solomon Islands, nor did he recommend a favourite restaurant. But he did roll up his pant leg to show me the bullet wound in his calf. The scar was the size of his thumb and the texture of tire rubber. "I am going to kill the man who did this," he said. "Fucking kill him." I didn't reply. I just stared into the deputy mayor's mouth, which was like nothing I had ever seen. His teeth were the colour of rotten cedar and his tongue lolled beneath a worrying gob of pinkish fibre. A drop of red juice had dried at the corner of his mouth, like something from a Transylvanian nightmare. This was the mouth of a betel nut addict.

I did not want to be breathing recycled air with the deputy mayor. I wanted to be crashing north towards Nukapu aboard a cargo vessel, a mission ship, a yacht, a canoe, crossing the ocean that Henry Montgomery had once crossed, whipped by salt spray and nautical hardship. It should have been easy to arrange a passage to the Solomons from Vanua Lava: Sola is the last jumping-off point for boats travelling north from Vanuatu. In theory, the two nations are just a day's sail apart. Less than 150 kilometres separate Hiu, the most northerly of Vanuatu's Banks and Torres Islands from Vanikoro, the most southerly of the Santa Cruz Group, of which Nukapu is an outlier.

But each time I shook awake the customs officer in Sola—which I did every afternoon for nearly two weeks—he assured me there were no cargo ships bound for the Solomons. Finally, he lost his patience. Why would there be a northbound cargo ship? What in God's name would it carry? Didn't I understand, he asked, that after all the fighting, Solomon Islanders simply had no money left to buy cargo?

There were yachts, though: a sail grew out of the horizon every day or so. Vanua Lava sits smack in the middle of the trade-wind route that carries yachties from New Zealand and Polynesia to their storm season havens in the Gulf of Thailand. The Solomon Islands offer the next batch of good harbours on the route. With each new arrival, I would wait for the sails to come down, the anchors to fall and the dinghies to bob towards shore. I would shave and put on a clean shirt, and then I would catch the sun-ravaged yachties on the beach and tell them about my special island, Nukapu. We could be there in four days, I would tell them. They could drop me off on the reef and carry on towards Torres Strait or Papua New Guinea. The yachties were universally horrified by my proposal. Hadn't I heard about the guns? The blood feuding? The pirates? The awful Chinese food? "We're not bloody idiots, mate. The Solomons are no place for children," one yacht dad told me sternly.

It was September. The storm season was approaching. One by one, the yachties all turned west for Cairns. As I watched the last sail disappear, I realized that Sola was a dead end. My only hope of getting to the

Solomons was to backtrack: hop the mail flight south through Santa Maria, Espiritu Santo and Malekula to Port Vila, then catch the weekly shuttle east to Fiji, then loop northwest again, three hours by 737 from Fiji to Honiara, on Guadalcanal. After that 3,600-kilometre detour, after trading the rolling uncertainty of the open ocean for the crystalline detachment of the stratosphere, I would try to reach Nukapu from the north.

Which is how I met the deputy mayor of Honiara, whose first act upon reaching his homeland was to spit a stream of crimson mucus onto the tarmac of Henderson Field, the Solomon Islands' international airport. Betel nut juice is apparently great fun to spit, which is why the most striking thing about the airport was that everything was spattered blood red. The arrivals hall looked like the scene of a mass murder. It begged to be hosed down, scrubbed, relieved of bloody memories. The rest of the city was the same.

I was met at the airport by Morris Namoga, the manager of the national tourism bureau. Morris was a jovial man with a big moustache and a rugby player's physique. I had faxed him from Port Vila, promising to write happy stories about the Solomons if he helped me. I felt a pang of guilt as soon as I saw his generous grin.

Morris drummed the steering wheel and hummed the Canadian national anthem as we drove into town, trying to distract me from the storm of dust and refuse, the plastic bags that rolled like tumbleweeds across the road, the heaps of garbage that smouldered like castles after a siege. And this, spray-painted across an abandoned building: Welcome to Hell.

"Haw! haw! Sorry about the mess," Morris said in English. "The municipality doesn't quite have the means, haw haw, to clean up any more."

Honiara was perfectly safe, said Morris, before I had a chance to ask. He also assured me that the deputy high commissioner of New Zealand had not been stabbed to death. She had fallen on her own knife.

The heat was unbearable.

"Morris," I said, "why don't we drive out of town and go for a swim in the ocean?"

"Haw haw! I don't think so. No, I don't think so. Well, of course *you* can go, but it would not be a good idea for me to come with you. Oh, no. Guadalcanal people are still being, haw, haw, shall I say, *assertive*."

Morris was from the island of Malaita. Malaitans controlled Honiara, a fact which displeased Guadalcanal natives so much they had launched a civil war in 1999.

We passed an open-air cathedral. I could see hundreds of people inside. "Funeral!" said Morris. "For the national Minister of Sport. Tsk, tsk. Very sad. Murdered two weeks ago. Father Geve—yes, he was also a Catholic priest—he went back to his constituency to talk to Harold. Not a good idea. You know about Harold Keke, of course."

I had been hearing Harold Keke's name for months. Harold the militant leader. Harold the Guadalcanal nationalist, Harold the warlord, Harold the madman. Keke was all these things. He had been hiding out on Guadalcanal's storm-battered southerly Weather Coast ever since the peace agreement had ended the civil war in 2000. I was told that someone had convinced a gang of eleven lads from the Malaita bush to go looking for Keke. The boys were given guns and a boat, and they buzzed around the Weather Coast until they found Keke. Or rather, until Keke found them. He killed them all. That was three months before my arrival. People were starting to think Harold had cooled off, but then he went and put a bullet in Father Geve's head.

"Harold thinks the war is still on, which it certainly is not," said Morris, wiping the perspiration from his neck. "None if this is good for tourism. Haw! Sorry about the mess."

Morris left me at the Quality Motel, a fortress of steel mesh and barbed wire overlooking the port. That night, I sat with the motel's guards—there were five of them, earnest young men with broad chests and billy clubs. We watched a gang fight in the orange glow of the street lights below us, and we listened to the radio. The news was read both in English, the official national language, and Solomon Islands Pidgin, which floated in a linguistic swamp between Bislama and English. On the news: Harold Keke had sent a message from the Weather Coast, saying Father Geve had died from "lead poisoning." Lead poisoning! Everyone got a chuckle out of that. Other news: four people were dead and six wounded in a shootout on an oil palm plantation east of the airport. Police suspected the combatants were neighbours. (But how would they know? The Royal Solomon Islands Police had been too scared to drive beyond the city limits for months.) Last item: the police had made a formal request for citizens to please stop stealing government trucks and vans.

The brawl on the street below us ended abruptly when the power failed. Honiara was left in darkness punctuated only by garbage fires and the sparks that rose out of them like fireflies. I heard one disembodied voice howling and bawling late into the night. "Go home," it cried. "Go home, oh please go home."

CHRISTIANITY WAS supposed to save the Solomon Islands from its dark side. So promised Selwyn and Patteson on the *Southern Cross*'s first tentative foray into the group in 1856, when this was the most feared corner of the South Pacific.

"The Melanesian Mission did not reach the Solomon Islands a day too soon," wrote Austin Coates in *Western Pacific Islands*, a Colonial Office–sponsored summary of British rule in the region. "This was a society in a state of rapid disintegration, due principally to an appalling, and evidently rather recent, spread of cannibalism, head-hunting and black magic." Coates breathlessly catalogued the nineteenth-century outrages that begged British intervention. Village longhouses were piled high with the skulls of enemies and slaves. The natives delighted in large-scale cannibal feasts at which every guest risked becoming a part of the meal. Men killed and roasted children with indifference; newborn babies were a particular favourite. A mother who lost her baby to a feast would simply offer her breast to a suckling piglet. Slaves were kept handy in case they were needed for sacrifice: they were useful for throwing into the postholes of new houses or for laying down on the beach so war canoes could be launched over their bodies, crushing them. Assassins, whose job it was to carry out revenge killings or collect bodies for feasts, were revered. One murderer on Santa Ana was noted for fattening his captives before slaughter. "Brutality had reached such a pitch that it was brutality no more; it was normal," concluded Coates. The chronicler cannot be judged too harshly for his hysterical assessment: his thesis was rooted in the reports of the white invaders. They were the ones who kept the diaries, and the things they claimed to have seen and heard were undoubtedly horrific.

Other outrages added to the collection. In 1844, a British trader arrived on Eddystone Island just after its men had returned from a war expedition. The village canoe house was strung with skulls, ninety-three of them, gathered on the successful raid. A travelling mission historian named Tippet reported that two hundred heads were taken in a single expedition and hung from the branches of trees. The skulls of white men were especially in demand; at the turn of the century, one trader on New Georgia reported that sixty-two Europeans had been murdered in his district in the space of a few years. Attacks on passing ships were a monthly occurrence.

The resident trader, John C. MacDonald, claimed to have witnessed a canoe-launching ceremony in 1883 at Nono Lagoon, during which a slave boy was dunked underwater until exhausted, then decapitated. The child's body was paraded around the village canoe house until the blood ceased to pulse from the neck. At that point, the body was cooked along with a pig. Alone among the headhunters, MacDonald could only watch in horror. Two years later, the trader's young son shot and killed the son of a Santa Ana chief with an arrow. MacDonald reported that he avoided the revenge-killing of his own son by buying a slave from another island to serve as a substitute victim.

Compounding all this indigenous violence were the white traders who had reached the archipelago before the missionaries. The traders were often of dangerously poor character, wrote Henry Montgomery. They armed the natives with axes and guns. They taught them Western bad habits. Worst of all, they persuaded natives not to have anything to do with the new teaching. "Mission work has no greater enemy than the ungodly white man, for the foes within the household deal the most deadly blows," despaired the bishop.

A favourite rumour among the missionaries was that traders were dabbling in headhunting as a means of obtaining plantation workers. Since labourers from New Georgia were considered the best workers, and since chiefs from that island were quite happy to send their sons off to the plantations in exchange for human heads, some labour recruiters were arriving in New Georgia with bags full of fresh heads—lopped off en route by their cunning native crews. Heads for bodies: the free market at its most exuberant.

Whether true or not, such stories convinced right-thinking British that the Solomons needed both God and discipline. The former was delivered by the Melanesian Mission, the latter by the Royal Navy. A story pieced together by my great-grandfather illustrates the double-whammy effect that evangelical zeal and naval power had on the islanders.

By 1880, the mission had attracted a handful of followers in the Florida Islands, but most of the natives remained hostile. That year, the British naval sloop HMS *Sandfly* cruised into the Floridas. The ship's commanding officer, one Lieutenant Bower, took a boat and four oarsmen and landed on the islet of Mandoleana, which he assumed was uninhabited. He was right, but his landing was noted by Kalekona, a chief on nearby Nggela. Kalekona had various personal grievances, and though he had no specific quarrel with the crew of the *Sandfly*, he wanted at least one white head in order to make things right again. Such was the *kastom*. He sent a party, led by his son, to ambush the sailors. They attacked with axes, killing three of the sailors. Unable to catch Bower, the warriors made do by cutting off and carrying home the heads of the three dead men. The next morning, Kalekona's men found Bower hiding high in the branches of a banyan tree and shot him with one of his own rifles.

Enter the disciplinarians. The Royal Navy returned on an obligatory village-bombing foray, reducing several hamlets to ashes but notably sparing a mission village. More importantly, HMS *Cormorant* arrived the following year, with Bishop John Richardson Selwyn (son of the original missionary bishop, and Patteson's replacement) aboard. Selwyn cut a deal with Kalekona. The chief gave up the murderers—except for his son, who spilled the beans on the rest—and a "ringleader" was hanged from the banyan tree where Bower had made his last stand. Others were tied to the tree and shot. The incident did wonders for the mission. Floridans smashed their shrines, gave up their wars and joined the Church by the thousands. Coates surmised it was because the natives had seen the righteousness of the British teaching, a fusion of power with justice. But justice had not been done. Kalekona, the massacre's architect, was not punished, because he allied himself with the Church. The Melanesian Mission was clearly the political agent that could save islanders from the fury of the British man-of-war.

Sir Charles Woodford, a burly naturalist who had made three forays into the Solomons, lobbied for years for Britain to take the islands on as a protectorate. He insisted the islanders needed security and a "firm and paternal" government. They also, in Woodford's opinion, needed him as their resident commissioner. Woodford got his way. But there was more than magnanimity at work when HMS *Curaçoa* steamed into the archipelago and declared the British Solomon Islands Protectorate in 1893. The colonial scramble for Africa was simply being re-enacted in the South Pacific by Britain, France and Germany. Woodford arrived in the Solomons in 1897 with eight Fijian policemen and built himself a villa at Tulagi, in the Floridas. The Colonial Office was all for acquiring a new colony but was not keen to underwrite Woodford's venture. If Woodford wanted a government for his new protectorate, he would have to fund it himself. He needed plantations to tax, which meant wresting land out of native hands so that it could be sold or leased it to white planters.

Land alienation did not provide much of an ethical dilemma for Woodford, since he believed Melanesians were a deficient race whose impending extinction was "as certain as the rising and setting of the sun." Some planters did buy land from hereditary owners: one district of land was bought for £20, two thousand porpoise teeth, two hundred dog teeth, a case of tobacco, a case of pipes, a case of matches, one piece of calico, two knives and two axes. But elsewhere, Woodford simply annexed hundreds of thousands of acres of "unoccupied lands," most of which he had never seen, and licensed it out to planters. This did not go over well with locals, who quite accurately saw the move as land theft and grounds for war. Sometimes they attacked plantation owners or traders. Whenever they did, Woodford or his allies responded with lethal force. For a time, Woodford's efforts to "purify" the Solomons looked a lot like traditional Melanesian blood feuding.

In 1909, during an attempt to catch the warrior Sito on Vella Lavella, a government party shot and killed his wife and children. Sito responded by sending his men to kill the wife and children of a white trader on Mbava. In turn, Woodford sent a punitive expedition of government officers, "revenge-crazed traders" and a militia of Malaitans, who swept over Vella Lavella in a wave of random killing and destruction. The islanders, who were outgunned, learned that safety lay within the mission stations. Not only could the missionaries conjure up men-of-war, they could protect islanders from their fury. Congregations grew. Churches and mission schools sprouted in the coastal forests. Headhunting and the cycle of inter-island war gradually petered out. Coconut plantations flourished.

Why did Melanesians take up Christianity en masse over the next decades? It was one thing for boys like George Sarawia to be re-educated during months of intensive indoctrination at the mission school on Norfolk Island. It was quite another for an entire race of people to switch allegiances. Their conversion was not just a triumph of indoctrination, nor was it the result of a great revelatory miracle. What happened?

One theory is that Melanesians had always turned to their spirits and ancestors for pragmatic reasons: religion was a means for gaining power, social status, wealth and security. Since white men had more power, more wealth and, increasingly, more status, it was logical for islanders to assume that the white religion was more effective. They wanted their children to learn to read—a skill which many islanders regarded as a key to white power.

I was becoming more certain every day that the written word itself had brought about Melanesia's spiritual about-face. *Kastom* tales were colourful and exciting and laden with profundity, but how could the oral tradition possibly compete with the 66 books, the 1,189 chapters, the 788,000 words of the Old and New Testaments? The Bible's miracles were more splendid, the violence more panoramic, the God more thunderous and the epics more, well, epic, than any contained in the memories of even a hundred village storytellers. The Bible was simply too vast a mythology to ignore.

That's not what islanders said, of course. They insisted that the conversion of their ancestors went back to the promise the bishops made: that the new teaching would bring peace. In contrast to the old religions, which were inextricably linked to cycles of sacrifice and warfare, Christianity would free islanders from the fears and jealousies and horrific violence that waited outside the bounds of their villages. For a time, it did. A general peace among Solomon Islanders lasted for most of a century,

interrupted, of course, by World War II, a surreal two years during which
most of the British fled and islanders helped the Americans to drive the
Japanese invaders out of the archipelago.

The Americans were generous, handing out millions of dollars in food
and shovels and clothing, just as they had done in Port Vila. By the time
the British were ready to take charge again, Solomon Islanders had discovered that the power of white men was not inseparably linked to Christianity or the monarchy. They grew restless. There was a nationalist revolt
on Malaita. It failed, but the seeds of independence had been planted.
Thousands learned to read. Hundreds attended universities in Australia
and Fiji. Some became doctors and lawyers and teachers. They wrote
books, debated their future, elected their own governing council, and in
1978 they won independence. For a time, Solomon Islanders were opti-
mistic. The rich bought televisions and air conditioners and mobile
phones. They built cement houses with tin roofs in Honiara, and their
wantoks arrived from the provinces with sleeping mats and dreams of
prosperity. But after decades of peace, after everyone was convinced they
had built a modern democracy, after 95 per cent of Solomon Islanders had
embraced Christianity, after all these things, a new darkness began to rise
like a full moon tide.

Nobody could tell me exactly when the killing began. But the men on
Guadalcanal began collecting guns sometime in the mid-1990s. Some
borrowed hunting shotguns. Some found leftover World War II rifles,
which they oiled, polished and tested using salvaged ammunition. Some
made their own guns from drainpipes and auto parts. The gun collectors
claimed to be upset that the government had never paid for the land it
had used around Honiara. But they were especially angry that so many
Malaitans had moved to Honiara and prospered there. The Guadalcanese
didn't like Malaitan *kastom*. They blamed Malaitans for the murder of
twenty-five Guadalcanalese in the two decades since independence, including four who were hacked to death in a machete massacre on the outskirts of the capital. They wanted compensation: $20,000 per corpse, to
be exact. The Guadalcanalese militants had a vague but passionate notion
of "getting their island back"—even though most of them, including
Harold Keke, hailed from the remote Weather Coast. With their home-

made guns, their axes and spears and their anger, Keke and his *wantoks* crossed the island and rampaged along the north coast, chasing Malaitan settlers from their gardens and setting fire to their homes.

The prime minister did cut a cheque for the compensation claimants. It bounced. Chaos mounted. Thirty thousand refugees—a third of the residents of Guadalcanal—fled, seeking shelter in the heart of the capital or crowding onto rusty passenger ships and retreating to the provinces. Most were Malaitan. By June 1999, almost every settlement on the outskirts of Honiara had been trashed and burned. Nobody called this ethnic cleansing. Instead, one government minister put the trouble down to young people who simply wanted "a bit of fun and adventure." Fun: a Guadalcanal man visits a nightclub in Honiara. The next day his headless body turns up at the town market. The same day, Guadalcanal militants kill a Malaitan farmer and mount his head on a stick at a roadblock.

Such fun had only begun. The Malaitans had a plan for vengeance. During the previous decade, the country's leaders had grown increasingly nervous about a war that was already taking place on the Papua New Guinean island of Bougainville, just an hour's paddle from the Solomons' most westerly islets. The fighting had occasionally spilled across the border, so the Solomons government bought $10 million worth of guns from the United States, ostensibly to protect the country from invasion. The guns were never used on foreigners. But they *were* used.

A group calling itself the Malaita Eagle Force raided two police armouries and made off with two thousand of those machine guns. It wasn't hard, as three quarters of the police force happened to be Malaitan. The Eagles woke up Prime Minister Bartholomew Ulufa'alu one night and informed him he would not be leaving his house until he resigned. He complied. The Eagles transformed Honiara into a Malaitan fortress. The police didn't stop them, because the Eagles *were* the police. They ripped off a wide-gauge machine gun from the bow of a police patrol boat, mounted it on a bulldozer and *voilà*, they had built the islands' first tank. Meanwhile, their Guadalcanalese enemies, who now called themselves the Isatabu Freedom Movement, raided a gold mine and made off with four shipping containers of explosives and a dump truck which, with a little creative welding, became the country's second tank. The two sides blew up bridges and gas stations. They burnt down hotels, churches and villages. They strafed mission stations and they invaded hospitals and clinics in order to finish off the wounded. Neither group would admit casualties, but at least two hundred people were killed in the first half of 2000.

Finally, the two sides met at Alligator Creek, just east of the international airport. What everyone had called the "ethnic tension" had become a war. After a few days, the creek's sluggish waters were stained crimson with blood. The fighting let up only when a group of men wearing black shirts, black shorts, white sashes around their waists and copper medallions strung from their necks, marched to the middle of the bridge. The Melanesian Brotherhood had had enough of the killing. They held their walking sticks in the air: sunlight reflected off shards of inlaid abalone, white snake eyes glowed. The *tasiu* prayed for peace. Some fools actually shot at them, but witnesses all agree the bullets were deflected by those magic walking sticks.

AFTER A CEASEFIRE was declared in 2000, Solomon Islanders managed to elect a government. International aid was flowing in. Life in Honiara should have been getting better. It was not. Every month of peace brought more dysfunction, more anarchy, more bloodshed. The economy was in the toilet. Foreign businesses had packed up and left. The government was beyond broke. The villagers who controlled the capital's water source turned off the tap each afternoon to remind the government to pay its water bill. Machine guns were still floating around the countryside. Neighbours were settling scores in hillbilly-style shootouts. Schools had been closed. Hospitals were running out of medicine. Malaria was making a comeback. Money did not flow. Phones did not ring. Boats did not sail. Planes did not fly.

With its potholes, ruptured drains, dust, wire mesh, tree stumps and open sores, Honiara looked like a piece of suburban Mexico City. It had the crude aesthetic of an industrial park and the haggard air of a refugee camp. The sidewalks were crowded with hundreds of makeshift stands selling cigarettes and betel nut, the city's two favourite addictions. The ground was stained indelibly red, like the hands of Lady Macbeth.

I headed down Mendana, the capital's one avenue, past the bluff where the Spaniards had planted their white cross in the red dirt more than four and a half centuries before, past the yachtless yacht club, past the diesel generators that kept the air conditioners flowing in Honiara's three office buildings, past the video club where Chuck Norris beat the shit out of the Viet Cong again and again on a wide-screen TV, past the spit-smeared walls and unkempt grounds of the National Museum, past the Ministry of Finance, which cowered behind a giant slinky of razor wire. I stopped by the office of Solomon Airlines, where a relief map on the wall showed an airport at Nendo Island in the Santa Cruz Group. Nendo was three days' sail east of Honiara, but less than 60 kilometres from Nukapu, my grail, the centre of the Patteson myth. Sign me up, I said. Not so fast, said the agent. Santa Cruz was the Hotel California of flight destinations: a plane could get to the group, but it could not return. Nendo had run out of fuel months ago. The only way to get there now was by ship.

So I headed for the port. Two ships made the run to Santa Cruz. They were tied up to the same crumbling cement pier. One, the *Eastern Trader,* looked like hell: she was a garbage heap of grease, great flakes of exfoliating rust and flapping laundry, but her deck was stacked with fuel barrels.

"When can we go?" I asked her skipper.

"We wait," he said.

"For what?" I asked.

"For fuel," he said.

"But your ship is loaded with fuel," I said.

"That's the airplane fuel. We need diesel, and we don't have the money to pay for it just yet."

"So when will you have the money?"

"When our passengers pay us."

"And you've been waiting how long?"

"Not long. A month, maybe."

It was the same story with the slightly more reliable-looking MV *Temotu.* At least ships had run during the civil war. There had been money then. Now everything was grinding to a halt, and I was stuck.

So I wandered around and met the unhappy people of Honiara, who were not like the fresh-scrubbed, just-blessed innocents of Vanuatu. It was as though all ease and subtlety had been drained from them. Men told me things like, "Our country is fucked." Urgent women invited me to meet their daughters. Everyone was afraid: of ex-militants, rascals and extortionists, but also of the police. No wonder: after the armistice, as many as two thousand ex-militants had been enlisted by the Royal Solomon Islands Police as "special constables." This was supposed to be an incentive for militants to stop fighting, but putting them on the government payroll didn't convince them to turn in their stolen guns, nor did it reform those who had been responsible for all the torture, rape, intimidation and murder during the war.

People were afraid of Harold Keke, afraid that in a moment of utter madness the last of the Weather Coast militants might march across the mountainous spine of Guadalcanal and storm the capital. But they were even more afraid of Keke's enemies, men like Jimmy Rasta, one of the supposedly reformed Malaita Eagle commanders.

Freed from the ethnic crusade, Rasta had entered the post-tension market with a private army of former militants. His boys could be hired to rough up anyone you didn't like. Once, Rasta and his gang showed up at a political protest. Rasta dispersed the crowd with a blast from his machine gun, which he then used to bludgeon the protest leader, putting him in hospital for a few months. People whispered that Jimmy's boys had kidnapped two policemen from a nightclub and shot them. I met a shopkeeper who had once done a roaring trade in beer and soda. One afternoon a gang of Rasta's boys had demanded $5,000 worth of beer from him. The shopkeeper, who had already been quenching their thirst for months for free, lost his patience. He told the boys they weren't being fair—why didn't they pick on the Chinese stores? A few days later, they returned with machine guns and cleaned out the shop.

Now, Rasta ran his own bottle shop on the highway near the airport. I went there and asked the dull-eyed lad behind the counter to pass a note on to Rasta for me. I was curious to know if Jimmy thought he was going to hell. That's not what I wrote in the note. I wrote that I was meeting with all the most important men in the Solomon Islands.

I returned to the bottle shop three times. Finally, Rasta rolled up in a battered Toyota SR-5, reggae pumping so loud the car's doors rattled.

Rasta was about thirty. He was Bob Marley gone gangsta: thick dreadlocks, baggy jeans and a delicate gold wristwatch. He handed me a Sol-Brew and led me out back. We sat on a couple of beer crates by a pond of discarded oil.

Rasta, whose real surname was Lusibaea, told me that he had been a peaceful guy before the ethnic tension. But one night in 1999, some of Harold Keke's boys had burst into his village and shot up the place. Rasta's grandfather was so scared his heart stopped beating and never started again. Then the bodies of Rasta's *wantoks* started turning up in creeks and gardens. The police did nothing, so Rasta and his friends raided the police armouries and took their revenge. But all that was in the past, he told me proudly. Now that the tension was over, he ran a private security business, providing "employment" to more than thirty boys. No, they didn't use guns. How could they use guns? The boys had given all their guns back: all their SR-88s, their M-16s and their LMGs, long gone.

I wanted to say, "Jimmy, you're lying," but I was too scared. I sat and drank my beer, listening to him rant about his enemies, which included the Melanesian Brotherhood.

"The *tasiu* are false prophets. They *garem* no magic powers. Look, they stopped at my headquarters one day, trying to cause trouble, and my boys went and broke two of their walking sticks. Has anything bad happened to us since then? No. Nothing. *Mi no fraet long olgeta tasiu.*"

This was not the story most people told. They said that the boy who broke the walking sticks was now crippled. His hands had shrivelled up.

"Some people think you should be in jail," I said quietly.

"What?" Rasta barked.

I chickened out. "When will your country have peace?" I asked.

"Peace? We *garem* peace. Look, my store is open. Business is good."

He winked at me, beamed, slapped me on the knee.

"Look, I'm a Christian boy. South Seas Evangelical Church. Are you a Christian boy?"

"Um ..."

"Well if you are, then you know that everything happens according to God's plan. From the day we are born, God knows what will happen to us. He has a plan for us. All will be well, my friend. All will be *gud tumas.*"

But all was clearly not good in Honiara. The tension still ebbed and flowed like the tide. When it rose, you could feel it. It was thick and heavy, and it covered everything with a dark, sticky film, like betel spit. That's when you watched your step. That's when you looked into people's eyes, not too long but long enough to check their intentions. I left Rasta and caught a minibus back into town. The streets were full of excitable young Rambos, bored mongrels with betel-stained lips, teeth razor-sharp with rot, wandering between the garbage fires in packs or squatting in the dirt, spitting red, smoking, waiting. A bright-eyed lad caught my eye and called to me cheerily across the street: "You watch out!"

The trouble came quickly: the sound of distant shouting, then the pop-pop of gunfire. Suddenly, we were all stampeding madly for cover. I hid behind a shipping container. There was the lad, giggling.

"What happened? What happened?" I asked breathlessly, peering out at the empty street.

"Mi no savve," he said, husking himself a betel nut. *"But long Honiara, taem olgeta pipol run, yu run olsem."*

I scurried back to my veranda at the Quality Motel to wait for the pressing heat and the unease to lift. The afternoon breeze came like forgiveness. It brought rain, and also the national Minister for Peace and Reconciliation.

Nathaniel Waena lowered his fleshy frame into a deck chair on the veranda and set down his grass handbag. He had come to explain the country's troubles to me. He spoke in Cambridge English. His voice boomed with authority. But he was at a loss to make sense of what he insisted on calling the "ethnic tension," or its lingering consequences. Perhaps it was all the Malaitans' fault. Or perhaps it was the fault of the British for sewing together a country out of such discordant fabric, for drawing people away from their home islands to the illusory riches of Honiara. Or maybe, said Waena, running his fingers across his spongy afro, squinting as though trying to suppress a headache, the crisis was a riddle handed to the people by God Himself. That was it.

"We will never be one country, one people. We will always belong to our own islands, the places where the Creator meant for us to live and survive," he bellowed. He threw his arms in the air. "But I ask you, why did God create the Solomons the way they are? Why has He bound and separated us by the sea? Why has He made us so different from each other? What is it that the Lord is saying to us?"

I was speechless. Waena brought his fist down on the table, spilling his glass of bush lime juice. A drop of sweat dribbled down the left lens of his thick glasses. He lowered his voice. "We have been wrong in our ways. We have so many riches. So many millions of dollars in international loans. Where did all those riches go? What is wrong with us? What does God want us to do? How can we know His mind?"

Waena wasn't the only one who was baffled by the fate of the Solomons. Everyone was sad. Everyone was angry. Everyone except Harold Keke and Jimmy Rasta felt as though they had been abandoned, or perhaps were being punished, by the Almighty—or, worse, by the spirits of their ancestors. As the weeks passed, and as I came to know the islanders and their mess, I began to see that, in a way, they were right. The root of the crisis lay not in politics or logistics but in the soul of the nation. The bond between islanders and the *kastom* that once ruled their lives had been so frayed by rootlessness and change and greed that it had simply snapped.

Kastom had not fared well in the Solomons. For a century, missionaries had run a system of residential schools which removed children from their home villages, stripping them of their *kastom,* the teachings of their parents and the stories of their ancestors. Take, for example, the age-old *kastom* of compensation: islanders had relied on grand feasts and the ritual exchange of pigs, shell money and favours to create bonds between clans and to reconcile all kinds of disputes. But this *kastom* had been perverted by the cash economy into a grotesque caricature of itself. People were demanding mountains of cash for bride price, for injuries and for affronts real and imagined. Swear in front of a woman and her brothers will demand money. Spoil the reputation of a politician and Rasta's thugs will come looking for cash. The compensation for killing a man? Once upon a time, it was a life for a life. But now it was cash: $20,000 per corpse. If you had a gun you didn't need any justification for your compensation claim.

Compensation became a national obsession. Hundreds of people returned to Honiara from the provinces to demand payback for land, property or relatives they had allegedly lost during the conflict. The grieved parties did not sue their attackers. Instead, they harassed members of parliament for compensation money. The government was broke, so it sent ministers to Taiwan and Japan to beg for development loans, which were granted like the miraculous fulfilment of a cargo cult fantasy.

Two years after the declaration of peace, the rot had eaten deeply into the nation and the compensation booty was running out. People felt so defeated, so abandoned by their ancestors, so without power to heal their wounds—so without *mana*—that some were carrying cargo thinking to its final frontier. They were demanding more than money or cargo from foreigners. They wanted strangers from beyond the horizon to come and make things better with more guns. It was shameful, but it was exactly where their deepening crisis was leading them.

ONLY ONE STORY gave islanders hope. It had many versions, many plots, but it always featured the same band of heroes and it always ended in a miracle. I heard one chapter of it from Robert Iroga.

I had hoped that the *Solomon Star*'s "ethnic tension" reporter would give me a sober analysis of the crisis and its architects. But even the paper's hard news man seemed to prefer myth to political scoops. I caught up with Iroga at the Mendana Hotel, the once swanky resort where politicians and ex-militants now drank Johnny Walker together at the pool bar. The militants wore Hawaiian shirts. The politicians wore camouflage sun hats.

There were fresh bullet holes in the ceiling of the hotel lobby. Nothing serious, said the waiter. A few of the special constables had had a party on the weekend and brought their machine guns.

I bought a jug of beer to loosen Iroga's lips. Explain the madness to me, I asked him. Whose fault was it?

Iroga was a strapping young man but he was nervous. He glanced around the room, nodded here and there, and looked back at me gravely. He assured me it was not uneducated men like Jimmy Rasta and Harold Keke who had instigated the tension. No, no. The trouble didn't bubble up. It trickled down from the educated "elite," from lawyers, parliamentarians and businessmen. But Iroga would not tell me the names of the rascals. The one thing you didn't do in the Solomons was lay blame on people.

"Look at our newspaper," he said. "Sometimes we are so careful, we don't even print the news. For example, the Malaitan boys who went to catch Harold Keke on the Weather Coast: I know those boys are dead, I know Harold killed them, and I know the *tasiu* buried them—the brotherhood even sent me a fax to confirm it! But we could never run that story. If we did, the Malaitan leaders would come and demand compensation from us for spoiling the reputation of their boys."

Everything in Honiara was broken, he said. Nobody could be trusted. Except for the Church, of course. Except for the Melanesian Brotherhood. The country would have torn itself to bits if it weren't for the *tasiu*, who walked between the armies, who were now endeavouring to collect guns from the ex-militants and who, with God's help, would lead islanders back to the light.

Iroga had agreed to meet me because he was interested in studying journalism in Canada. You would think he would try to impress me with his objectivity and his journalistic detachment. You would think he would at least feign a degree of rationalism. But now he took a deep pull on his beer and launched into the story he really wanted to tell.

Once, while on assignment in south Malaita, Iroga was being guided through the bush by three members of the Melanesian Brotherhood. At some point, the travellers' path was blocked by a river too deep to ford and too swift to swim across. They looked for a canoe but couldn't find one, so the three *tasiu* came together and prayed for God's assistance. They had barely said their amens when a crocodile rose out of the murk. It was huge, as wide and long as a canoe and, one *tasiu* noted, the perfect size for riding. This was the answer to their prayers. One by one, the travellers climbed onto the croc's back and, one by one, they enjoyed a gentle cruise across the river. When all four men had safely reached the far bank, one of the brothers pulled a copper medallion from his bag. It was not the same medallion the *tasiu* wore. This one was reserved for the generous and pious individuals who pledged to support the brothers in their work. They hung the medallion around the crocodile's neck and told the monster it was now a Companion of the Brotherhood.

I laughed.

Iroga sipped his beer solemnly.

"I'm writing this down. You rode on the back of a magic crocodile," I said, hoping to make it clear to him that we were going to make a fool of him together.

"It takes great faith to perform miracles," he said.

Now, it is one thing to believe a thousand-year-old parable or to accept that a miracle has happened to a stranger, or even for a rumour to gain wings after being passed on a hundred times. But Iroga was not joking, nor was he passing on an ancient myth or an urban legend. This was his own story, and he was utterly serious.

I know and you know that wild crocodiles do not offer men rides across rivers. I know and you know that if Iroga believed his own story he was deluding himself. And if he did not believe his story he was lying to me, either to test my gullibility or, perhaps underestimating my scepticism, to boost his cachet. Either way, there was an annoying gap between Robert Iroga's actual experience on Malaita and the story he was spinning. It was equally annoying that every time I told Iroga's story in Honiara, people nodded in recognition. "Happens all the time," they said. "Didn't Jesus walk on water?" they pointed out. "Why do you fight so hard against these things?" they asked. "The *tasiu* might save us all."

I wanted to scream, to jump up and down, to shake the people of Honiara awake from their delusions. I don't feel that way any more. I can't scorn any of the people who wrap their wars, triumphs, crises—even business deals—in tendrils of magic, because I have begun to understand the power of stories to transform nations. I can't dismiss those stories and then ask anyone to trust me, or at least trust that I am doing my best to be honest when I tell of the strange things that finally came to me from the darkened sky and the warm depths of the sea, and which readied me for my own journey with the Melanesian Brotherhood. There is more than one way to hear a story. That's what I began to understand in the Solomon Islands.

15

THE BISHOP OF

MALAITA

Solitude lies at the lowest depth of the human condition.
Man is the only being who feels himself to be
alone and the only one who is searching for the Other.

OCTAVIO PAZ, *The Labyrinth of Solitude*

SPENT MY DAYS at the port in Honiara, looking for a passage to the Santa Cruz Group and
thence to Nukapu. The *Eastern Trader* was al-
ways on the verge of sailing. So was the *Temotu*, its competitor. Neither
ship budged.

I watched them from the veranda at the Quality Motel, and I dozed,
so I barely noticed when a sturdy-looking tub took on a load of passengers, pigs and rice, then chugged away with a puff of black smoke. I was
furious when I learned the *Endeavor* was bound for Santa Cruz. I was less
furious when I learned its fate. The *Endeavor* ran out of oil halfway to
Nendo. Someone had pinched all the ship's spare engine lubricant, so the
engineer poured coconut oil into the gearbox, fouling it completely. The
Endeavor drifted west towards the Coral Sea, where the swell grew so big
and so steep that the pigs began to slide across the deck. The rice was
lashed down, the pigs were not. Each time a pig went overboard, sharks

charged out from under the ship to rip it to shreds while the horrified passengers looked on. It took a week and a half for someone in Honiara to scrape together enough money to send the Royal Solomon Islands Police patrol boat out to rescue the passengers and the last of their pigs.

Nukapu would have to wait. Fine. I wanted heathens. I wanted magic. The nearby island of Malaita promised both.

Malaitans are fierce. Malaitans are warlike. Malaitans are mysterious. These are points on which all people in the Solomons agreed, especially the Malaitans themselves. It was Malaitans who made the last great stand against colonialism in 1927, when they smashed the skull of a British tax collector and murdered his fourteen assistants. It was Malaitans who controlled the police, who had outwitted and humiliated the Guadalcanal militants, who had the government under their thumb. It was Malaitans who still offered blood sacrifice to the sharks and octopuses that prowled their lagoons. It was Malaitans, or at least a few thousand villagers in the island's Kwaio highlands, who still refused the Church and the authority of the government.

It was the mountain Kwaio people I was keenest to meet. They were not like the heathens back on Tanna; they were not recycled heathens. They had never succumbed to the missionaries' charms. They had never abandoned their *kastom*. They did not put on dances for tourists. They were notoriously hostile towards outsiders. When coastal Malaitans joined the dance of blood and anarchy in Honiara, the mountain Kwaio went on tending their gardens and sacrificing to their ancestors as they had been doing for thousands of years. I wondered what stories the Solomons' last pagans told each other about the fractured world beyond their mountain home.

Malaita and Guadalcanal are less than 75 kilometres apart. On a map, they resemble two slugs crawling slowly northwest, parting just enough to make room for the amorphous Florida Islands. Once upon a time, ships departed Honiara for Malaita every day. Now there was a problem. A fibreglass canoe carrying eight men from the north end of Malaita had disappeared and then been discovered, half submerged, off the coast of the Florida Islands. Its bilge plug had been yanked out. The passengers were never found. The north Malaitans suspected their *wantoks* had been ambushed and killed by rivals from Langa Langa Lagoon. Since it was Langa Langa men who built and sailed the ships on the run between Honiara and Auki, those vessels had become fair game in the feud. Being north Malaitan, Jimmy Rasta had taken it upon himself to pirate one of those ships, the *Sa'Alia*, and sail it back to his base east of Honiara. Now the rest of the fleet was afraid to make the journey.

So I lingered on the docks and was seduced by the port with its great silver oil tanks, its dust, its crumbling cement piers, its corrugated-iron warehouses, its milling crowds, its possibilities, its roughness. The waterfront was not delicate or charming. There were none of the gleaming sailboats that populated Port Vila's harbour, only working craft: coastal freighters, iron barges, wooden hulks dripping diesel from their seams, second-hand ferries that still bore Chinese signage from their days on the Pearl River Delta. There was the *Ramos II*, whose clumsy steel frame bled rust where it had taken bullets on its last trip to the Weather Coast. There was the *Kangava*, all bulbous hull, flapping canvas and black smoke, forever chugging between Honiara and the old colonial capital on Tulagi. There was the *Liufagu*, which, with its two storeys of carnival blue–painted weatherboard, looked like a Mississippi riverboat without the paddlewheel, or perhaps a floating tree fort.

The port was a crossroads for the Western Pacific. There were fair-skinned, straight-haired Polynesians; barrel-chested pygmies; dwarves with spiral tattoos on their cheeks; fragile-looking Malays and Indonesian fishermen; jet-black men with violently red hair or sun-bleached afros; bony women with skin the colour of licorice and eyes of mud. The Malaitan sailors were the most curious-looking and the most handsome. Their skin was like cinnamon and covered in blond down. Their cheeks bore scars from ritual cutting: spirals and stylized sun designs etched forever into soft flesh, so that Malaitan *wantoks* would always recognize home in each other's faces.

Some evenings, I wandered out past the candlelit betel-nut stands to look at the *Eastern Trader* straining at her lines and her crew lounging like cats on the rails or slumbering in hammocks, strong arms dangling, fingernails tapping the grimy deck. They were bored. They twisted their frizzy hair to resemble the dreadlocks they had seen on TV at the video cinema before their money had run out. Their bare feet were grotesquely callused. Their teeth were crimson with betel stains, but their smiles were pure and generous. When we talked, the sailors would reach for my hand, grasp it, squeeze and refuse to let go, even when our conversations ended. They craved beer. They told me their ancestors came from Africa, like Bob Marley. They weren't sure how old they were. They smoked sweet black tobacco rolled in notebook paper. I would listen to them and breathe in the scent of their hard work, and I would let my hand be squeezed, tentatively at first, but later I would squeeze back, and I would wonder about the rest, and I would allow something resembling loneliness to leave me, let it drift away across the sound, up into the sparkling fullness of the night sky.

Back at the height of the civil war, the only ships to ply the waters around Guadalcanal without fear were those run by the Church of Melanesia. The rascals and militants would never dare harass an Anglican ship. So it was that I was finally helped across the water by a band of church ladies. The Anglican Mothers' Union had planned a congress on Malaita long before Rasta's gang had paralysed the seas, and they had no intention of being waylaid. After all, they had booked a mission ship.

The mothers, dozens of them, arrived at the port in T-shirts and skirts. They squawked and huffed and dropped their bags of sweet potatoes into the hold of the *Kopuria*, a cute wooden tub named for the founder of the Melanesian Brotherhood. The *Kopuria* was all of 20 metres long and painted honey-bee yellow. We chugged off at eight knots, heading straight for the Florida Islands, Big and Little Nggela, which lay directly between Honiara and Auki. The sound was absolutely calm, its glassy surface broken only by our bow waves and by the flying fish that exploded from them. Their rainbow fins beat like the wings of hummingbirds, leaving trails of shivers across the water.

I stood in the shadow of the wheelhouse and listened to the captain's whistling. By midday, a knobby collection of low crags, lush islets and palm shores had spread itself around us. In a distant cove, I saw a great white ship on stilts. The captain gazed at it longingly. He told me that was the ship he should have been sailing. He had helped build her back in '91. She had two screws and could handle rough seas masterfully. Oh, and she had a cabin fit for a bishop, because she was the flagship of the Church of Melanesia. She was, of course, the *Southern Cross*, the seventh-

or eighth-generation (nobody was really sure) descendant of the vessel my great-grandfather had sailed through the Nggelas in 1892. But this *Southern Cross* was being fitted with a new hull, explained the captain sadly. She would be out of the water for at least a year.

The Nggelas are separated by a serpentine passage of black water and dozing crocodiles. We followed the passage until it was as narrow as a river. The hills closed in around us. The forest thickened. Creeping vines tumbled down water-stained cliffs and covered the trees like a great heavy net. After an hour, the hills parted and we emerged on the eastern shore. Long white lines of surf ripped across the outer edge of the reef. We threaded our way along a channel marked with bamboo poles and pushed out into the swell. Across the strait, Malaita's mountainous spine carried a heavy load of storm clouds. We reached Auki harbour at nightfall.

I hadn't given much thought to where I would sleep. Everyone else had. The Bishop of Malaita was a Canadian, said the mothers. He was my *wantok;* he was bound by *kastom* to take care of me. In fact, they said, the bishop acted like everyone was a *wantok.* His house was overflowing with de facto *wantoks.*

That night we gathered in the bishop's yard. The mothers cooed and fussed over the bishop. They placed a flower garland around his neck. The bishop said grace in Solomons Pidgin and reassured the mothers that, even though they were on Malaita, they need not be scared. Then he plunged into a plateful of pig fat and mashed yams, scooping the food into his mouth with his fingers while they watched approvingly.

"There is no helping it," the bishop told me, licking his fingertips. "The women refuse to serve themselves unless I have started eating."

I didn't trust the bishop at first. I suppose I had decided even before we met that he would be a strange exile living a colonialist fantasy. His very presence on Malaita made him suspect: after all, his mission included the quashing of Melanesia's most resilient pagan enclaves. Why had he come to Malaita, if not to bear the torch of cultural imperialism?

I studied him, looking for Victorian anachronisms, conspicuous paternalism, shades of my great-grandfather. But Terry Brown offered none of these things. He was a gentle, slightly awkward man who stumbled through small talk and lurched through his house in a threadbare T-shirt which read "No Fear." His trunk-like legs shook the floor with every step.

He seemed always to be rustling through papers, chasing some new administrative emergency, peering through his thick glasses at the ceiling, pondering, pondering. Sometimes his face bore a look of vague shock, as though seized by the first tremors of a heart-stopping epiphany.

The bishop kept a stained map of Malaita on the wall of his office. He had pressed coloured pins into the map to show where the Church had spread across the island. There were congregations all along the seashore, clustered in coves and strung out along the road that ran from Auki up the west coast. There were pins scattered through the northern mountain ranges. But in the dead centre of the island, across a ragged mess of creeks and peaks and topographic contours, the map was pristine and unpierced: Kwaio country.

"That's where I need to go," I said.

The bishop hummed thoughtfully. "We can get you to the edge of the Kwaio bush, but our influence ends there," he said. "You just don't wander into Kwaio country without an invitation."

"But aren't you evangelizing up there?"

"Well, the Melanesian Brotherhood has certainly tried. But the Kwaio aren't interested in the gospel. They only come to the brothers asking for medicine or for help finding lost pigs. The brothers are getting a bit sick of it, actually."

"Why aren't you up there converting them?"

The bishop looked over the top of his glasses at me. He knew I was baiting him. "Because they do not wish to be converted. And, to be honest, I'm sure they could teach our Christians a few things. They are humble. They are generous. Their communities are strong. People support each other. Look, the Seventh-day Adventists have been trying to evangelize these people for a hundred years, but the bush Kwaio have been quite happy to go on killing pigs for their ancestors. If some of them decide to pack it in and get baptized, well that's fine, we'll take them, but I'm inclined to just, oh, live and let live."

"But if they die without being baptized, then aren't they bound for hell?"

"Ah! There's the question that we Christians have been asking ourselves for a century. Some Christians feel that traditional culture is demonic and must be overturned—you'll hear that from the Adventists. On the other end of the spectrum, especially in the West, people are saying that salvation is possible, um, yes, without any knowledge of Christ whatsoever. Universalism, they call it. The idea is that good Muslims and Buddhists and yes, even ancestor-worshippers, can go to heaven, too. So there is less of a drive to evangelize."

The pagans were the least of the bishop's concerns, anyway. He had his hands full with his own flock. It was Christians who were running around with guns, stealing boats and trucks, robbing their rivals' stores, burning down each others' houses. The bishop was going to have a serious talk with Jimmy Rasta for starters. But his biggest beef with his flock was theological. Malaitans still believed in *mana*. They believed that *kastom* chiefs had *mana*. Rich men had *mana*, too. Most of all, they believed the clergy had *mana*. People asked the bishop to bless tree bark, oils, potions and *kastom* medicine. They asked his priests for holy water to pour into the radiators of stalled cars. They pinched the bishop's dictionary of angels, believing that if they knew the "secret" names of those angels, they could control them, calling on their powers to bring them wealth or kill their enemies, just as the Kwaio called on the *mana* of their ancestral spirits. They were sure that God's power could be diverted, focussed, distilled and put to work for themselves.

And then there was the Melanesian Brotherhood, who had the most *mana* of all, said the bishop.

After performing an exorcism in a village near Auki, a group of *tasiu* had built a small stone cairn by the road to "protect" the village. Not long after, a drunk walking home from a party stopped to empty his bladder on the cairn. "According to the story people told later, that guy only got about a hundred yards before—pow!—he was struck by lightning, or an invisible bullet or, well, something. He died, or so the story went. I never saw any proof of any of this, of course, but the message is that one shouldn't mess with the brothers. All this is all rather problematic for Christian theologians. I'm very, very concerned."

"But don't you believe in miracles?"

"Of course I do. But our relationship is supposed to be directly with God. People here are trying to use angels like they once used their ancestral spirits. They are still trying to accumulate and direct *mana*. There is almost no reference in this to Christ at all. Christianity is not about wielding power. It's not about personal charisma. It's not about *mana*. It is about meekness. Jesus gave up his power in order to die, weak and helpless, on the cross. This idea is repeated over and over again in Corinthians: *Strength is made perfect in weakness!*"

The bishop encouraged his priests to focus on the New Testament, on Jesus and resurrection through love, but Malaitans seemed to crave the battles and divine favouritism of the Old. In fact, they cherished the myth and miracles of the Old Testament so much they extrapolated them, drew them out through the centuries and across the oceans to include their island. Many Malaitans firmly believed they were descendants of one of the lost tribes of Israel, said the bishop. A few hundred generations ago, a descendant of the Hebrew tribe of Levi supposedly journeyed around the world, washed up on the shore south of Auki and started again. The theory made a strange kind of sense: traditional Malaitan *kastom* paralleled the *kastom* of the Israelites, the ones given to Moses and written down in the Book of Leviticus. Rules around the impurity of menstruating women, the sacredness of worship sites, the details of blood sacrifice . . . Malaitans had followed them all, long before Europeans arrived. Somewhere along the way, the Malaitans had simply substituted their ancestors for Yahweh. The biggest sticking point in this theory concerned those blood sacrifices: the Israelites sacrificed lambs to their god, but there were no sheep in Melanesia, so the lost tribe had no choice but to switch to a less than kosher alternative. Pork.

The lost tribe theory had gained momentum during the civil war, particularly when Malaita Eagle commanders circulated a treatise whose author used quotes from Genesis and Deuteronomy to "prove" that Malaitans shared their pride and aggressiveness with the sons of Jacob. Malaitans, who had never gotten along with each other, suddenly had a myth to bind them: they were different from the primitives across the water. They were bound by history and collective superiority. They were the lost tribe! It worked until the armistice was signed in 2000. Then Malaitans turned their guns and machetes on each other again.

All this saddened the bishop. Christianity was supposed to free the Malaitans from their fears and their restrictive *kastom* rules, but *kastom* was enjoying a kind of perverted resurgence. Various Christian sects were bringing the old *tabus* back, especially rules regarding women. They forbade women to wear shorts. They demanded that women remain in isolation during menstruation. They jacked up the price of brides to include hard cash as well as the traditional exchange of shell money. One breakaway priest had a vision which told him that women should not be permitted to wear ribbons in their hair.

The bishop put me up in the spare room of his tin-roofed bungalow. I studied him, his household and what I had wrongly thought was his exile. In 1996, Terry Brown had been living in Toronto when the Church of Melanesia announced it needed a new bishop for Malaita. He had spent a few years teaching in the islands, so why not put his name forward? He was elected in a unanimous decision by a committee of Melanesian clergy. He came to Melanesia alone, but his aloneness was not tolerated. The bishop's Melanesian predecessors all had installed their extended families in the official residence, but Terry Brown did not have a family. It didn't matter. The residence was like a sponge. It gave him one.

There was George, a bright-eyed Polynesian teen who had adopted the bishop as his father. George's function in the house seemed to be to prance Pan-like about the house and hold guests' hands. He had discovered glitter paint at a church dance. It sparkled from his eyebrows the night I arrived.

There was Derrick of the deep facial scars and dark moods. One afternoon, Derrick asked to borrow the stick of underarm deodorant he had found while digging through my pack. I said fine. Then he rubbed it through his beard. Derrick had once been Auki's Casanova, but he had fallen in love with the wrong girl. Her family demanded fifteen lengths of common shell money, two metres of red shell money, two thousand dolphin's teeth and a whopping $6,000 in bride price, all of which was taking Derrick years to raise. The bishop paid him to drive his truck.

There was sluggish Thomas, who arrived for tea and toast on the bishop's veranda each morning, and whose wife would invariably come searching for him by midday. Thomas was very skilled at driving race cars on the bishop's new computer.

Then there was gentle Tony, who took care of the bishop and quietly nagged the others to do their dishes.

"Melanesian society is corporate," the bishop explained to me one night as he cooked sausage stew for the gang. "There are no individuals here. You are either part of the community or you are quite simply considered something less than human. I have never been alone here—I am not permitted to be alone."

The bishop's residence reminded me of a fraternity house. Dirty dishes were stacked high. Walls were flecked with dried tomato sauce. People came and went without knocking. Strangers lurked in the kitchen, poked their heads into the refrigerator, then froze when they spotted me watching through the screen door. There was a note tacked to the bishop's bedroom door: "Please don't search through drawers and take things that aren't yours." The boys in the house were not servants. The bishop did all the cooking. The boys borrowed his slippers and sweaters. They went to the market with his money to buy yams and returned with pockets full of betel nut instead. They played games on his computer late into the evening. They teased him. They rarely called him bishop. They yelled at him from the veranda. "Big B!" they shouted. "Come out, Big B!"

The bishop confided to me that at first he had been shocked by the touching, the familiarity, the closeness, the relentless communalism of Melanesian life. Now it made him smile. He wanted to write a book to convince people in places like Toronto that this was a better way to live.

For a time, I thought the bishop was being taken advantage of. Perhaps he was, but no more than any other Solomon Islands big man. This is the essence of the Solomon Islands *wantok* system: if you are a big man, you are obliged to share your wealth. If you have food, your *wantoks* will come and eat it. If you have money, they will ask for it. If you start a canteen store, they will clear the shelves before you can sell anything. Clothes they will borrow, permanently. If you join the government and move to a house in Honiara, your *wantoks* will move in with you and pester you until you divert some of that government cargo their way.

The boys planned my invasion of the Kwaio bush over tea and biscuits on the veranda. George grabbed my hand excitedly: we could climb over the spine of the island and surprise the Kwaio! Nope, said the bishop. Too dangerous. Better to start from the Seventh-day Adventist mission on the east coast. A dirt road crossed the north side of the island; from there, I could catch a canoe down the coast to the mission. The road hadn't been maintained since the start of the war, but Derrick insisted that with him at the wheel, the bishop's truck could make the crossing. I told him I knew that "road" didn't really mean "road" in Melanesia.

On Sunday, I went with the boys to the tin-roofed cathedral where I saw the bishop finally transformed into the Victorian version of himself. He towered above his congregation, a giant in cream robes and shining tassels. He wore a honey-gold high cap and clutched a great curled staff. He swung a silver censer full of incense, and the smoke drifted around him as he prayed. The bishop's magnificence carried me back to my childhood, to the morning of my father's death, to the Bishop of Tasmania gazing down at me from his portrait, noble, good, at peace with God. Now the choir rose, and the cathedral echoed with the sound of pipe drums. Two dancers appeared, teenaged boys with bare shoulders shining and stone discs clattering on their chests. The boys stamped their feet and shook their rattles. The cement floor vibrated as they punched the air and charged up the aisle towards the bishop. In their wake came two girls, breasts bound with strands of shell money, arms straining under the weight of a wooden tablet. The tablet was decorated with flowers. On it was an open Bible. The girls brought the Bible to the bishop. He lifted it and he kissed it.

This was not the moment that revealed the bishop to me. He had not imposed all this Anglo-Catholic ritual on the islanders. It was they who had preserved it since Victorian times and only recently layered it with *kastom*'s drumbeat. It was they who had provided the bishop with his finery and insisted that he read at least part of the liturgy in English, rather than Solomons Pidgin. No, I saw the bishop most fully after the service.

Raindrops thundered down on the tin roof, but still the people poured out of the church onto the lawn. There, the drummers were joined by a pipe band. The pipers blew on hollowed sections of bamboo. The drummers smacked at the open ends of sections of pvc pipe with their flip-flops. The rhythm was playful. People formed a circle and began to dance under the flowering trees. They surrounded the bishop, who had changed back into T-shirt and shorts. They took him by both his hands and pulled him in among them, and they shrieked with joy as he lurched about, elbows high, eyes raised ecstatically to the sky. "Look at B! Look, he dances like a frog!" George shouted. And the rain fell on the bishop, and mud squeezed out from the lawn and splattered his great calves, and flower petals fell from the trees, and the big man closed his eyes and giggled like a tickled child.

This bishop had not come to Malaita to rule. He did not love Malaitans because they revered him, deferred to him, waited on him or obeyed him—for they did none of these things. This bishop loved Malaitans because they bossed him around. They harangued and chided him. They yelled at him. They invaded his house, asked him for favours and money. They were not afraid to touch him, not afraid to pat him on the shoulder while he was cooking, not afraid to grasp his hand tightly, without reservation and for no particular reason at all. He loved them because they ate his stews, and when they were finished, they leaned back and belched at him in unselfconscious contentment; because he had lived in a northern metropolis and he knew what it was like to rub shoulders with thousands of people and still feel an immense, crushing solitude. He loved Malaitans because they surrounded him like water, because they made him know beyond any doubt that he was not alone.

16

A SHORT WALK
IN EAST KWAIO

The supernatural power abiding in the powerful
living man abides in his ghost after death,
with increased vigour and more ease of movement.

R.H. CODRINGTON, *The Melanesians*

THE DEFINING moment in Kwaio history came on the morning of October 2, 1927. The British colonial district officer, William Bell, arrived to collect taxes at the base of the mountain headwall marking the eastern edge of the Kwaio bush. Two hundred warriors marched down the mountain to meet him. By the end of the morning, Bell and fourteen of his party were dead, and Melanesia's toughest, proudest, most feared pagans had set themselves up for a fight they knew they could not win.

Most battles on the frontiers of the British Empire were recorded only in the accounts of white colonizers. Britain's enemies were remembered as mythical savages, sometimes cunning but more often pathetic, and always doomed. Such were the tales that drifted around the world after the Malaita massacre. The Kwaio side of the story would have been forgotten outside the bush if survivors had not passed on their history to a sympathetic researcher half a century later. The American anthropologist Roger

Keesing lived among the Kwaio for sixteen years and wrote down their version of the chain reaction of violence from which they have still not fully recovered. The story, recounted by Keesing and colonial historian Peter Corris in *Lightning Meets the West Wind,* went like this:

William Bell was a tough bastard with a booming voice and a hot temper. After twelve years on Malaita, his face had been baked to a copper hue and his eyes pressed into a constant squint by the tropical sun. As district officer, Bell's job was to pacify the Malaitan warlords, a job at which he excelled, using a combination of intimidation, negotiation and brutality. Bell ordered an end to the blood feuding that had continued for centuries on the island. He arrested and hanged murderers. He ordered Malaitans to give up the guns they had acquired on distant plantations, but he armed a constabulary of Christian converts to do his own rough work.

Bell respected the Malaitans, but he had hardened with the years. If natives were impertinent in his court, he flogged them with his walking stick. If he felt they were lying, he punched them in the face. He developed an aura not unlike that of the warrior strongmen who ruled the Kwaio bush. "Missa Bello," the Malaitans said, was the strongest white man in the world. Years later, one Kwaio elder told Keesing: "Mr. Bell's words blew like the smoke from a fire across the island. 'You have killed, but the killing is over. Even though you have the rifles you have got from Queensland and Fiji and Samoa, even though you have killed a thousand people with them, it is over. Now the law has come to forbid it.'"

The colonial government wanted more than peace. The resident commissioner demanded a yearly head tax—in pounds sterling, no less—from most able-bodied men. Since islanders were still trading in shell money and pigs, the tax forced them to work on white plantations, which was exactly why it had been introduced.

The men who ruled the Malaita bush saw the tax as a direct challenge to their rule. These men were not chiefs. They were *ramo,* warrior leaders whose power and wealth lay in their ability to collect and distribute blood money. The *ramo* were frequently assassins, quite willing to commit murder in order to exact vengeance on wrongdoers, to enforce the rigid codes of Kwaio conduct, or simply to collect bounty. They were generous feast givers and sacrificers, and therefore favoured by the ancestors.

The most powerful *ramo* of all was Basiana, a warm and constant family man who happened to have executed a score of people. Basiana killed adulterers and thieves. He killed when he was insulted. He killed a cousin because the man had wrongly eaten part of a sacrificial pig. Like Bell, Basiana was proud, stubborn and ruthless. Like Bell, he had gathered a band of rifle-wielding henchmen around him. Like Bell, he was supposed to be infused with supernatural power. Bell and Basiana knew each other's reputations. They were destined for a confrontation.

As Bell's power and notoriety grew, people chided the Kwaio *ramo*. Missa Bello will make women of you all, the coastal people said. Basiana watched as neighbours to the north and the west were subjugated. He watched them forsake their ancestors in favour of the white man's god.

Then, in 1926, the Kwaio *ramo* came down to the water at Sinalagu harbour and paid Bell the five shillings head tax the government had demanded. Basiana handed over four shillings, and a shilling-like disc he had carved out of a piece of sacred pearl-shell jewellery. Bell called Basiana a bastard for his trick but took the shell coin anyway. The next year, word drifted down the east coast of Malaita that Bell was returning and that he wanted not just head tax but also to confiscate the rifles of the *ramo*. This was too much to ask. Not only were rifles sacred (Basiana's had been consecrated to a warrior ancestor), but Bell had already armed the coastal headmen who were loyal to the government. The loss of their rifles would render the Kwaio *ramo* impotent and would mean the end of their sovereignty.

Basiana called his fellow *ramo* together and made his case for an attack on Bell. Those who had travelled into the white man's world begged him not to do it. "The white people aren't the same," warned a man who had been in prison in Tulagi. "If we kill them, our homeland will be finished. No child will be left, no woman will be left. They'll destroy everything."

Basiana would not be denied his last stand. He reminded the *ramo* of the strength of their ancestors. Weapons were gathered, and priests killed dozens of pigs to enlist the ancestors' support.

Word of the impending attack tumbled down the mountainsides. When William Bell arrived in Sinalagu harbour, his coastal allies warned

him to stay on his ship. Just shoot the bush men on sight, suggested his
Malaitan constables. Bell insisted he would not cower on his boat, nor
would he draw first blood. He went ashore, arranged the constables in
and around his tax house, sat down behind a table at the front of the
building and opened his ledgers. A long line of warriors carrying rifles,
clubs, spears, bows and arrows appeared on the mountainside above.
Basiana's men numbered at least two hundred. They screamed fearfully,
but everyone knew that only two or three of their rifles were actually capable of firing and that Bell had a modern arsenal of two dozen rifles and
two revolvers.

Bell called out to Basiana. He promised not to take his gun away. He
asked the *ramo* to order his men to put down their weapons. Some did.
Basiana and his warriors formed a line in front of Bell's table. While
Basiana paid his tax, his men crept to the rear of the tax house and cut the
cane lashing that held fast the wall panels. The circle of warriors tightened around the building. Basiana retreated, picked up his rifle and hid it
between his arm and his body. He returned to the tax line and worked his
way forward again, surrounded by his kinsmen. Bell looked up from his
scroll just in time to see Basiana, who raised his rifle butt with both hands
and brought it down so hard that the district officer's skull exploded.
Bell's body went limp. Basiana leapt over it and charged into the tax
house, where he was tackled by the constables inside. This had the desired
effect of distracting the constables from their rifles. The unlashed walls
collapsed, and the Kwaio warriors swarmed, cutting down Bell's party
with a hail of spear, knife and axe blows. Within minutes, the district
officer, his assistant and thirteen loyal constables were dead. The clearing
was strewn with blood, guts and limbs. Only two of the attackers were
killed. It was a glorious victory for Basiana. It was also his last.

Enemies both white and black salivated at the chance to exact revenge
on the Kwaio. Hundreds of Malaitans volunteered to help avenge Bell
and the dead policemen. Dozens of white planters and traders came forward too. Within two weeks, an Australian warship steamed into
Sinalagu harbour. A punitive expedition of 50 sailors, 50 native police, 25
white volunteers and 120 native carriers marched into the Kwaio hills.
Villages were torched. Pigs were shot. Chemical defoliant was sprayed

onto vegetable gardens. The white volunteers fired a few shots into the forest, but mostly they got drunk, quarrelled and collapsed from malaria and dysentery. The Australian navals retreated to Sydney after six weeks. Justice was largely left to the native police, most of whom happened to be the Kwaio's bitterest enemies, Kwara'ae from north Malaita. Now the Kwaio apocalypse began in earnest.

The native police did not limit themselves to the hunt for Bell's killers or tax evaders. They used their new authority and firepower to exact vengeance for grievances going back generations. Dozens of Kwaio were shot, including thirteen women and girls. The female relatives of Bell's killers were gang raped. Some police hacked off the hands and feet of the dead, piled them on the bodies, then called out tauntingly to the victims' ancestors. Sacrificial stones were defiled. Ancestral relics and drums were smashed and burned. Skulls were taken from shrines and thrown into women's menstruation huts. This humiliation of Kwaio ancestors was the most devastating crime of all. Everyone knew that angry ancestors punished only their own descendants.

Basiana and his fellows eventually surrendered. Basiana's two sons were forced to watch their father hang along with five others. How many Kwaio died as a result of the Malaita massacre? More than sixty were shot or hacked to death and thirty died of dysentery in jail. But Kwaio storytellers later put the death toll in the hundreds, because after the destruction of their shrines, the Kwaio were effectively abandoned by their ancestors for generations. Sacrifices stopped working. People fell ill. Taro stopped growing. Hundreds of people starved. The apocalypse was both physical and metaphysical.

GETTING TO EAST KWAIO was not easy. The bishop's truck sank like a hippo in the red clay along the road that, as I had suspected, was not a road at all. At each hill, I got out and pushed along with Tony and Thomas and the dozen-odd hitchhikers we had collected en route. Derrick would stomp on the gas, the tires would fling great gobs of dough-like mud at our faces, and the truck would lurch from rut to rut, groaning more emphatically with every new bluff. Finally, it refused to advance any farther.

The boys were outraged and shamed at the thought of my carrying on alone, but they felt better after they had cajoled one of the hitchhikers into guiding me to the coast and carrying my gas jug. (I had brought along 20 litres of fuel because there was none left on the east side of Malaita. Without fuel, it would be a long paddle down the coast to the Adventist mission at Atoifi.)

"Oh no," I told the hitcher weakly. *"No, yu no kari petrol blong mi,"* and then I handed the jug to him. He glared at me and strode off with it. I scurried behind. An hour later, he dumped the jug on the road, accepted a month's wages for his effort and disappeared on a side trail. Then I was alone. I balanced the gas jug on my shoulders, above my backpack, and carried on. The overcast sky began to lose its late afternoon glow. The mud stuck to the soles of my sandals until they were as heavy as ski boots. I slipped, swore, pulled off the sandals and trudged on. Tall grass grew like an endless hedge down the middle of the track. I walked through the end of twilight, expecting to see lights around each new bend. But there were no lights, and no sounds other than the rustling of the forest. I pulled out my headlamp and walked into the night. I cursed the road and the disappearing hitchhiker and Solomon Islanders for going to war instead of keeping up their roads. I cursed myself for not simply waiting a week and catching the supply plane to the Atoifi mission.

But finally I saw a faint glow and followed it until it became a lamp in the window of a plywood shack. A sign outside the shack announced: Peace Monitoring Council. That was good. The PMC had been formed to lobby militants to give up their guns. Three people answered the door when I knocked: a grandfather, a thickish woman and a quivering young man. It was too dark to see their faces, but I knew they were good people because they made me a hot cup of tea and offered me a bed and a mosquito net for the night. What a coincidence, they told me when they heard my story: they would be taking a canoe down to Atoifi Mission in the morning.

The young man, whose name was Patrick, announced he would tell me a funny story from the time of ethnic tension. (Why did nobody ever just call the civil war a civil war?) Once upon a time, Patrick had worked with his best friend, Chris, at the Shell Oil station in Honiara. When the tension began, Patrick joined the Malaita Eagle Force, but Chris joined the Guadalcanal side, the Isatabu Freedom Movement. That was a real scream, said Patrick, because the Eagles had machine guns while the poor IFM boys had to make do with machetes and homemade pipe guns. Patrick insisted that he and his friends had killed at least sixty-eight Guale boys in Marau, thirty-eight in Kakabona and twenty-five more in Kombule. He met his best friend again after the fighting was finished. "Chris said to me, 'Hey, if you had seen me at the battle of Alligator Creek, would you have shot me?' I told him, of course I would. And it would have been easy, because I had my SR-88, my machine gun, and Chris had to make do with his homemade pipe gun and his prayers! Ha!"

"Prayers?"

"Yes, they were all begging their ancestors to protect them from us. It didn't work. How could magic work against our machine guns?"

"So you guys didn't try using magic?"

"Some of the Eagles did. An old man once came to our bunker with a powerful black stone from Choiseul. He said it would stop the IFM's guns from firing. That didn't work, so we decided to pray to God instead. We prayed every morning before our battles."

"Surely God wouldn't help you kill people!"

"I know, I know," Patrick said, barely able to contain his laughter. "We didn't ask Him to help us win. We said, 'God, we know you are against what we are doing here, but please can you wash us with the blood of Jesus Christ? Can you make us clean again?'"

"Asking for forgiveness even before you sinned," I said. "That's cheating."

"I know, it's crazy isn't it? *Funi tumas!*"

Morning came, or something like morning. A deep grey glow crept beneath the belly of the overcast sky. It was not bright enough to penetrate the forest along the trail or to transform the oily black hue of the cove, which we reached after an hour's walk. The sun never did appear in East Kwaio. When I look back and try to remember scenes from the next few days, the mountains, the people, the mission, the machetes ... all these things return to me in a muddy twilight of charcoal, rotting mahogany and leaden shadows. It was like moving through Atlantis, a world made heavy and cut off from the truth of things by a hundred fathoms of murky jade.

The peace monitors had arranged for a *kanu*, which was not a dugout canoe but a fibreglass skiff. We slid out through the mangroves and headed south across still water, skirting the inside of a long barrier reef. East of the reef, there was nothing; we were tracing the rough edge of the world. The sky took shape underneath the vast overcast: a storm front billowed like a sail, then swept over us. The sea exploded with raindrops. I hid under my windbreaker and watched the shore. As we droned south, the mountains grew taller and pushed out through the coastal plain so that eventually they thrust directly from the edge of the mangroves. Their slopes were not pristine: the jungle was cut and torn like a mangy scalp, a patchwork of cultivated fields, burnt patches and bare red earth. There might have been a melancholy beauty to the place, but that is not what I felt at the time. What I felt was an immense hostility, as though the bush itself was urging me to keep my distance.

The Seventh-day Adventist Mission appeared on a bluff above the ocean, its tin roofs glistening like broken glass in the dull light. We tied up to a pier made from a heap of coral rock and hiked up towards the mission and its hospital. The Adventist compound was a jarringly ordered collection of offices, verandas and hedgerows, not at all a part of the tangle of vines and gardens that cradled it. A generator thrummed somewhere out of sight. A line of children in white shirts filed out of a cement-brick church.

The screen door of a bungalow swung open, and a white woman emerged, her white dress billowing around her ankles. "Come in! Come in! Your lunch is ready," she bellowed.

I obeyed, and the door slammed shut behind me. The Adventists had been expecting me: I had radioed before leaving Auki, hoping to track down an Australian reputed to have strong connections with the Kwaio. This was not him. This was Geri, wife of one of the volunteer doctors at the mission hospital. I was immediately transfixed by her. She was mountainous. Her face was flushed with the heat. She glowed with good intentions. We held hands as Geri said grace. Lunch was a hallucination from daytime television. Heaps of Kraft Dinner glowed a vibrant orange.

There were squeezable bottles of ketchup and processed cheese on the table, and a plate of chocolate chip cookies. It was heaven.

"We're here for three months—you don't think we're gonna eat yams the whole time, do you?" Geri said, squeezing a glistening slug of cheese onto her plate. "I had our food flown in, all the way from L.A."

I told Geri I wanted to head into the Kwaio bush. She reached for my wrist and shook her head sadly.

"The pagans," she said. "Such a shame. Those *poor* people are so close to the mission, but they *reef-yoos* to change. They *reef-yoos* to progress. And do you know why? They are too scared of their *devil-devils*, that's why." Anyway, it wasn't a good time to go see the pagans, Geri said. Better to stay at the mission. There would be eight hours of worship tomorrow, it being Saturday.

"But why is it a bad time to see the pagans?" I asked.

"Lordy, where do I start?" said Geri. "First, they've got a dead *devil* priest to deal with up there. Then there's the Italian mess. You heard about the Italians, didn't you? They were fools, as far as I could see. They had it coming to them. And, oh look, here's our David."

David MacLaren looked as though he had been plucked from a Queensland cattle station: all scruffy beard, crow's feet and sharp blue eyes. He quivered with nervous dingo energy. He glanced at my Kraft Dinner and gave me a knowing wink. Then he closed his eyes and said a whispered grace.

David was my connection. He had been popping in and out of East Kwaio country for a decade, first to work as chief pathologist at the hospital, then as part of a touring open-heart surgery team, and now to study the place as part of his master's thesis in public health.

The Adventists ran the only proper hospital on Malaita, David said, but they had a problem. They offered most medical services for two Solomon dollars (about the price of two coconuts), but the bush Kwaio still could not afford to set foot in the place. Why? Everything about the hospital—its architecture, its procedures, its toilets, its staff—violated Kwaio *kastom*.

Some examples: the hospital was a two-storey building, but the ancestors forbade Kwaio men from walking under any structure where women had walked. Men's rooms happened to share the same roof as the maternity ward; this was an outrage, as a Kwaio man should never enter a women's delivery house. The hospital toilets were impressively hygienic, but they were also under that same roof; asking a Kwaio to sleep in such a building was like asking him to sleep inside an outhouse. Then there was the issue of bodily fluids: the Kwaio knew that sink water, which contained human saliva, mingled with toilet water in the hospital's drains. Fluid from one's mouth could not be mixed with *shit-shit*. No way. If a Kwaio entered such a sacrilegious building, he would insult the ancestors so much that they would withdraw their magic protection: gardens would fail, misfortune would spread through his village, sickness and disease would follow. He would have to sacrifice a dozen or more pigs to placate the dead. A hospital visit could cost a decade of accumulated wealth, not to mention future favours.

David had spent the last three years trying to figure out how to build a hospital wing that the Kwaio would actually use. He had won the trust and friendship of the pagan chiefs. That's why he could not let me just wander up the mountain. Not now.

"Because of the *devil* priest," said Geri.

David smiled the smile of a teenager whose mother had embarrassed him. "A *kastom* priest has died," he said. "They will be killing pigs up there, putting on a mortuary feast. All my contacts will be mourning. Nobody is allowed to travel in the district. It's a matter of respect. That's one thing."

"The other?"

"Well, you don't just wander into Kwaio country without the permission of a chief."

"Like the Italians did," said Geri.

"Who are these Italians?"

David sighed. The previous month, he said, a party of white men and women had arrived on the mail plane. They said they were doctors and were here to help. They found a guide and headed for the hills. It didn't go well at all. The doctors didn't heal anyone, but they did break all kinds of *tabus*. The worst thing they did was to carry toilet paper into the villages. It was unused, of course, but the unclean association was a screaming affront to the ancestors. The bumbling Italians made it back down to Atoifi, but a mob of angry pagans cut them off en route to the airstrip. The Italians tried to negotiate. Big mistake. The machetes came out. One Italian was sliced pretty badly—he almost lost an arm, said David. Finally, the visitors agreed to compensate the Kwaio. They held a ceremony and took the next plane out.

"You have to understand the pagans are incredibly suspicious of outsiders. They still haven't gotten over the 1927 massacre."

"So what am I going to do?" I asked, simultaneously irritated and vaguely relieved.

"Well, the next plane should come through in four days. You could stay here and talk to our patients," David said.

"We have worship tomorrow," said Geri hopefully.

David watched me grimace. "Or you could get out of the district. Get out of the area of mourning, steer clear of anywhere the Italians walked. There is a Christian chief in Sinalagu who might help you. Peter Laetebo. He worked with Keesing back in the sixties."

"Sinalagu!" Geri sang out. "The youth group is putting on a worship there tomorrow. You could go with them, 'specially if you paid for their gas."

I would have retreated to Honiara the next day if there had been a plane out. I felt crushed by the sodden sky, harassed by the mountains that seemed to want to push the entire mission into the sea. It was all wrong, this place, and my being here. But the plan was set. I would follow the ghost of William Bell into Sinalagu harbour.

I LEFT ATOIFI at dawn in an aluminum runabout loaded with ten scrubbed Christians and one portable karaoke machine. We pushed through the barrier reef and headed south. The heavy sky had pressed the ripples out of the sea. Six black dolphins leapt in the distance. We skirted a series of ragged limestone cliffs which eventually ruptured, providing a passage into a vast, diamond-shaped lagoon. The boatman deposited the Adventist youths at the north end of the lagoon, where coral grew in the shallows like giant clumps of rotting cauliflower. Then we headed for the southern corner of the harbour, where the mountains were higher and steeper. The boatman pointed to a low bluff. "Mister Bell," he said. "That's where they killed him."

He cut the outboard engine and lifted it from the water. We poled through the shallows towards a cluster of huts on stilts. This was Gounabusu. I hopped out and sank to my knees in muck. The boatman went home. The villagers ignored me completely until I found Peter Laetebo, the chief. He was an ancient and vaguely muddled fellow. He had wrapped a dirty yellow dishtowel around his waist like a sarong, and his belly trembled above it like a deflated balloon. He took me to someone's hut, where we sat on a wooden bench and I tried to explain myself to a rapidly expanding jury. One by one, the village men came in, and I handed out my business card, which said "journalist." The chief smiled and nodded knowingly. On his right sat a burly young man who wore a thick, shell money necklace and a Pearl Jam T-shirt; he had bleached his hair blond. Pearl Jam was silent but I could tell he was my ally. Things were going quite well, I thought, until the one-eyed man arrived.

The one-eyed man didn't say anything at first. He just gazed at me with that one angry eye while pus oozed from the other. He wore a bandana around his head and an army fatigue vest. He slapped his thigh with his machete. It looked sharp. He stroked the hairs on his chin.

"White men are millionaires," he said in Solomons Pidgin.

"Pardon?"

"I want to know why you *stap* here."

The other men fell silent. I explained myself again and threw in a blurb about promoting tourism or something. I watched the one-eyed man's fingers tighten around his machete.

"This is my land. Those gardens up there on the hill belong to *mifala*. We don't need white men to come and steal the stories *blong mifala*. We don't need another Keesing to make himself rich from our culture."

Keesing? How strange, I thought, as blood rushed to my cheeks. The anthropologist had spent two decades mucking about the bush with the pagans. He didn't get rich, and he wasn't particularly interested in the Christians down here on the coast. I didn't say any of these things.

The one-eyed man held my business card up with both hands, then slowly ripped it in two. We all watched the pieces flutter to the floor. I thought about William Bell seated at his tax-collecting table, and compulsively I stood up, perhaps shaking just a little. This was a Christian mission village. Christians didn't chop visitors to bits.

"Um," I said. "Sorry. Um, there must be a mistake. I must have made a mistake."

"Yes! You sorry! You should have asked before coming here. You no ask. *Yu mas stap insaed long kanu blong yu and go nao.*"

I had decided that looking at the one-eyed man was a bad idea, since I could not keep my gaze from shifting over to that right eye socket, where sometimes, a tiny bloodshot sliver of eyeball did appear. I looked instead at the floor, wondering why the chief and the others weren't helping me. It felt like hours until the one-eyed man finally stomped down the stairs and trudged away across the dirt.

"Everything is fine, mate," said my ally with the bleached blond hair. He spoke in English with an unmistakable Aussie accent. "I'll take you into the mountains tomorrow. But now, you should come to my house. Right now."

The chief nodded gravely.

My ally introduced himself as Roni Butala. His house was a tin-and-timber shack on the other side of the village, past the South Seas Evangelical Church. I made myself small on Roni's veranda and accepted a cup of tea from his mother. Roni called together a few cousins, then disappeared. The cousins remained. Two of them carried long bush knives. One had a bow and arrow.

"Maybe you should *stap* inside," Roni's mother said nervously.

An hour later, Roni returned with the one-eyed man, who had adopted a more diplomatic aspect.

"Everything is fine," said Roni.

"You are welcome here," said the one-eyed man, whose name was Samuel. "*Yu savve walkabaot.*"

"Thank you," I said.

Samuel offered me his hand.

"Come back inside *long* house," Roni's mother called to me, urgently now.

I accepted Samuel's hand. His palm was sticky, like wet tobacco. He shook mine aggressively. He sneered at me, then retreated.

"We will have to give him some money before you leave," said Roni.

"Roni!" squawked mother from the veranda. "Oh Roni! Why did you let *fren blong yu* shake the hand of Samuel? This is bad. Oh, this is bad *tumas.*"

THAT NIGHT, Peter Laetebo joined Roni and me on the veranda. The chief had put on a button-down business shirt. In the lamplight, I could see his facial tattoos shine beneath his white stubble. They looked like unfinished games of tic-tac-toe. The chief wanted to *storian.* Gounabusu village was entirely Christian, he bragged, and had been long before William Bell and his constables came to Sinalagu. And it was all because of Florence Young.

Back in the days of the *ramo*, the elders had sent their sons off on the blackbirders' ships. They ordered the boys to come back from the plantations with tools, tobacco and guns. Many did, but the ones who met Florence Young did not. Young was the wife of a Queensland plantation baron. She would come early each morning to the Malaitans' barracks in the sugar cane fields, wake up the workers, sing them hymns and tell them stories from the Bible. She was persuasive. When the boys returned to Sinalagu as men, they brought her South Seas Evangelical Church with them. This made the elders furious. "We told you to come back with guns, and you came back with Bibles!" they said. Christian teachers and their converts were harassed and sometimes assassinated. They banded together in coastal villages like Gounabusu for protection. The pagans stayed in the mountains.

Peter Laetebo had been a pagan priest when he met Keesing, the anthropologist, back in the 1960s.

"But you're a Christian now," I said.

"Hem i tru tumas ia," the chief said, slapping his knee proudly. "When I was a heathen, life was good, but it was expensive. Every time my *pikinini* got sick, I had to give up money and pigs to the *devils . . ."*

"Ancestors," said Roni under his breath.

"One day *soniboy blong mi* got sick," said Peter. "Fever, *belly-run.* I was tired of sacrificing so I brought the boy down to the mission here. The pastor put his hands on *soniboy* and prayed: not long, two, three hours, *nomo.* Then the boy woke up and started to cry. I said, *'Disfala God, hem i tru wan stret ia!*' My other gods they ate all my money and pigs. The Christian god, he works, and he is altogether free! Ha!"

Peter moved his family down to Gounabusu and learned to follow the new *tabus*. The South Seas Evangelical Church forbade alcohol, tobacco and betel nut. It forbade any kind of ancestor tribute. Women had to cover themselves. Those things were a bother. But Christian life helped the chief to save money: he could keep all his pigs for himself, and he didn't have to spend weeks in isolation after sacrifices. The erstwhile pagan priest had now become a church elder.

Peter couldn't talk for long. His son, another son, was gravely ill. He would be sitting at the boy's side for the rest of the night.

"What about you, Roni? Are you a Christian?" I asked.

Roni looked at his mother and hesitated. "We have church in the morning, mate," he said. "I'll take you up the mountain after that."

I went to bed—or rather, to my grass mat—and hoped, silently, that Roni would rescind his offer. I longed to leave East Kwaio. There was a diffuse hostility to the place, something beyond the heat, the stickiness, the constant drip and rot, beyond even the one-eyed man's anger. I felt it spreading through my joints like a poisonous ache. I felt it in the damp night air as I lay awake on the floor of Roni's house. I felt it through the sleepless night, and then I felt it amplified by the sound of a church bell, which began clanging long before dawn.

My legs and feet had been scratched countless times during my trek across the island. What began as nicks had developed into spectacular abscesses. Purple blisters spread out under my skin. They were streaked like marble with faint intrusions of pus. An unexplainable boil had risen on my little toe and was threatening to erupt. My head throbbed. What was it I wanted from the pagans? I couldn't remember. What could they possibly have to say about the spiritual crisis of the Solomons? I couldn't imagine.

Roni's mother greeted me on the veranda. "Oh no!" she said when she saw me. "Oh Roni! *Mi tellem yu finis for no lettem Samuel for touchim disfala fren blong yu!*"

Roni put a hand on my forehead. "Fever," he said. "Now you *must* climb the mountain with me. It will take *kastom* medicine to fight a curse like this."

I wanted to tell Roni that it was not Samuel who had made me sick. It was the bad air, the unwashed hands, the mosquitoes, the septic sludge that dribbled into the harbour, the sickening heaviness of the air. It was climate and biology that had got to me, just as it had got to Europeans for centuries. The Australian navals who had charged into the Kwaio bush looking for Bell's murderers in 1927 experienced the same thing. Many were carried back down to their ship on stretchers, covered in septic ulcers, shivering with malaria and dripping with diarrhea.

The hothouse fertility of these shores had ended writer Jack London's attempted circumnavigation of the globe in 1907, infecting his crew with sores and fever. This led London to declare in his travelogue, *The Cruise of the Snark,* that in the Solomons, "I really and for the first time in my life comprehended how frail and unstable is human tissue."

Just to spite Samuel, we put on clean shirts and attended Sunday mass, which was a show of pure evangelical anarchy. Hands waved. Eyes rolled. Men reassured God. They shouted that he was the greatest, the mightiest. "Hallelujah!" they wailed. "Hallelujah!"

Roni and I slipped out mid-program. We followed a trail that zigzagged up the mountainside, through sweet potato gardens, limestone rubble and fallow patches choking with woody brambles. The slope was steeper than the tin roof of the church. The air was dead calm and cruelly hot. My clothes were soaking wet.

"You were loud in church this morning," I said to Roni. "So you are a Christian."

"When in Rome," he said, gazing up into the forest.

"Come on, Roni, which side are you on?"

"I am on the side of my ancestors, that's which side."

Roni had grown up in Gounabusu. He was a smart kid. He had won a scholarship to Massey University and spent four years in New Zealand. That's why his English was so good. The Kiwi girls loved Roni, but he was startled by their *kastom.* One white girl invited Roni home to meet her parents in the suburbs. When she put her arm around him and told her father, "This is my boyfriend," Roni screamed and fled. Later, the girl explained to him that in New Zealand it was an honour to be introduced to your girlfriend's father. Roni told her: "If your father was Kwaio, he would have taken a knife and killed me."

Roni had studied plant science and fraternized with the granola crowd. He returned to Malaita as an environmentalist. He also carried a new sense of Kwaio otherness and took to wandering up into the hills, and into the past. He smoked and storied-on with the patriarchs and pagan priests. He grew dreadlocks—not matted like Bob Marley's but braided as he imagined his ancestors' had been. (Roni's dreads were gone now. His mother had finally ordered him to cut them off. She was worried the ancestors would recognize Roni as one of their own and try to influence him.) Now he was helping to rebuild the traditional school that Keesing had once established on the mountainside, a place for the pagans to pass on their *kastom* religion and to learn to write down the names of their ancestors as well as to study mathematics, so they would know when the Christians were trying to cheat them.

"So you really are a pagan," I said.

"I went to Christian school. I believe in God. I know he is powerful. But if I had to choose," he said, "I would choose the ancestors."

"I don't understand. If you believe in the Christian God, then you must believe he is more powerful."

"Look. Up there," he said, pointing to a nearby ridge. Most of the land had been cleared, but a clump of trees had been left on the crest. "Those forests are *tabu*. That's where people keep their ancestors. Now imagine you lived here. When you died, your children would take your skull and put it in the *kastom* hut so your grandchildren could make sacrifices to you, and so you could stay with your own land forever. That's our *kastom*. That's what I want."

We pushed on, climbing up into the shadows of the rain forest. Roots splayed out from great tree trunks like webbed feet. Vines trailed overhead. Condensation dripped from ferns. We splashed up a creek bed, past tiny clearings thick with taro and papaya. We climbed into the soft belly of a slow-moving mist. It was cooler there. I forgot my headache, forgot the malevolence of the mountain, didn't think twice when a face appeared through the leaves, then disappeared with a rush of breath.

We rounded a bend and stepped into the stone age. The clearing was all blackened palm stumps, smashed limestone and fresh-churned mud through which pigs rooted vigorously and women dashed, bare breasts swinging. The women ducked into the doorways of thatch huts and watched me from the shadows. I could see the glowing embers of their tin pipes. The face from the mist appeared at the top of the clearing, a teenaged boy in soccer shorts, now wielding a machete the length of his torso. Beneath him, sitting on a white rock, cross-legged, stoking a pipe and smiling like a garden gnome, was Roni's friend, Diakake Doaka, who was sort of a chief but more of a priest, and who liked to be called Jack. He had the same worn sun hat as Henry Fonda in *On Golden Pond*. Jack had an even worse grasp of Solomons Pidgin than I. Much of what I pass on here is Roni's translation of our conversation.

Jack was pleased to see Roni. He was particularly relieved to see me. He told me he had had a dream about me the previous night. "The grandfathers told me you were not welcome in Gounabusu," he said. "You must never sleep there again. The Christians will try to poison you."

Jack seemed gratified when I told him that I was ill and that I was keen to see the *kastom* doctor Roni had promised me.

"Soon," said Jack with a satisfied chuckle. "The *lamo* is on his way."

In his book *Kwaio Religion*, Keesing wrote that the Kwaio world view is reflected in the social geography of their settlements. The men are literally on top. Jack's village matched Keesing's description. This was clearly not a great place to be a woman.

The highest point in the village was dominated by the priest's hut, where sacred things were kept. (There were skulls inside, but I didn't see them. Being sullied by my time in Gounabusu, I wasn't allowed to so much as peek in the doorway.) It was a quaint cottage, the only one in the village surrounded by plants and a bamboo fence. Next down the slope was the unmarried men's clubhouse. This was my favourite: a fort raised on stilts two metres off the ground that looked like the kind of playhouse an investment banker might build for his kids. It had a neat, pitched roof and a timber floor, on which were scattered pieces of a radio. (A functioning radio would have been useless anyway, because the price of batteries had tripled since the tension began.)

In the middle of the village were a couple of communal huts, where women cooked and children rolled in the dirt. Smoke rose from one thatch roof like steam from a wet lawn. The communal huts had special rooms just for pigs. "Our *pik-piks* are important," said Jack. "We love them almost as much as our sons. No good suppose somebody steal 'em." Farther downhill were the women's communal sleeping huts, which were austere. At the bottom corner of the village, where all the mud and pig piss eventually trickled, was a tiny hovel, not much bigger than a dog-house. A shy girl peeked out from behind. I tried not to gawk at her. This was the place where women waited out their monthly menstruation time.

David MacLaren had explained this geography to me and insisted that it shouldn't be taken literally. The Kwaio didn't really think that women were lowly and impure and that men were more holy. No, they both had their own sacredness, and the menstruation hut was a kind of earthly mirror image of the priest's house. But everyone knows that sewage flows downhill. And here in Jack's village, it was the women's place to wallow in it.

The village was only a hundred days old. Apparently, the commu-nity—which consisted of an extended family of about twenty—had moved to avoid a spiritual catastrophe. A man had fallen ill at their last settlement. He was near death when Jack received a dream in which the ancestors revealed the cause of the illness. A woman had urinated, or per-haps begun her menstruation cycle, in one of the village huts. Jack knew that the grandfathers' displeasure about this defilement could only be re-lieved by moving and starting again. So here they were in the fresh mud.

JACK'S WIFE—nobody told me her name—was using a stone to smash a heap of gnali nuts she had collected in the forest. They tasted like al-monds. Mosquitoes rose in the late afternoon haze. Jack and his wife were highly amused to see me spread insect repellent on my legs. "White man weak *tumas*," I explained, and Jack nodded in agreement. I was miserable. My joints felt as though they had been battered with a pig club. The boil on my toe had ruptured obscenely. I wrapped it in duct tape. Where was the damn *kastom* doctor? It was not that I imagined any sort of magic could heal me. I was quite ready to give up on magic at this point. No. I wanted to see the *kastom* doctor in the same way a tired mountaineer wants to see the top of Everest. The doctor's arrival would mean the be-ginning of my journey back out of East Kwaio.

"I think you have a good life here," I lied to Jack.

He nodded and explained that life in the Kwaio bush was good because he and his family still obeyed the rules that a giant snake had im-
parted to the ancestor Ofama, 125 generations before. Respect the
ancestors and their shrines. Don't steal pigs or women that aren't yours.
Don't kill without a good reason. Take care of your own ground, your pigs
and your taro gardens. Be tidy. Don't use your house as a toilet. All quite
reasonable. Oh, and men must never eat from a plate used by women. Men
should live and shit uphill, women downhill. Women and the things they
touch should never, ever, gain more altitude than men. Men's bathing
water should be diverted so it doesn't mix with women's pollution somewhere downhill. Priests should offer extravagant sacrifices of burnt pig to
the ancestors, and the meat should be eaten by the priest alone. Et cetera.

My feminist friends nod when they hear these stories. They tell me
that *kastom*, myth and *tabu* are tools of the patriarchy, of powerful men
pushing everyone else down, especially women (i.e., in the menstruation
hut). That may be true, but I was less interested in the politics of the rules
than I was in their mythical origins. Were the Kwaio's myths really com-
municated by ancestors, or were they invented and fabulized in order to
lend sacredness to the rules they supported?

The Bishop of Malaita had introduced me to the theories of French
linguist Maurice Leenhardt, who had lived on New Caledonia between
1909 and 1926. Leenhardt concluded that Melanesian myths were not
fictions plucked from the ether so much as they were an expression of
lived experience. By this (I think) he meant that though Melanesians
could not control their natural world through technology, their myths
provided tools to help them adapt to it. Every day they saw how the order
of the world depended on the standards of their conduct.

In some ways, Leenhardt's theory seemed to fit here in East Kwaio.
When the ancestors were honoured and their rules obeyed, life generally
went well. But when the rules were broken, people got sick, crops failed,
and women became infertile. Sometimes natural calamities occurred
without warning, but the Kwaio always seemed to find a reason (a shrine
disturbed, for example, or a house fouled by urine) to connect these
events to the ancestors' wrath. Things could be made better only by
offering a sacrifice to manipulate the forces of the supernatural realm in
their favour, or at least to placate them.

I couldn't see how the edicts of Melanesian ancestors differed from the exacting rules that Moses had handed down to the Israelites in the Book of Leviticus, or the bizarre prohibitions—no consumption of fish without scales, for example—still maintained by the Seventh-day Adventists. Humans crave structure. We crave rules. Where few are required, we extrapolate; we tease them out of our myths. Obey, or the gods will exact vengeance. Obey, or you will burn in hell. Obey, or the taro will rot in the ground.

Anyway, all Jack Doaka had to do to reinforce his faith was to look at the world beyond the Kwaio hills. It was going to hell in a handbasket. Jack had no doubt that all the great evils of Solomon Islands life stemmed from Christian transgression. War? That's what Christians did; it's what the government—which was really just an arm of the Church—brought to East Kwaio in 1927. Sexually transmitted diseases? They were spread by Christians who defied the old sex *tabus.* Poverty? That came from dishonouring the ancestors, which Christians were always keen to do. Christians were greedy. They chased money and forgot their place in the world.

Not only had Christians rejected their grandfathers in favour of one from a faraway island—how crazy was that?—but they had followed the missionaries to the coast and given up their ancestral lands. This was the biggest crime of all, said Jack. Most Christians, he said, couldn't even find their own land any more. How coule there be peace when men were living on other men's land? "The *grannies* warned me that one day the people would rise up and start killing each other over the land," said Jack. "See what happened to the Malaitans who didn't listen, the ones who left the land of them and went off to Guadalcanal. *Bigfala trouble nao!* We don't have those fights here, because we listen to the *grannies* and we stay close to them. We stay on the land *blong mifala nomo.*"

It was clear that the Christians' luck had run out, said Jack. They had completely fallen out of favour with the ancestors, and now they were paying for it. They had no power. Just look at Peter Laetebo, the chief down in Gounabusu.

"What about him?" I said. "God saved his boy's life. That's why he became a Christian."

Jack thought that was hilarious. While he cackled and wiped tears from his eyes, Roni explained the joke. Just yesterday, Chief Peter had paid Jack a load of shell money so that Jack would sacrifice a pig for the sake of his other sick son. The young man was sick because he had gone and cut down a tree near a pagan gravesite. The ancestors were naturally furious.

"Years ago, Peter could have made this sacrifice himself," said Jack. "But now that he is a Christian, he is unclean. He has lost all his power. He has to come ask *mifala* if he wants a favour from the ancestors."

So much for spiritual fidelity. Roni gave a satisfied smile. He said that Peter was so impure, he wasn't even allowed to enter the pagan villages. But Roni could. The pagans knew *he* wasn't a real Christian.

Jack did not mean to be disrespectful. He was sure that Jesus was a strong ancestor. It was just that he was an ancestor from another island; it was natural that his power would be weak here on Malaita. The only Christians Jack knew who actually wielded power were the *tasiu*. Yes, said Jack. The Melanesian Brotherhood. They had *savve*.

I CANNOT REMEMBER the *kastom* doctor's face. Later, Roni explained that this was part of his magic. I do remember that he was a tall bony man and that he wandered out of the forest carrying a black umbrella and a woven handbag full of betel nuts. He did not introduce himself. Nobody said hello to him. He reminded me of a crow. The doctor squatted on a log and watched us silently for a time. He husked a betel nut with his teeth. He pulled out a bamboo container from which he spooned a finger of lime into his mouth, along with the betel. He chewed until the pink juice dribbled down his chin. Finally, he let out a bored sigh, lifted himself up and strode towards me on those long, scaly legs. He paused in front of me, cocked his head and cooed softly.

"Take your shirt off," translated Roni.

I took my shirt off, then realized the whole village had come together to watch the spectacle. The only people not paying attention were two teenaged boys, who were engaged in picking through each other's scalps and eating whatever it was they found.

I sat still. The doctor paced around me as though inspecting a show dog. He nodded and hummed knowingly. He ran a hand along my shoulder blades. I shivered. He kneaded the skin on my shoulders and along my spine. That was quite nice. Then I felt the doctor's breath on my right shoulder blade. I couldn't see him, but my nostrils quivered at the mulch-like scent of betel nut on his breath. I could feel both his hands cupped against my shoulder, and I could hear the rush of air as he sucked and blew through them. As the exhalations came harder and faster, I could feel spit striking my skin and I could hear the terrible cough and gurgle of the doctor's effort, which reached a troubling crescendo and then ceased with a loud pop.

The crowd gave a communal "Ahhhh."

"What? What?" I said.

"Lookim!" said Roni, pointing to the doctor, who had retreated a couple of metres. The doctor was retching and holding his throat. Then he let out a tremendous cough, and something came flying out of his mouth, much like a hairball might issue from the throat of a cat. He picked the projectile out of the dirt and showed it to me. It was a tiny wooden disc. It was red, but dusted with lime.

"That is what made you sick," the doctor said quietly. "Some *rubbish* man down in Gounabusu put this inside your skin." He bit a corner off the disk. "There. Now I have killed the *swear*.* You'll feel better tomorrow."

The doctor warned me not to spend another night down in Gounabusu. I was not welcome in the Christian village, he said. I could have told him that. Then he extended his black umbrella and strode off into the forest.

THE RAIN FINALLY CAME, and so did night. We took shelter in the communal hut with the women, who served us unseasoned taro steamed inside lengths of bamboo. We ate with our hands. Everyone mumbled and joked quietly. I lay down on a wooden rack uphill from the women and watched them poke at the coals of the little fire glowing on the dirt

---

* *Swear* is the Solomon Islands Pidgin word for "curse," a translation that reveals the cultural gap between Melanesians and Europeans. If swearing—or cursing—at someone is the same as wishing them ill, then it makes sense that Melanesians view those words as parallel. It also shows their inherent belief in supernatural power. For example, a British copra trader who yelled "God damn your eyes!" at an islander wasn't actually attempting to blind the man. He was just swearing. But for Melanesians, an invocation is an invocation. There is no difference between a curse and a *swear*.

between us. I could hear pigs grunting softly behind a leaf wall. I began to feel better. Not from the doctor's cure, of course. Oh no. The doctor and I both knew that his little bark disc had come not from under the skin of my back but from his handbag. Still, I did feel strangely comforted and unthreatened here among Jack's clan. The air felt lighter than that on the coast. The mountain, when you were on it, was not hostile. Despite the outward chaos of pigs and mud and burnt forest, I felt an ethereal, ordered calm. The wounds on my calves were beginning to dry out in the smoky air. The ache began to subside.

It struck me that the mountain Kwaio led a peaceful life. It was paganism without the bite.

"This is a far cry from the days of blood feuding and those *ramo* assassins," I whispered to Roni. "So peaceful."

He translated for Jack.

"*Ramo*..." said Jack. "*Ramo*... Ah, *lamo!*" The Kwaio, I remembered, substituted "l" for "r" when they spoke.

"*Ramo!*" exclaimed Roni, and they both laughed.

"What's so funny?" I asked.

"You think the *lamo* are gone? Every village still has a *lamo*. If someone seduces one of the daughters here, or steals a pig, or murders someone, Jack will gather a bounty of pigs and shell money so he can pay the *lamo* to go kill whoever did it."

"Tell me more," I said.

"Why didn't you just ask the *lamo* when he was here?" said Roni.

"Wha—you never introduced me to a *lamo*!" I complained.

Roni translated, and Jack laughed so hard tears came to his eyes.

"The *lamo* was here all afternoon, but you ignored him, so he just healed you and went home," said Roni.

The doctor was the *lamo*. The doctor was the assassin.

Six months after I left East Kwaio, a new administrator arrived at the Atoifi Adventist Mission. He hiked out into the forest to measure a plot of land. He did not know that the land was the subject of an ownership dispute. A *lamo* met the administrator at the plot and cut off his head. The Kwaio have always been passionate about their land. The severed head was recovered. The assassin was not.

17

RAIDERS OF THE
NONO LAGOON

I shall define cannibalism as a cult construction which
refers to the inordinate capacity of the Other to
consume human flesh as an especially delectable food.

GANANATH OBEYESEKERE,
"Cannibal Feasts in Nineteenth-century Fiji" in
Cannibalism and the Colonial World

THE BELIEVER never forgets his first miracle.
Mine remains utterly clear. It came to me high
on a forested ridge above the skull grottos, the
sacrificial slabs and the vast cradle of New Georgia Island's Marovo Lagoon. That's where I disobeyed the chief of Mbarejo and performed my
ritual in the dead calm of afternoon. I made trees shake and birds take
flight. I transformed muggy stillness into a maelstrom of tearing wind,
groaning tree trunks, hot raindrops and churning mud. Let that be my
story. I did make it rain, and for a good cause, too.

It was never my intention to explore the lagoons of the Solomon Islands' Western Province. The *Southern Cross* had ventured as far west as
New Georgia in 1866, but the Anglicans did not have the gumption to
leave any teachers there. "New Georgia has been known to the Mission

chiefly as an island inhabited by bloodthirsty head-hunters and cannibals," wrote my great-grandfather in explaining the mission's timid approach.

I was carried west by a moment of serendipitous frustration. A few days after returning from Malaita to Honiara, I was assured of the imminent departure of both the *Eastern Trader* and the MV *Temotu*, and had hauled my pack down to the port, ready for the five-day journey to Santa Cruz and my Nukapu.

"You go when?" I asked the mate of the *Eastern Trader.*

"Taem disfala Temotu *hemi i go,"* he said.

"You go when?" I asked the engineer of the MV *Temotu.*

"Maybe next week," he said.

"You liar," I fumed. "You have said the same thing for a month."

He just laughed.

A curtain of rain swept across the pier. It lifted the betel husks and the garbage, carrying them in slow-moving streams around my feet. I had had enough. I would not be shackled to Honiara any longer. I marched to the next pier.

"You go when?" I asked a sailor who was leaning on the rails of the first ship I saw.

"Mi go wea?" he replied.

"No," I said. "I don't care *where* you go. I'll go anywhere as long as it's today."

"Cranky waet man," he said. *"Mifala go neva. Sip, hem bagarup."*

I tried the *Compass Rose,* whose steel deck was fully loaded with oil barrels and rebar.

"You go when?" I asked a fat woman sitting with her children on the open deck.

"Good question," she said.

I tried the *Isabella.* It would leave for Santa Isabel the following morning.

Then the *Baruku.* It would leave for somewhere someday.

Then the *Tomoko,* a once sleek ferry that looked as though it had been pelted with rocks. The *Tomoko's* engines were rumbling. A sooty cloud was erupting from its smokestack. People were tossing babies, bags of rice and grass mats into arms that reached out from its long passenger decks.

Those arms were as black as beetle wings, the colour of New Georgia skin. If the *Tomoko* was going anywhere, it was heading west, to New Georgia. Santa Cruz was east, but I didn't care.

"You go when? You go when?" I hollered. The bowline went slack.

"*Mifala go nao!*" a voice yelled back, and a muscular hand dropped down from the upper deck. I reached for it and was pulled into a crowd of steaming bodies.

"First class! First class!" I shouted. The owner of the hand that had pulled me aboard led me through a passageway—the floor was a slippery paste of oil, spit, crushed insects and a disturbing slurry that seeped from the ship's head—and then, to my shock, through a door which read: VIP CABIN. It was a miracle. One bunk was piled high with old computers. The other was mine. I smashed six cockroaches, blew air into my mattress, lay down and let the ship carry me away.

Through the porthole, I watched the sea and the sky merge into night. Somewhere beyond the eastern tip of Guadalcanal, we hit the Coral Sea swell, which was not violent. Tarpaulins swayed. Doors knocked. Cockroaches crept into the folds of my clothing. The ship rolled me gently to sleep.

I was awoken not by the light and bustle of dawn but by stillness. The *Tomoko* had stopped moving completely. The cough and rattle of the engine had settled to a restful hum. I listened. Finally, there came a shout in the distance, followed by a hoot from the bridge. Then, splashing water. I felt my way out onto the deck. A searchlight shot from the bridge into the blackness. It was reflected back by a dozen pairs of eyes, which drifted close and became men in slim dugout canoes. They paddled alongside the ship and passed baskets of yam, taro, and bushels of betel nut up over the rails. Flats of tinned meat and sacks of Delite Flour were passed down. The trade was carried out in murmurs until the *Tomoko's* engine rumbled to life again. The ship pushed forward. For a while, the market men clung to our side, their canoes pulled along like lampreys on a great shark. Then we left them behind.

As the stars faded, islands took shape around us. To port: dark coves wrapped in jungle, ridges climbing towards clouds and the red edge of dawn. To starboard: a low band of shadows stretched into the distance like sections of a long, crumbling wall. We had entered Marovo, the first of the great lagoons that surround New Georgia Island and its smaller neighbours like a series of enormous moats, protected from the open ocean by a series of narrow barrier islands that extend along the north coasts of Ngatokae, Vangunu and New Georgia. These lagoons were once among the most feared waters of the South Pacific. The New Georgian "savage" had taken on a mythic aspect in the eighteenth-century European imagination after seafarers told shocking tales of the headhunters and their gruesome trade. The lagoon chiefs went beyond the sporting skirmishes practised by villagers back on Gaua, far beyond avenging grievances and defending territory. White traders only had to count the skulls to confirm their worst fears.

In 1843, the English trader Andrew Cheyne sailed the brigantine *Naiad* down from Hong Kong in search of bêche-de-mer and tortoise shells. His tour of New Georgia left him in a constant state of mortified outrage, according to his diaries. After visiting a village on one New Georgia outlier, Cheyne noted: "The first thing that met my view was the wall plates of a large canoe house strung with human heads, of both sexes, and apparently of all ages. Many of them appeared to have been recently killed, and the marks of the tomahawk were seen in all. I was horrified at the sight and felt quite sick until I got away again."

The New Georgians attacked with rocks and arrows whenever Cheyne sent his crew onto the reefs to collect bêche-de-mer, so the trader attempted to ally himself with local chiefs, a task which he found excruciating. "They rubbed noses and hugged me in anything but an agreeable manner, their persons being exceedingly filthy, smeared as they were with ochre and cocoanut [*sic*] oil," Cheyne wrote of two chiefs who boarded his ship. "It was evident by their gestures that they took us for supernatural beings, and considered our dress a part of the body. They threw themselves down on the deck, and kissed it repeatedly."

Cheyne eventually took on board a dozen-odd men from Eddystone Island as bêche-de-mer divers, but when the ship encountered canoes from other tribes, the Eddystone men leapt overboard and attacked their rivals before Cheyne could trade a thing. The Eddystone chief later explained to him that the attack was a reprisal for an earlier massacre carried out by his rivals, who didn't think twice about roasting and devouring women and children. Cheyne's Melanesian trading partners were always eager to detail the viciousness of their neighbours. "Monsters in human shape," he concluded.

The New Georgians' ferocious appetites were apparently felt as far away as the coast of Santa Isabel, about 90 miles to the east. In 1880, a trader reported that he had sighted more than a thousand canoes on the annual raid. The raiders slaughtered entire villages, leaving hundreds of headless corpses in their wake. After touring Santa Isabel's west coast aboard the *Southern Cross,* Henry Montgomery wrote: "The people have either been wiped out and eaten, or else they have migrated to safer quarters." The survivors, who lived in a constant state of dread, sought refuge in tree houses or in hilltop fortresses.

These days, post-colonial theorists can't agree if such early accounts of headhunting and cannibalism in the South Pacific were based on fact or the fantasy that inhabited the European imagination of the time. Revisionist historian William Arens proposed in *The Man-Eating Myth* that the cannibals who always seemed to inhabit the edges of the Western world were largely the product of intellectual conjuring. He argued that explorers, missionaries and anthropologists constructed their cannibals using second-hand stories and the glue of their own primordial fantasies. Twenty years later, a Princeton anthropologist named Gananath Obeyesekere tore apart the so-called eyewitness accounts of great cannibal feasts in Fiji, concluding those stories were merely seamen's yarns written to please a public hungry for a taste of tropical savagery. The cannibal fantasy was a projection of European psychoses rather than an accurate representation of history.

The revisionists did have a point. Take Andrew Cheyne's diaries, for instance: they served to magnify the headhunting myth back in imperial London, but Cheyne never actually saw any heads lopped off, never saw anyone roasting babies. The horrific stories his island allies told him about their neighbours could easily have been propaganda to keep the Englishman away from competitors who were eager to trade with him. Cheyne left New Georgia appalled and aghast but absolutely unscathed. He was clubbed to death, but that happened two decades and 2,000 miles away on Palau. Not bad for a man who made a career of stealing tortoise shells and bêche-de-mer from other people's reefs.

The revisionists aren't suggesting that headhunting and cannibalism never happened but rather that cannibal tales reveal more about their believers than they do about the people they describe. Europeans wanted to believe in man-eating headhunters as much as they wanted to believe in their own heroes. Both provided psychological fodder for empire-building.

The colonial historian Austin Coates characterized New Georgia as the centre of an "epidemic" of headhunting and cannibalism which had spread west from Papua New Guinea and had been depopulating islands since the early nineteenth century. He used his stories to justify British intervention in the Solomons, but a perusal of early reports reveals his theory as backward. Yes, the New Georgians told Europeans that human heads contained concentrated *mana* and that the raising of a canoe house, the launching of a war canoe, the honouring of ancestors, all required skull offerings. Yes, traders and missionaries saw hundreds of skulls decorating the walls of canoe houses, lining ancestral shrines and hanging from trees. But for all the supposedly unchecked carnage, some historians suggest that the New Georgians may have established a kind of steady state of feuding, trading and head-taking. Their raids were carefully planned annual affairs, steeped in ritual, magic and communal work. Expeditions took weeks of planning and travel, but involved barely a few hours of fighting, the grand finale of a yearly cycle of preparation, feasting, carving, gardening and trading.

If there was ever an outright explosion of headhunting in New Georgia, then it was triggered by the white man's arrival. First, the traders armed their allies with axes and guns. Although European governments had agreed to ban the sale of firearms to islanders in the 1890s, apparently only Germany, which controlled Santa Isabel, enforced the ban. The result was disastrous for the residents of Santa Isabel, whose tree forts were not much protection against lead shot. The well-armed tribes of New Georgia were rendered superhuman compared to their rivals. That was one factor.

The other was European tinkering with the supply and demand of skulls. If skulls represented concentrated *mana*, then to destroy them was to rob their owners of power. In 1891, HMS *Royalist* steamed into the New

Georgia lagoons, intent on punishing the headhunters for the murders of a few white traders—and ostensibly to pacify them in anticipation of the establishment of the British Protectorate. The navals burned all the villages in the western end of the Roviana Lagoon and destroyed 150 war canoes, but more importantly, they smashed hundreds upon hundreds of skulls. This caused a crisis of *mana*, triggering a sudden feeling of vulnerability, a lack of confidence in power and wealth that had taken decades—perhaps centuries—to accumulate. The Roviana chief, Ingava, sought redemption through warfare. He put together the greatest war machine the region had ever seen—hundreds of warriors, hundreds of breech-loading Snider rifles and at least two European whaleboats—then spent much of the next decade replenishing his stock of skulls.

Yet the lagoon population only really began its downfall *after* the Royal Navy had put a stop to all the raiding. The pioneering anthropologist W.H.R. Rivers noted a spectacular drop in birth rates among communities on Vella Lavella and Eddystone islands in the first two decades of the twentieth century. Upon further investigation, he discovered that people had stopped getting married and having children. Rivers concluded that this reproductive lethargy was, in fact, triggered by the ban on headhunting, which was essential to the fabric of religious and community existence. Without headhunting, islanders simply lost their zest for life. They grew bored and listless. Communities were dying from *tedium vitae*. The only hope, he felt, was for Melanesians to embrace Christianity with the same passion and vigour they had their old beliefs. Rivers, who did much of his travelling aboard the *Southern Cross*, would likely have suggested the Church of England as a cure but it was far too late for the Anglicans to set up shop in New Georgia; Methodists and Seventh-day Adventists had gained a foothold in 1902, and their charismatic worship turned out to be just the heartfelt substitute for cannibalism that Rivers had prescribed.

A century later, it was clear that New Georgia had got its groove back. There was no shortage of children in the village of Seghe, the *Tomoko*'s first landfall. We pulled up to a coral rock jetty and all hell broke loose. Passengers tumbled over the rails and scrambled away from the ship as though it were on fire. It might as well have been. The head had been overflowing like a fountain all night, transforming the ship's passageways into a frothy slough of gastrointestinal horrors. The cabin air was an unbearable stench of sewage, diesel smoke and rotting meat. We all hustled to shore and washed our hands in the sea. I bought a coconut in the market that had sprung up at the foot of the jetty and stared at the *Tomoko*, glumly considering three more days aboard—that's how long it would take for the ship to make its circuit through the lagoons. I sat under a tree, sipping the sweet milk from my coconut until the *Tomoko* pulled away. The market disappeared too, carried away on the backs of women with shining skin and frizzy hair bleached surreally blond by the sun. Seghe fell silent. I picked up my pack and wandered through the palms.

There was a tin-roofed church on a hill, and a line of plywood shacks strung between the sea and a vast lawn, which steamed in the morning sunlight. That lawn, it turned out, was all that remained of the airfield the Americans had built during the war. There was a red shack beside the field. I went inside and found the air agent yelling into a radio phone. The only point of interest in Seghe, he told me, lay in the lagoon at the end of the runway, where there was an American fighter plane from the war. It shone in the depths like a great silver fish.

"You could fly back to Honiara," he said. "The plane will be in this afternoon."

"Skulls. Maybe I could look for skulls," I said.

"There's a girl you could have. Over at the village rest house," he said.

"Or crocodiles. I could look for crocodiles," I said.

He shrugged and pointed through the chicken wire of his window to where a few men were lying under a tree. "That boy will help you. He has a *kanu*. Hey! John Palmer!"

John Palmer was the tallest Melanesian I had ever laid eyes on, topping out at about two metres if you included his hair: his head was shaved except for an island of braided dreadlocks on the crown. He had bound the strands together so their splayed ends resembled the fronds of a palm tree. He wore army fatigue shorts. He had the wide eyes of a child, but to be accurate he was not a boy. He was at least twenty-five.

(I had thought that the Victorians in Melanesia were being patronizing when they referred to men as "boys." But had the missionaries really regarded Melanesians as children? During my own travels, I discovered that when Melanesians said *boy* in pidgin, they meant "unmarried man." I quite liked calling men *"boys."* It made them seem friendlier.)

The air agent told John he should quit whatever mischief he was up to and take me away to look for skulls and crocodiles. I could come back to Seghe and catch the plane out in a week.

John suggested I come stay with him on his island. If I had strong legs, he could also show me the Nonotongere.

"Nonotongere?" I asked.

The air agent interrupted. "Crocodiles, fine. Skulls, fine," he barked, then poked me in the chest with his finger. "But don't you lead John Palmer astray. Don't you put his Christian soul at risk. Leave that stone alone." I left it for the moment.

I was suspicious of John Palmer. I wasn't sure why he was so willing to help me. "You want money?" I asked.

"You savve pem petrol long kanu blong mi," he said hopefully. Gas money.

"And . . ."

"And nothing."

John left to hunt for fuel, and I waited with the boys by the airstrip. In the afternoon a Twin Otter buzzed in, released a trio of Asian men in gumboots and polyester business suits, then took off again.

"Loggers," said one disapproving onlooker. His name was Benjamin. He told me there was a time when he thought he could make a living from eco-tourism—in fact plenty of people in the lagoon had the same idea after the World Wide Fund for Nature told them how special the place was. The United Nations was on the verge of declaring Marovo a World Heritage Site. People constructed bungalows with stoves and raised beds for tourists. Benjamin had opened his own lodge on a remote corner of Vangunu. But then the tension came, and the government withered, and the tourists disappeared, and the Malaysian Chinese showed up with their suitcases of money.

One by one, the lagoon's chiefs had been selling their forests in return for cash and tin roofing and outboard motors, and the red scars had crept up the hillsides, and the guts of the forest seeped into the lagoon like blood, and the coral choked and turned white in the silty half-light, and fishnets began to come up empty.

Sometimes people didn't want their chiefs to sell off the forests. They burnt logging trucks and stole chainsaws. Back in the nineties, islanders had tried to work with groups like Greenpeace to start their own village-based "eco-forestry" ventures, but the foreign loggers had guns, guards and friends in high places. At least one eco-activist got his neck broken.

According to the Central Bank of the Solomon Islands, raw log exports were running at nearly three times the sustainable level by the mid-1990s, about the same time that various government ministers' bank accounts were mysteriously being topped up. The then–prime minister, Bartholomew Ulufa'alu, tried to clamp down on corruption and unsustainable forestry, but his work ended abruptly when the Malaita Eagle Force arrived on his doorstep with machine guns. Now, things were back to normal in Honiara. "The loggers' work is much easier now that the government is broke," said Benjamin. "They bribe the government agents and the chiefs, then cut as fast as they can."

New Georgia's wealth, its *mana*, was being sucked away and delivered raw to mills in Malaysia and Japan. Meanwhile, Benjamin's eco-lodge was empty, so he had started a canteen beside the airstrip, where he sold crackers and warm beer to the loggers.

A woman from the village came to warn me about John Palmer. She said he was the sort of boy I should avoid. He was a *rubbish boy*. He ran with the rebels from across the water in Bougainville. And worse. "What kind of worse?" I asked. "Just worse," she said, staring at the dirt, then stomped off without another word.

John returned after dark with the last two jugs of gas in Seghe. We jumped in his *kanu* (another flimsy fibreglass runabout) and headed west to Nono Lagoon. The stars were out, but their light was nothing compared to the halo of phosphorescent sparks that flowed around the bow. Our wake glowed behind us like the tail of a comet. There were other lights, too: yellow nebulae, waving and pulsing under the surface of the lagoon.

"Divers," said John. "Collecting bêche-de-mer."

Sometimes John would ease the throttle and shine his light into the clear water, and then it was as though the belly of the lagoon had been split open and its entrails had floated up in great bubbles, stopping just short of the surface. Coral. Thousands and thousands of kilograms of pale green and purple coral. Within its folds I could see the bêche-de-mer, the mottled sea slugs that had excited Chinese palates and lured traders to these waters for two centuries. Some were as big as footballs.

Islands drifted past like shadows on shadows. Then a violent constellation of industrial orange emerged from behind a curtain of palms. It was a ship, anchored in the middle of the lagoon. It must have been fifty times bigger than the *Tomoko*. Floodlights shone down from two steel cranes. The lights illuminated a stack of raw logs on the deck below. The cranes jerked and twisted frantically, like great metallic birds arranging a nest of sticks.

The curtain of islands closed again. We rounded a point and steered towards a single spark of light. The light grew into the warm glow of an oil lamp, which sat on the porch rail of a cottage on the shore. We tied up to a heap of sharp rocks and were greeted by six shirtless young men. They all wore dreadlocks, and they all smoked long cigarettes rolled from magazine paper. John introduced them as his *brothas*, which didn't tell me much because that might mean "brother" or "cousin" or "uncle," or some more distant relative. These *brothas* were Sam, Laury, Oswold, Allen-Chide, Namokene and Ray. The island was called Mbatumbosi, but John preferred to call it Bad Boss, because that name made it seem tougher. The island did feel a bit like a gang hideout at first. The brothers smoked and wrestled and lay about in hammocks. There were no women, no sisters, no scolding parents.

"We are alone," said Allen, as he brought our dinner—a pot of plain rice—to a boil on a gas stove on the porch.

"We are free," said Ray.

"We are raiders," said John.

"Raiders," I said encouragingly, "like your ancestors?"

"No, man. Raiders *blong luv. Olsem* Casanova!"

John explained how raiding worked. The brothers would take their *kanu* over to the hamlets that dotted the edges of their lagoon, and they would whisper beneath the young women's windows: "Come out, come out and play." And the girls did crawl out their windows and disappear with the brothers into the shadows. The Methodist village of Nazareth made for poor hunting, but the girls on Mbarejo, which was Seventh-day Adventist, were always eager.

"So you are creepers," I said, recalling the rascals who had harassed Sabine back on Vanua Lava.

"Yes!" said Allen.

"No!" said John. "The girlies, they come to us. They tell their daddies that they are going fishing on the reef. Then they paddle straight to Bad Boss."

Ray said that it was the marble trick that attracted the girls more than anything. The boys had learned the trick from Japanese fishermen. John had one marble. Ray had two. What you did, explained John, was smash a glass mug and file down a small piece of the handle until it was perfectly round and smooth. Next you took an old toothbrush and filed the end of it to a sharp point. Then you got your brother to pull out a pinch of skin on the shaft of your penis, so you could poke a hole through the skin with the sharp end of the toothbrush. You used the toothbrush to push the marble into the hole. In with the marble, out with the toothbrush, a splash of Dettol and *voilà*, you had transformed your penis into a sexual novelty. John unzipped his fly and, squirming with pride, exposed just enough of his penis to prove they weren't lying. There was indeed a roundish lump just under the skin.

"*Lookim,*" Ray said as John pushed the lump with his finger, "*hem roll all-abaot!*"

Then we all bowed our heads and Ray said grace beneath John's framed portrait of Princess Diana.

The brothers may have been raiders. They may have been vagabonds. They may have been naughty. But they were not alone on Bad Boss by choice. John's parents lived in Honiara and so had he, before the tension.

The problem, he said, was the colour of his skin. John was tall and lanky, like his great-grandfather, one of the lagoon's first white traders. But John's skin wasn't white or black or even a Guadalcanal shade of peat brown. The Guadalcanal militants wouldn't believe John had Guale blood in him, so they chased him and beat him. Then, when the Malaita Eagles took their revenge in Honiara, John got a second round of beatings.

That's why he was hiding out on Bad Boss. Not because his father had caught him hanging out with Bougainvillean exiles. Not because he was in hot water for hiring a car and helping his friends in the Bougainville Revolutionary Army round up a trunkful of machine guns. No, said, John, he was a refugee, and it had been three years since he had sat in a car or tasted chocolate.

WE PASSED DAYS LANGUIDLY on the lagoon. We paddled through the estuary of the Choe River looking for crocodiles, but there were none to see. We took John's boat out through a gap in the barrier islands to spear fish for our lunch, but all we caught were rainbow-striped minnows.

We climbed among the limestone cliffs on the barrier islands. The rock was an amalgam of petrified coral and giant clamshell, and impossible to walk on with bare feet. We found the first skull under a cracked slab. It was surrounded by fractured bones, doughnut-sized rings of carved rock and bits of shattered clamshell jewellery. I picked up the skull. It was warm. A spider skittered along its jaw. Startled, I let the skull slip from my hands. It struck the ground and lost a tooth.

"No problem," John said. "This is not one of my grandfathers. This is someone my grandfathers killed, probably some weak *fala* from Roviana."

Back on Bad Boss, John led me to three skulls tucked into a shady ravine behind his house. He picked up one and lovingly rubbed the mildew from its forehead. Its eye sockets were cracked and imploring. This, said John, was one of his great-grandmother's people. Those folks were tough, but apparently not tough enough. They had migrated west to Bad Boss to escape the marauding tribes of Roviana Lagoon. Then they were chased away again.

"So you come from a long line of refugees," I teased John over dinner.

He assured me that his ancestors had killed many people. They had raided from Roviana all the way to Isabel. And besides, the Tagitaki were no ordinary enemies. They were giants who wielded clubs so heavy it took six ordinary men to lift them. That's why the ancestors were scared of them. The Tagitaki had once lived on the mountain ridge across the lagoon from Mbarejo. That ridge was *tabu* now, said John.

"Because of the ghosts of the Tagitaki?"

"Ha! Of course not."

"Then why?"

"Because of the Nonotongere."

Once upon a time, long before men hunted for heads, said John, a giant serpent had prowled the lagoons. The snake was thicker than a sow and as long as the airstrip at Seghe. One day, the snake fought with a giant lizard. It didn't go well for the snake. The lizard ripped it to pieces. Parts of the snake's body now littered the foothills of New Georgia, but its head, which lay on the crest of the ridge where the giant headhunters once lived, had managed to retain its *mana*. If you disturbed that snake head, shouted at it or even so much as blew on it, the *devil* inside it would answer you with a meteorological hissy fit. It would bring wind, rain and thunder.

"Didn't the air agent in Seghe tell us to stay away from the Nonotongere?" I said.

"Maybe," John said and smiled mischievously. "Would you like to go say hello to it?"

John was not one for following rules. He told me he was not afraid of the *devil* stone. Sometimes he hiked up the ridge and blew on it, just for the sheer joy of watching rain sweep across the lagoon below, knowing that the drizzle and cool breeze would enliven the young women. He imagined all those damp T-shirts clinging to all those young breasts.

"Mmmm, yes, Nonotongere, hem gud tumas," said John, closing his eyes, drawing deeply on his cigarette.

Right. Another magic stone. Melanesians were like my great-grandfather: they waxed mystically about supernatural power. They were big on stories. But good luck if you wanted proof. I did not bother to pester John for a demonstration of the Nonotongere's power. I just crawled into bed and went to sleep.

JOHN LIFTED MY MOSQUITO net and shook me awake before dawn. He whispered in my ear: *"Day blong Nonotongere!"*

I decided that John either had guts or he didn't mind being humiliated.

Under the soft belly of an overcast sky, John, Allen and I motored over to Mbarejo to pick up Jimmy, a jittery, distracted fellow with one functioning ear. We needed Jimmy because he was on good terms with the chief of Mbarejo, who owned the mountain where the Nonotongere waited. We stopped at a waterside canteen and bought supplies for the expedition: three sticks of tobacco and a pad of notepaper for rolling. Then we headed for New Georgia.

There was a logging camp in the bay across from Mbarejo. The camp sat in the middle of a dismaying smear of red-brown mud. It looked as though the hillside had caught some horrible skin disease and its flesh had rotted right down to the muscle. Trucks roared out of the forest one by one, but the mud near the lagoon was so viscous they had to dump their logs on the top of the hill. Bulldozers dragged the logs through a deepening trench of slick clay down to a bark-strewn pier. A gang of kids slipped in and out of the trench, cheering each passing log.

The chief of Mbarejo had given the Malaysians permission to log the mountain. John wasn't sure how much the loggers paid the chief, but the old man had been handing out canoe engines, chainsaws and other bits of cargo to his *wantoks* for the past year. John had managed to score some tin roofing. He said he felt slightly guilty; he knew the loggers were spoiling the lagoon, but it was nice to have that tin roof on his house. And anyway, what choice was there? Everyone knew the Malaysians would get the logs whether the lagoon people wanted to sell them or not.

We tied up to a rock near the pier and found the chief up to his fat ankles in mud. John negotiated. Jimmy gazed at the sky, which was thick and disapproving, and cooed at it.

"Fine, fine. I give you permission to see our *kastom* sites," the chief bellowed over the roar of the bulldozer. But don't you disturb that *devil* stone. Don't you dare!"

"I promise I will respect your *kastom*," I said to the chief.

"*Kastom?* I am *wanfala* Christian, not *wanfala* heathen," he replied. "That stone means nothing to me. But look at this mud! We don't want any more rain around here. No more rain, do you understand? Don't you so much as touch that stone!"

The chief trudged over to Jimmy and yelled in his good ear. Jimmy yelped like a kicked dog. The chief pointed at the mountain and yelled some more. Jimmy leapt in the air and charged up the log trench. We followed. At the edge of the camp, we were intercepted by a distressed-looking Chinese man in gumboots. "You not from Greenpeace? You not hippie?" he said to me. I shook my head.

"You not taking photos of logging?"

"No, no, of course not."

"Our security man, he will go with you."

We all climbed into a rusted pickup, John, his brother Allen, Jimmy, the security man and I. Everyone insisted I sit in the front seat, so I did. The truck driver's name was Foo. He told me he had a wife back in Kuala Lumpur. Every year, he got a month's vacation and took his wife to a casino hotel in Tenerife. He despised New Georgia. I told Foo the only Cantonese phrase I knew, something like *"Lohk gau si."—It's raining dogshit.* That made him laugh.

We slid through the muck, past a platoon of miserable-looking young men with chainsaws on their shoulders. Instead of shell money, the men had engine gaskets and chains and sprockets strung around their necks and wrists.

It wasn't the missing trees that struck me the most. It was the ground. The red earth had been unbound, freed from its protective weave of roots and bush. It was crumbling, collapsing, sliding all around us; now seeping away like hot lava, now spilling over the roads; filling the gullies like wet cement, overflowing from creek beds, leaving the mountain thin and wasted like the victim of a sorcerer's life-sucking curse. This was a landscape being drained of its life.

We had driven for fifteen minutes when Jimmy banged on the roof of the cab, and Foo stepped on the brake. Through a hole in the floor near the brake pedal, I saw the tire lock and skid. I remembered another common bit of Cantonese: *"Sihk yah ng-jouh yah, jouh yah dah-laahn yah."—You consume everything but make nothing, and whatever you touch, you spoil.*

Foo laughed again, sadly this time. "A mess," he said. "Sure. A real mess." Then he drove away with the security man.

The rest of us followed Jimmy up through the slash, which was as dry as kindling and crusted with baked-on mud. The forest, when we reached it, was cool and damp. We bushwhacked towards the ridge crest. The guys swung at the undergrowth with their machetes. I remember the rocket-ship trees and their splayed roots. I remember the soft leaves that left welts where they brushed my ankles. But I can't remember much else about that forest, because I was trying to keep up with Jimmy, who was charging through the bush, oblivious to our screams for him to slow down. His hoots and squawks echoed through the canopy. Finally, he paused alongside a tremendous, spiralling tree trunk, spray-painted with the letter *T* in orange. The mark stood for *tabu*. The loggers could cut down the forest until they reached that mark. Directly below the *T* was a heap of ruins: a tumbled-down wall, a stone terrace and the remains of an earthen oven. Most of these rocks were the remains of the city of the Tagitaki, shouted Jimmy above the silence.

A faint path wound along the ridge crest. We followed it until we reached a roughly polished sandstone slab and a heptagonal pillar, about the height of a lectern. This ruin was John's favourite. He said the slab was for special occasions, those times when the Tagitaki managed to bring home one of their enemies' children. When the Tagitaki caught a baby, they would keep him for a while, fatten him up on taro and gnali nuts. After a few months, the giants would get together and play catch with the toddler. That helped soften the meat. Then they would lay the child on that sandstone slab, slice him open and eat him raw. Nobody seemed to know what the pillar was for.

The people of New Georgia loved their baby-eating stories even more than colonial historians did. Everyone had one. Weeks later, a sweet old lady on Marovo Island showed me an ancestral firepit behind her house and recounted how it had been used to cook children.

These stories made me wonder if the cannibal-myth doubters had ever bothered to consult Melanesians about their historical revisionism. It was hard to dismiss the cannibal stories when the locals themselves were such adamant believers in the savagery of their ancestors.

But why did New Georgians treasure their baby-eating stories? The simplest answer would be that the stories lent their tellers a kind of primordial cachet. They were a reminder, for example, that John's forebears had been kick-ass warriors and that the only tribe tough enough to chase them were, in fact, baby-gobbling giants. But I think the horror stories served another function. Just as white men had used cannibal stories as a kind of moral armour to justify their interventions, the Christianized New Georgians had employed them to reassure themselves that the new way was the best way, that they were following a better path than their ancestors. The old stories were entertaining, but they also served to remind the lagoon people of the darkness that lurked within their own souls, the darkness that required vigilance. If the cannibal story is mythical—which is to suggest that its main function is to hint at truths of the human soul—then its historicity (like the historical accuracy of the Bible) is of secondary importance. The key to mythical truth is not bones and ruins, but belief itself.

This is the tug-of-war between historical and mythical truth, and it occurs among tellers of tales of horror and magic alike. The stories my great-grandfather brought with him to Melanesia—the miracles and resurrection of Jesus, the almightiness of God, the fires of hell, the glories of everlasting life—these were the shimmering images that had convinced islanders to turn their backs on their ancestors, just as they had convinced my own forebears to relinquish their Nordic gods.

Faith, rather than veracity, gives stories their power. And thus charged, stories confer power on their believers, whether that power is simply the strength of certainty, spiritual clarity or something more. In this, there is not much difference between a story of ancestral horror or a story of magic.

In Honiara, people assured me I would be in no danger from black magic, even if a sorcerer waved a handful of *mana*-charged cobwebs in my face, because my disbelief was stronger than *kastom* magic. But when you fall towards mythical thinking, when you rub up against the rough edges of it long enough, it can enter you like a virus, and the world changes. There is more danger, but there is more possibility. Events present themselves symbolically. They wrap themselves in magic rather than coincidence, and their circumstances assume direction and purpose.

Faith is a decision, of course. But it can be precipitated by certain conditions. A story, say, about the connection between a mythical snake, a lump of rock and a storm, is presented. Context, something like a battle between natural goodness and industrial exploitation, provides a foundation. The landscape might reflect these things: it might be ravaged or it might seethe with its own fragile power. The air might take on a certain quality, perhaps a kind of pregnant heaviness. There might be an eerie silence. These things might prepare you. They might lead you to the readiness I began to feel as I followed one-eared Jimmy up the ridge, through the jungle, past the ruined fortresses of the giants, towards the leaden sky.

I paused, finally, to wring the sweat from my T-shirt, only to realize that Jimmy's grunts and whoops had ceased, and the forest had gone suddenly silent. The silence wasn't complete. It was punctured by the whine of chainsaws in the distance and occasional squawks from longbills up in the canopy. Nothing moved. The grey sky glowed. The forest waited expectantly. The stillness was crushing.

I found Jimmy, John and Allen in a glade at the top of the ridge. They were crouching near a mound of cut stones. "Nonotongere," said John, nodding towards a hunk of weather-blackened limestone in the undergrowth.

For all its notoriety, the snake stone should have been as big as a house. It was not. It was about the size of a medicine ball. From a certain angle, with the shadow beneath its angled jaw, with its angry temples and blunt snout, the stone did look like the head of a snake. A hole the thickness of a broomstick had been carved through its cheeks. The hole ends could have been eyes. I reached out and ran my fingers along its jaw. The rock was warm.

"Careful! Careful!" sputtered Jimmy.

"Sorry," I said, and stood up.

John looked at me and winked. *"Bae-bae yumi checkem olgeta skull,"* John said to Jimmy's good ear, and we tromped to the far side of the clearing where the rocks had been piled into a squarish vault. On top of the vault were several thick slabs, sprinkled with bits of broken shell. Jimmy hacked away at the shrubbery around the vault. John caught my eye again and winked. I got it.

"I'll make lunch," I said.

I stepped back to the snake head, keeping an eye on Jimmy and his machete. It's not like I would be risking an earthquake. Nobody would be hurt.

I crouched down, pursed my lips, blew a quick puff of air across the snake's snout, then jumped to my feet.

A shriek rose from the far side of the clearing.

"What's wrong?" I shouted.

"We just knocked some bones. Jimmy, he's worried," said John. No-body but me seemed to notice the trembling in the canopy, the gentle rustling of leaves, the faint breeze that whisked through the glade and disappeared into the stillness of the afternoon.

We ate in the cradle of a rocket tree. Allen cut up some papaya. I opened a can of spaghetti and a packet of shortbread biscuits I had brought from Honiara. Jimmy collected some gnali nuts and hammered them open with a rock. John cut some leaves and spread our food on them. We used the biscuits to scoop up the spaghetti.

"If the chief is a Christian, why is he so protective of the Nonoton-gere?" I asked John.

"Because chief works for the Chinese," he said. "Suppose we make rain: then the whole operation must shut down, and chief won't get paid."

"*No! Hem i becos chief hem i no likem for yumi sick from olgeta devil,*" said Jimmy, who was fidgeting nervously again, cocking his good ear towards the vault as though someone were calling to him. "*Nogud yumi tochim ol-geta bones. Yumi mas go out from disfala place!*"

Jimmy couldn't see the Nonotongere from where he sat. It lay behind our picnic tree. I excused myself to pee. But I didn't do that. I snuck be-hind the tree and knelt down by the snake head. I cupped that warm stone in my hands—gently, tenderly—then I took a deep breath and blew a lungful of spaghetti-scented air into the snake's eye hole. I took another breath and blew even harder. I blew again and again. I blew until I was dizzy, and then, as soon as I could stand, I stumbled back to our picnic. John watched me sit down and gave me a conspiratorial grin. Jimmy was trimming his fingernails with his machete. I reached for a piece of short-bread, then hesitated. My eyes met John's. We were ready.

The change came without warning, like a great wave breaking over the glade. It roared through the trees and flattened the brush. Leaves swirled and raced like swallows, then fell like green snowflakes. Tree trunks groaned. Longbills peeled from the highest branches like shingles torn from a roof and flew away, down into the valley. I could see the sky through a break in the ravaged canopy. The overcast was no longer flat. It was not distant. It did not glow. It was purple and heavy. It was collapsing, first in great sagging boils, then in translucent curtains, now in dirty grey stalactites, liquid spears of plunging pressure, all falling with the weight of exhilaration and relief.

Jimmy got to his feet, began to shout and moan, then dashed towards the stone vault.

"What is he doing?" I said.

"He is telling the ancestors he is sorry *tumas*," said John. "Jimmy thinks he brought the rain. But it wasn't Jimmy. It was you, wasn't it?" John grinned from ear to ear. It was the smile of a teenaged shoplifter, a lagoon Casanova, a first-time car thief.

"*Yumi go nao!*" wailed Jimmy as the first drops of rain exploded on his forehead.

"Yes, we go!" John shouted. "No good the *devils* find us and follow us home!"

"We go!" shouted Allen.

"We go!" shouted I.

The rain came thick and hard. It exploded on the forest canopy like thousands of firecrackers, then poured through in tiny rivulets. Everything vibrated with the impact. Water cascaded from broad leaves and tree trunks and rock walls. It collided with itself, gathered in glorious torrents and gushed down the trail.

Drenched, we charged down the ridge, splashing through the runoff, leaping deadfalls and sacrificial stones and lines of panicked black ants. We burst out of the forest into the logging slash. The road was not a road any more. It was a river. It bubbled like hot chocolate. Trucks stood abandoned. A line of young men trudged towards a hut in the distance. They carried long-blade chainsaws on their shoulders and left a trail of rainbow-swirled gas stains in the puddles behind them.

The rain streamed down my face, and I could not wipe the smile from it. I knew I was beaming like a fool, because John looked at me and burst out laughing himself. But he didn't know the truth behind my smile. It wasn't because we had disobeyed the chief like a couple of rascals. It wasn't because we had tricked Jimmy. It wasn't because I had conjured a tempest from the eye of the Nonotongere. (A storm! I had made it rain! Don't tell me I didn't.) It wasn't because, for the first time in weeks, the deadening heat and the fog of lethargy had loosened thier grip on me, and I could run and breathe and feel my skin again. It was because, in that moment, I let myself imagine that empire had not stolen all the *mana* from New Georgia, that for a few hours or days, or perhaps just for those few seconds, magic could halt the crushing engines of industry. The trucks were stuck. The fallers and the drivers were under cover, smoking and making plans to paddle back to their families. Foo was dreaming of Tenerife. The chief of Mbarejo was pacing back and forth in the mud, cursing. And there was mud between my toes.

If you summon a storm and your call is reinforced by an idea about the power of a stone or a god or a spirit, and then the storm does fall on you, surely you should honour the moment with faith and not bury it in scepticism. Surely you should wrap it in mythical truth, rather than explain it away. The Nonotongere drew the tempest down from the sky. I would let that be my story. It was a good one to believe, much better than the one with John complaining that it rained every afternoon on New Georgia.

The readiness came more thoroughly after I accepted these things. It began to course through my veins like a drug. It held me. For a time, it nourished me. But it always demanded more.

18

UNDER THE

LANGA LANGA LAGOON

*The supernatural power abiding in the powerful
living man abides in his ghost after death,
with increased vigour and more ease of movement.*

R.H. CODRINGTON, *The Melanesians*

THE AIR AGENT in Seghe knew that John and I
had played with the forbidden Nonotongere.
He was terse with me, but he did sell me a
ticket, and I flew back to Honiara with a planeload of loggers and their
bodyguards. We raced through the clouds, which seemed different now.
Everything seemed different after my storm: mist, rocks and trees seemed
infused with personality, willpower, potential energy. The world vibrated
with *mana*, and I could feel it—I could almost see it flowing through the
air. I was terrified of losing my new vision. I wanted to feed it. I wanted
another miracle.

The islanders who were recruited by the *Southern Cross* assured the
missionaries that ghosts and spirits lurked everywhere, but that the most
powerful and mysterious place in the world was the sea. The creatures
that lived in salt water always held the most *mana*. Alligators, sea snakes,
bonitos and frigate birds: any of these animals might be inhabited by a

tindalo, the soul of a dead man. The most sacred sea creature and the most frequent abode of ancestors was the shark. The people once loved and respected their ghost-sharks. A chief on Savo regularly swam out from his beach to make sacrifices to a shark *tindalo,* and that shark would come to him and accept his offers of food. At Ulawa, south of Malaita, villagers made offerings of porpoise teeth to their local man-eater. If that sacred shark tried and failed to eat a man, the people would be so afraid of the shark's anger that they'd throw the man back into the sea to be drowned. Sometimes, before a man died, he announced that he would return as a shark; his *wantoks* knew the deceased had returned when they spotted a shark remarkable for its size or colour. That's what they told Codrington.

Islanders still credit sharks with all kinds of magic and favours. A friend told me that he was once stranded far out at sea with another fellow who happened to be from Langa Langa Lagoon, the nexus of shark worship, when their outboard engine conked out. This might have been the end of them, but the Langa Langa man took control. He jumped into the water and waved around a bit. Then he instructed my friend to go to sleep under the deck cover. "I didn't sleep," he told me. "I lay there and listened. Soon I felt waves breaking off the bow. We were moving quickly through the ocean—it was as though we were being pushed by an engine. After an hour, I got up and looked around. We were back in the harbour! Then that Langa Langa man, he swam to shore. He collected some coconuts, brought them back to the boat, chopped them up and threw them in the sea. That's when I knew it was his shark granddaddy who had pushed us home."

Everyone had a story about the shark men of Langa Langa. In the old days, a shark-caller could summon a favourite shark to sink his enemy's canoe. The shark would then drag the victim back to shore so he could be chopped up. Priests on Laulasi regularly called sharks to their island. In exchange for bits of pork, the shark ancestors would allow young boys to ride across the lagoon on their backs.

I wanted shark magic. I told my friend Morris Namoga at the national tourism office that he should promote sacred shark tourism; maybe he could supply the shark priests with pig guts so they could toss them in the water and convince their ancestors to entertain paying customers, like me. Morris insisted that Christianity had put an end to shark worship back in the 1970s. The descendants of the shark people now went to church instead of praying to the ocean. They sipped the blood of Christ instead of slaughtering pigs and dumping the entrails in the sea, so naturally the sea spirits had abandoned them.

"But don't be sad," said Morris. "The MV *Temotu* is back in port! You will be leaving for Santa Cruz next week." Morris seemed to be right about the *Temotu*. The ship's purser even agreed to sell me a ticket to Nendo. Five days to go, he promised.

But I was sure that Morris was wrong about the shark-callers. I had found my connection. Her name was Veronica Kwalafa, and she ran a faith-healing clinic near the Quality Motel. (God had given Veronica the power in a dream back in 1987. He had shown himself as a bright star— just like the one the prophet Fred had seen before his return to Tanna Island. For $4, Veronica would hold your hand or massage your back, and because she had something like a television in her head, she could see your troubles and help fix them.)

I had met Veronica weeks before. She had assured me there was one shark-caller left in the Langa Langa Lagoon. He was her brother, of course, and he was the boss of the underwater world. He could talk to the sharks. He would caress them lovingly from the edge of his island. They used their magic to help him walk for hours on the ocean floor. Veronica had said she'd take me to the shark-caller if I promised to tell the world that her services were available via mail and that people with any kind of sickness could contact her through Mary Manisi, PO Box 93, Honiara. Veronica cured a woman with a terrible stomach ulcer an hour before my arrival. She's got magic hands. Write her! There. That's done.

Anyway, whenever I returned to the faith-healing clinic to seal our deal, Veronica's door was locked, and so it was on my return from New Georgia. I jumped up and down, slammed my palm against the hot paint, but that did no good either. Honiara never rewarded impatience. So I did what everyone with disposable income and time to kill did in the capital: I went to get smashed at the pool bar of the Mendana Hotel.

That's where I met the saltwater men. They were stone drunk and not doing a good job of keeping their heads off the table. I knew they were from the lagoons of Malaita because, when they did lift their heads, I could see geometric engravings on their cheeks.

They called to me: could I please ask the bar manager to turn up the music? He would listen to a white man. The music was already loud. It was playing the New Guinean hit *"Mi dae long yu."—I'm dying for you.* The Malaitans sang along:

> O daling, mi misim yu,
> O daling, mi luvim yu,
> O daling, mi dae long yu.

I pulled up a chair and told the saltwater men about the shark-caller of Langa Langa Lagoon. They said they belonged to Lau, a lagoon on the northeastern tip of Malaita.

"The Church wiped all the sacred sharks from Langa Langa, and from our lagoon too," said the most sober of the three. His facial scars reminded me of the Nazca lines. There were two concentric circles with streaks shooting out from them like sunbeams. "It's *tabu* for people to try to talk to sharks. Dangerous for the soul. We are Christians now."

"Ah, so then you wouldn't mind a little shark's fin soup."

"Don't say that! The sharks are our ancestors."

The first man looked at me sternly. *"Yu blong wea?"* he asked.

"Canada."

That brought a chorus of disapproving grumbles.

"We once had strong *kastom* at our home in the Lau Lagoon," the first man said. "An octopus. He took care of our ancestors. If they were lost at sea, he would bring them home. If they were drowning, he would save them."

"What was its name?" I asked.

"We cannot tell you that. It's a secret. Anyway, the octopus is gone now. Gone! And it was a *wantok* of yours, one man-Canada, who stole him from us."

All three men were fully awake now. "Maranda," they said together.

"Maranda, this thief, now he is showing our octopus to tourists in Canada," said the second man.

"He is making lots of *sellen* from our ancestor," said the third, rubbing his thumb and forefinger together in front of my nose.

"What do you mean? He took the octopus on a plane?" I said.

This was apparently a wildly stupid question. The men laughed. I bought more beer. And the story came.

The sacred octopus was inhabited by an ancestor of the villagers at Foueda, an artificial island constructed from hunks of coral out on the Lau reef. The octopus had indeed been helpful to people, but he demanded sacrifices in return for his patronage. Sometimes the octopus would crawl right up out of the sea into a man's canoe to let him know it was time for a sacrifice. It would crawl onto land, too. If you left a basket of food outside your door, the octopus would plunk himself down on top of it and engulf that *kai-kai*. He would change the colour of his skin from red to black to show he was pleased. He preferred pig guts to fruit.

To communicate with the octopus or sacrifice to him, you had to know his secrets. And the only men who knew these things were the *kastom* priests of Foueda, who had been handing down the sacred knowledge for centuries.

The octopus's troubles started when the missionaries arrived. They called the octopus a devil. Young people became scared to learn the sacred *kastom* knowledge. The priests were left with no one to whom they could pass on their sacrificial rituals. The last of the octopus priests were growing old when the white man named Maranda climbed ashore on Foueda. The priests refused to let him into their *tabu* hut, but Maranda was resourceful, said the first man. He tied a tape recorder to a stick and poked it through the door of the *tabu* hut while the priests performed their sacrifices. That's how he stole all their secret incantations. That's why, when Maranda got on his boat and went back to Canada, the octopus followed him. Now the people of Foueda had no octopus to protect them from the perils of the sea.

"But what about the *kastom* priests? Why couldn't they stop the octopus from leaving?" I asked.

"Dead," said the deep-scarred man. "All gone now."

"And there are no new priests to take their place?"

"There can be no priest without the secret knowledge."

"So there are no priests."

"Don't you see?" he cried. "*Maranda* is the only octopus priest!"

"But Maranda, he was not so smart," slurred number two. "He spoiled his sacrifices. He made the octopus very angry, so it made him sick. And it killed his wife."

I eventually tracked down the alleged octopus thief, who turned out to be the acclaimed cultural anthropologist Pierre Maranda, now an associate professor of anthropology at Université Laval in Quebec City. Maranda and his wife had lived among and studied the people of the Lau Lagoon from 1966 to 1968, and they did record the sacred knowledge of Foueda.

I e-mailed Maranda an account of my conversation with the saltwater men. In his response, Maranda admitted falling deathly ill after his first fieldwork in the lagoon. After he got sick, he said, the islanders made a sacrifice on his behalf, and he did recover, "which made them very happy." But Maranda insisted his illness was not a curse but a bout of falciparum, a nasty strain of malaria. As for his wife, she didn't die until more than a decade after the octopus's disappearance. Maranda told me he had assured the Lau people that he did not have their octopus in his swimming pool, but to no avail.

It's fitting that Maranda should be immortalized as part of the octopus myth, but he doesn't deserve to be characterized as a trickster-villain. In fact, he has done the Lau people a lasting favour. When Maranda returned to Foueda in 1975, Laakwai, one of the island's two high priests, lamented that the old *kastom* was "finished." The priest's sons were refusing to take on his duties after his death. They had caught the Christian bug. The other high priest, Kunua, had the same problem. Ten years later, both priests had given up hope. Laakwai dove under a woman's canoe, knowing he was committing a fatal reversal of high-low energy. Kunua purposefully botched a ritual. Both men died within weeks. It was suicide by metaphysical transgression. Thus, Maranda had become the sole keeper of Foueda's sacred knowledge and the default *kastom* priest, a legacy he holds to this day in his office on the far side of the world. I suspect Maranda's relationship with the myth is deeper than professional. When I asked him the name of the sacred octopus, he refused to tell me. The name, he said, was a secret he could only divulge to a Lau successor.

My encounter with the saltwater men at the Mendana Hotel filled me with an even greater sense of urgency. With beer on my breath and sea spirits on my mind, I stumbled back across town to look once more for the faith healer, Veronica Kwalafa.

The door to the healing clinic was open. I walked in to find no lights on and the ceiling fan cruelly immobile. The power was out. I could hear Veronica humming quietly behind a curtain at the back of the office, where she had shown me the tools of her trade (a crystal ball, a Bible and a Hello Kitty ruler).

Veronica's husband, Philip, was fast asleep on a wooden desk in the reception area. I cleared my throat. He didn't stir.

"You promised to take me to the shark boss and then you disappeared," I said.

Philip lifted his head. It took a moment for the arc of saliva between the desktop and his slack lower lip to break. Veronica appeared. I liked Veronica. She was soft. Her white hair had the texture of candy floss. I did not like Philip. He was a lazy slug of a man. Veronica did the healing. Philip guarded Veronica's box of money. She was big enough to crush him, but she called him Daddy.

"We are very busy. We cannot guide you to Langa Langa," said Philip.

Sweat rolled down my back. I imagined taking my chair and breaking it over Philip's head. It was the heat that made me feel such things. I ignored him.

"I want to help you," I said to Veronica. "I want to show the world that your brother still has the power."

"He does! He does have the power," she said.

I had a plan. With five days to go before the *Temotu's* departure for Santa Cruz, I didn't have much time, but Solomon Airlines advertised daily Twin Otter flights to Auki. Malaitans could afford to fly; they had all that compensation money to spend. I could fly, too. I had my credit card. It would be a treat for Veronica.

"Wouldn't you like to go see your brother?" I said to her.

"Oh, yes," she said.

"We'll fly to Auki together tonight. I'll pay. Then we can look for your brother in the morning. But the thing is, we can only stay for four days."

How could she resist?

"Daddy," she said quietly, "what do you think? Should I go?"

Philip ignored her. He was doodling on a scrap of paper and sucking his lower lip like a spoiled child. He was jealous of Veronica. I was beginning to despise him.

"Daddy?"

Finally, Philip looked up at me. "You say you want me to go with you to Langa Langa? I'll go. Yes, I'll go."

I was too horrified to speak. Veronica studied the floor. Philip assured me that four days would be more than enough time for the shark boss to produce his shark.

OUR PLANE DID NOT LEAVE for Auki that evening. The pilot had disappeared. The following morning, I returned to the airport with Philip. A Twin Otter was waiting on the tarmac, but still no pilot. We caught a cab back to the pilot's house to wake him up, but in our absence, another pilot arrived at the airport and flew our Twin Otter to New Georgia. I could feel the hours, my shark hours, rushing past me. I swore at some people in the departure lounge. It was the heat that made me do that. The heat in Honiara was not like heat at all. It was more like a great weight pressing down from the glaring sky and squeezing you until you oozed fatigue and sweat like honey from a sponge. My skin itched. I could feel the previous day's SolBrew seeping through my pores. Philip swore too. He told the air agents we were on an important mission. Then he asked me for some spending money so he could buy a carton of cigarettes for his in-laws in Langa Langa. He smoked those cigarettes as we sat in the betel-stained terminal.

"If we had just taken the boat, we would have reached Malaita by now," I said.

Philip pawed my shoulder and gave a phlegmatic chuckle.

"I have three days now, and I'm running out of money. Maybe God doesn't want me to go to Langa Langa," I said.

In the afternoon, by stunning coincidence, both a pilot and a plane appeared on the runway. The plane was an Islander, which was a step down from the usual Twin Otter: more like a go-kart with wings. There was room for six of us. From my front-row seat, I gazed down over the pilot's shoulder at the cockpit, which resembled the console of my brother's 1968 vw Bug, in that it seemed to be held together by a collage of duct tape. But the plane flew well enough. A half-hour later we skidded to a halt on a grassy corner of Malaita, and a half-hour after that Philip was leading me through the market to Auki harbour, where I had landed on the *Kopuria* three weeks before. We headed for the pile of rubble where the saltwater people landed their boats. We bartered for space on a fibreglass *kanu* with ten other people and their groceries. It was a heavy job for the 25-horse outboard. The engine screamed. We headed down the coast at a walking pace.

Langa Langa Lagoon began just south of Auki Town, and stretched for 30 kilometres along Malaita's mountainous west coast. Its surface was absolutely calm, protected from the chop of the strait by a string of barely submerged reefs and patches of mangrove. Of the reefs, only a few gnarled chunks of storm-tossed coral were visible, poking out of the sea like rotten teeth. The mangrove roots were splayed above the water like the bare legs of so many thousand old women, leafy skirts hauled up past knees in order to wade through the shallows.

The saltwater people must have wanted very badly to live away from Malaita, because, in the absence of natural islands, they had built their own from rocks dredged from the sea bottom. These man-made islands, some of them centuries old, were everywhere. Here was a pedestal with barely enough room for one shack. There, an abrupt plateau the size of a baseball field, rising head-high above the tide line and brimming with bungalows and palm trees. There were docks and long piers. There was a soccer pitch! It was a rough-edged Venice, fashioned from the skeletons of coral.

Why did the saltwater people go to all this work when dry land lay a half-hour paddle away? Some say they fled the hills because they weren't tough enough to defend themselves from the Kwaio warlords. I think they had a much better reason. There were no mosquitoes out on the lagoon.

We zigzagged from island to island, dropping off passengers to scale the rock walls of their villages. Nearly every island had a cathedral-sized barn in which rose the frame of a half-finished ship. The saltwater people were the Solomons' boat builders; half the wooden ferries that chugged in and out of Honiara were born on the shores of Langa Langa. But now, with Jimmy Rasta's boys terrorizing the sound, nobody was in any hurry to finish a ship, so the half-completed craft languished like the skeletons of beached whales, their great beams and ribs bleached as white as bone from years of waiting.

The day was fading when we pulled up to a muddy beach. There were a few huts among the mangroves, but this settlement could hardly be called an island. Most of the huts stood on stilts, and the high-water mark showed as a filmy ring around their ankles. Unfinished rock walls, foundations and pathways stood just barely above the patchwork of sand and mud. Philip led me across the island, handing out cigarettes as he went. Crabs skittered like rats out of our path and into sandy burrows.

I spotted the shark boss sitting in the shadows of an open cookhouse. I knew it was him, even before I got close enough to see his eyes. And it wasn't just because he had Veronica's frizzy blond-white hair. There was something about him. He ... well, he glowed. His leathered skin was translucent, as though the light of the fading sky were shining right through the gridwork of tattoos on his face. He wore a broad smile. I remember his eyes were blue. (But Melanesians have eyes the colour of burnt almond—how could his have been blue?) He was surrounded by children. A wooden tray on the bench beside him contained hundreds of rough red discs. He was carving shell money.

"I knew you were coming," said the shark boss, whose name was Selastine. "Last night I saw you in my dreams."

Amazing!

"Yes, I saw you sleeping in Auki," he continued.

"Well, we slept in Honiara last night," I said.

He paid no attention. "I know why you are here, and I will help you. For how many weeks will you stay?" he said.

"Weeks?"

"You have come for the shark, no?"

"Yes, that's it. For the shark. But I have to leave in three days."

Selastine looked at Philip and chuckled. "It takes many days, many pigs, to call the shark to shore," he said. "You must buy pigs. We must sacrifice. You must stay for weeks. Months."

"But Philip said . . ."

And then I stopped. Philip was already tucking into a dish of Selastine's fish and taro, refusing to look up and acknowledge my glare. Philip had duped me. He had wanted to fly in an airplane. He wanted a vacation. He wanted to sponge off his in-laws. That's why we were here. I imagined sharks tearing into his bulging stomach.

"I must leave in three days," I said, quietly, and then mumbled something pathetic about Bishop Patteson and Nukapu, about having to catch the boat to Santa Cruz.

"No worries. We can still *storian*," said Selastine, looking at me sadly.

I felt dumb with disappointment and anger. I wanted to thrash Philip, or perhaps humiliate him in front of his in-laws. But mostly I wanted to cry. My frustration was deep and wide. It was about more than Philip's deception, more than tricks with sharks. It pulsed through me. It was fuelled by the readiness that had come to me during the tempest on New Georgia, but it was bigger than that. It stretched across oceans, years and generations. It was a longing for something just out of reach. It was a story wanting an ending.

"I should just leave. I should leave right now," I said.

"No kanu long naet," muttered Philip through a mouthful of mashed taro.

"You stay," said Selastine softly. "We can fish out on the reef. We can dive."

Evening settled on the lagoon and the village. A half moon crept up through the mangroves. I pulled out the food I had brought and piled it on the bench. Instant noodles, bread, peanut butter and a bag of candies. Selastine handed out the candies to his grandchildren, of which he had dozens. His daughter set a pot of water to boil on the fire. She served us noodles topped with peanut butter.

I didn't speak. Selastine began his tale. I only jotted it down later, when I realized that the story was part of the shark boss's gift to me. I may not have all the details just right. But the truth of myth isn't in details.

Once upon a time, a young woman of Lalana Point got *bubbly*, which is to say pregnant. She was unmistakably *bubbly*, and there was no sign of any father, and her shame was great, so the woman left her village and travelled around the lagoon. When the time finally came to give birth, she settled in Binafafo, where she had twin boys. The first of these twins was not a boy but a shark, so the woman filled a giant clamshell with water and slipped the shark-boy into it. Her second child was a regular boy.

When the brothers were old enough, the woman let them play together in the shallows of the lagoon. She would throw sticks into the water, and the boys would fight over them. The shark-boy grew bigger and bigger. So did the man-boy. So did the sticks their mother threw for them. One day, when the brothers were fighting over a stick, the shark-boy bit the man-boy's hand right off. The man-boy swam to shore and bled to death. His mother was angry and bereaved. She told the shark-boy, whose name was Bolai, that the only way to atone for his terrible deed was to swim into exile over on Guadalcanal.

Bolai did as his mother told him. He swam west across the strait, and when he reached Guadalcanal he immediately gobbled up three more boys. That was at Bobosa River. The people at Bobosa were understandably cross with him, so Bolai swam along the coast to Logu. He ate some people there too, and the Logu people vowed to kill him, so Bolai swam on to Simui, where he ate a few more children. The Simui people built a barricade of trees and sticks to trap Bolai in their lagoon. When he tried to swim through it, his leathery skin was shredded by the sharp sticks. The people caught Bolai and carved him up. Now it was his turn to be eaten. They gave his head to an old woman, who built a fire in order to smoke-cure it. But just as the fire crackled to life, the woman noticed that tears were falling from the shark's eyes. She took pity on the poor shark head, especially when it told her its sad story.

"Don't cry for me, old woman," Bolai said. "Just go and gather my bones from the village. Bring them back to me. Then you go up into the bush and watch what happens down here tomorrow morning." The woman obeyed, and sure enough the next morning, a giant wave rose up and swallowed the village of Simui. Bolai pulled together his bones and created a new body for himself. It was huge and as black as cooking charcoal. Bolai swam all the way back to his mother in Langa Langa and told her that he had made amends for killing his brother. She was pleased. She told Bolai to stay in the lagoon forever, and to be a good boy and cause no more harm to his own people.

"And that," said Selastine, "is why no one has ever been eaten by a shark in Langa Langa. Bolai is in control of the whole lagoon."

"And Selastine, he is the one who knows the shark. He is the shark boss," said a voice from the shadows. I realized the entire village had gathered around us.

"Yes," said Selastine. "The power of the shark stops inside me. I can use him. I call him to help me dive in the salt water. I can dive to fifteen fathoms. He gives me air. I can stay under the salt water for ten minutes!"

Selastine had a room full of corroded treasure he had pulled from the wreckage of sunken ships near a reef far off the coast. Nobody else could get at the ships because of the sharks that guarded them.

"Aren't you afraid?"

"No, no. Bolai protects me. He swims around me, guides me. He likes to rub his belly against mine. He is bigger than all the other sharks. Longer than this house."

The shack was as long as a limousine.

"Why you?" I asked Selastine.

"Because the shark's mummy was my ancestor. Only I know Bolai's secrets. Only I know how to sacrifice to him properly. And I pray to him too."

"Where?" I said. Perhaps there was a shrine, I thought.

"What do you mean, where? I pray in the cathedral. The Catholic church."

"What does your priest have to say about this?"

"He doesn't mind. He knows the shark is not a *devil*. He knows he is my ancestor and that he gives me good power."

By now, the women had disappeared. The old folks were receding into the blue-grey half-light beyond our oil lamp. Their cigarettes flickered like stars on the horizon. Philip had long fallen asleep, his jowly face collapsing into his chest. I was not so angry any more.

A few teenaged boys still lingered. They clambered over the half wall of the cookhouse and whispered. Selastine turned to me and spoke with the gentle voice of a holy man: *"Yu savve swim?"*

We took a couple of the boys and pushed Selastine's canoe into the lagoon. The boat consisted of three mighty planks pegged together a long time ago. There was room for twenty people in among the fishnets and sloshing fish-gut water.

The lagoon was still except for the dip and slice of our paddles. The half moon illuminated the thin veil of clouds which had spread itself across the entire dome of the sky. The hills of Malaita were the colour of licorice. The lagoon flashed with amoeba-shaped patches of reflected light, a glimmer here, an urgent flutter there. Hot white sparks erupted from each paddle stroke.

We glided to a halt. The water became like the sky. The stillness of the night was broken only by distant percussion. It began as a crude thumping, like the sound that grouse make in the Canadian bush. But the thumping grew and was joined by more thuds and thunks. It became a kind of melody, rising and twisting, flowing across the water from some distant hamlet. I recognized it as the sound of a pipe drum band, of boys striking bamboo tubes with the soles of their rubber flip-flops, as they had after the Bishop of Malaita's cathedral service.

Selastine stripped to his underwear and strapped on a pair of goggles, the kind you could buy for a couple of dollars in the Chinese stores back in Honiara. His white hair shone like a halo.

"Wait," I said. "Why did the shark have to go and eat all those people on Guadalcanal?"

The boys giggled.

"Because his mother told him to," said Selastine.

"Why the hell would she do that?"

"To make better the death of his brother."

"I don't understand. How could that help?"

"This is Malaitan *kastom*," he said. "If you want to avenge a death, you don't go and kill another person in your village. You have to go to another place to do it."

"But the shark-boy was the one who killed in the first place!"

"It doesn't matter who killed. What *kastom* requires is a life to avenge a life. If you killed my brother, for example, I would not need to come back and kill you. Anyone's life would do. And I wouldn't have to do the killing myself. I would pay someone to do it."

"Like a *ramo*?"

"Yes, that's it. Bolai was our first *ramo*. This is *kastom*."

It didn't seem much different from the cycle of payback that had exploded during the tension and that was still crippling the plains around Honiara. Payback was tradition. It was *kastom*.

Selastine picked up his speargun, which consisted of a wooden pole, a simple iron spear with a barb at its tip, and a rubber elastic with which to propel it. He pointed his flashlight into the water. There was nothing to see. He looked at me.

"You come now!" he shouted, then leapt into the water, disappearing in a cloud of bubbles and phosphorescent sparks.

"*Yu garem glass-blong-diver. Yu swim. Hem fun!*" said one of the boys.

I pulled on my mask and crawled over the gunwale. The water was warm. I poked my head beneath the surface and gazed down into the abyss, where there was nothing. I pulled myself close to the canoe and imagined bad things.

The calm was broken suddenly by the leap and crash of something big.

"Long-fish. Hunting," said a boy. "You go! You go!"

I imagined myself as seen from below: a soft bundle of exposed flesh. I flattened myself against the canoe, wrapped my legs around the hull. All this talk of indiscriminate revenge killing had filled me with a nauseating sense of vulnerability.

Another explosion of water, this time near the bow of the canoe. It was Selastine. He was like a breaching whale. He gasped and sucked at the air. "*Gudfala* moon! *Gudfala* night! Come now. Follow my light," he said. And then he took a long heave and slipped away again, leaving an expanding circle of silver ripples in his place. I saw the flashlight beam across the hull of the canoe, turn towards the deep and then descend until it was engulfed by a silty mist.

One of the boys pushed down on my head with his paddle blade. He hammered on my knuckles, making it hard to cling onto the boat. The boys thought I was afraid. Of course I was afraid! I was swimming with the bloody lord of the sharks. But the humiliation made me let go.

I took a breath, pushed off from the canoe and reached into the void with both hands. The effect was mesmerizing. Every movement, each handstroke, was followed by a momentary burst of blue-green light, as though I had released a handful of fireflies. I circled beneath the canoe, which, with its paddles pointing out, resembled a great black dragonfly hanging in the sky. I waved and curled my hands, kicked above me until my body was surrounded by a whorl of stardust, like the sorcerer's apprentice in *Fantasia*. I was laughing when I surfaced, and so were the boys, who knew what I had seen.

And I could stop here. I could let this be enough. But there should be more to this story. I do remember there was more.

I realized Selastine was still underwater. How long had it been? One minute? Five?

"Selastine," I said, and the boys just laughed. *"Hem go walkabaot. Hem fising."* I peered down and saw nothing. I took a great breath and dove, kicking at the sky, pulling at the deep, peering through the blackness.

There is a panic that comes when you hold your breath for too long. It's about oxygen, of course, and the thought of all that water pouring into your lungs. I saw the faintest glimmer of light beneath me, and I struggled against my buoyancy, but the panic turned me around. I kicked for the surface and emerged far off the bow. The boys paddled towards me. I grabbed the gunwale and took ten deep breaths, then dove again. I exhaled slowly this time. I ignored the sparks that peeled from my fingers. I saw the light and kicked hard towards it. It grew into a jaundiced circle of seaweed and sand. Perhaps there were coral rocks. I couldn't tell. A great, obscuring dust storm of silt was sweeping through the lagoon. I kicked farther and saw that the light was coming from Selastine. He was sitting cross-legged on the ocean floor, not moving, just sitting there. Occasionally, a bubble escaped from his mouth and floated like a nervous jellyfish up towards the steel glare of the night sky. Then the panic returned, obscuring my vision, screaming for me to surface, even as I struggled to make sense of the scene, which was somehow right and not right at the same time, and confusing, because I knew I should have been scared yet I was not.

Selastine was not alone. Between the halo of his flashlight and the impenetrable void, in the grey murk between certainty and imagination, I saw something like a great drifting shadow. It was sleek, as long as a car and as black as charcoal. And it was circling the shark boss, slowly, slowly, and if I could have pulled myself down just a little deeper I would have been able to give it a shape, but even as I gaped I was beginning to rise slowly back up towards the surface and the shark boss was becoming a blur, and his pool of light was shrinking and the great shadow was melting into the murk.

I wasn't certain at the time what I saw. And I never spoke to Selastine about it. When he bobbed to the surface a moment after me, he just smiled and said, "*Gudfala* moon! *Gudfala* night!" again, and I agreed. We paddled to the shallows and splashed around a bit, while the pipe drum band thumped away beyond the distant mangroves. We returned to the fire and drank hot water mixed with milk powder.

Selastine asked me to stay a week, so we could fish and dive on the reef. I told him I couldn't. I told him I was bound for the Santa Cruz group, to look for Bishop Patteson's ghost on Nukapu. He understood. Then he asked for my diving mask, and I gave it to him.

When I returned to Honiara, I didn't think about the shadow, not even when my friend Morris asked me about Langa Langa. Did I see the shark spirit? Did we have a tourist attraction? he asked. No, I told him. No, I told all my friends, though each time I told my story I felt it could have been more complete. And then, late one evening after the lights had failed and the rascals had fled the city, after the conversation of a dozen men had trailed away around me and there was no sound but the rustling of palms and the whirring of cicadas, as the perspiration seeped down my back and the circle of listeners drew close, I let myself say yes. Yes, I saw a shadow in the deep. Yes, it was big and it was as black as charcoal, and every sweep of its tail fin raised a storm of silt from the lagoon floor. Yes, that shadow had circled ever so slowly around my friend the shark boss, who was sitting cross-legged on a bed of crushed coral. Yes. And the story became whole. And I grew more certain every time I repeated it. Now there is no doubt. Yes, it was a shark. Yes, it was Bolai. Yes, the ancestor had not forgotten the saltwater people of Langa Langa Lagoon. Yes, I was a believer.

Myth, like love, is a decision. What it answers is longing. What it demands is faith. What it opens is possibility.

19

THE BROTHERS AND

THEIR MIRACLES

And the Lord said unto him, What is that in thine hand?
And he said, A rod. And he said, Cast it on the ground.
And he cast it on the ground, and it
became a serpent; and Moses fled from before it.

Exodus 4:2–3

THIS IS the beginning of the story that would transform the soul of the Solomon Islands.

In 1924, Ini Kopuria, a young corporal in the Native Armed Constabulary, suffered an injury while trying to arrest a bad man. His leg was torn open, or perhaps it was broken. Nobody remembered the details. It was the message that mattered. As he rested in hospital, Kopuria had a visitation from Jesus. "Ini," said Jesus, "you are not doing the work I want you to do." It took Kopuria several months to realize that what Jesus really wanted was for him to organize a fraternity of native missionaries to carry the gospel to all the dark places where people still clung to their heathen ways.

The Bishop of Melanesia, John Steward, encouraged Kopuria and, in 1926, ferried him around the islands aboard the *Southern Cross* so that he could recruit volunteers. By the end of the year, Kopuria had enlisted six men. They returned to his farm at Tabalia, on the northern tip of Guadalcanal, where they cleared the jungle and built a house for their headquarters. They called each other *tasiu*. They took vows of chastity, poverty and obedience to the Church. They adopted a uniform, which consisted of a simple black loincloth and a black belt, underneath which was wrapped a white sash. This was the start of the Melanesian Brotherhood.

The brothers travelled in pairs, trekking barefoot to the most remote pagan villages in the Solomon Islands. The brothers did not behave like other missionaries. They were humble. They only stayed in villages where they had been invited. When they did stay, they worked in people's gardens, slept in people's homes and spread the word gently. They also carried walking sticks, which they used to exorcise evil forces from bodies and places.

From the early days, islanders recognized that the Melanesian Brotherhood had a tremendous amount of *mana*. People said the *tasiu* were not afraid of *devils* or ancestral spirits. They could heal the sick and perform miracles. Their *mana* was similar to the power held by *kastom* priests, but it did not come from traditional spirits or ancestors. It came from God. What made the *tasiu* holy was their prayer, their devotion, their vow of poverty, their separation from material striving. People respected the clergy. But they revered the *tasiu*. Everyone knew that God worked through the *tasiu*, and that crossing them was akin to crossing God.

Everyone knew that when the darkness closed in on Honiara, when the city and its shanties were claimed by chaos, fear and dumb violence, it was the Melanesian Brotherhood—not the police, the government or foreigners—who brought back the light. In the year 2000, when bullets were whizzing back and forth between the barricades that surrounded Honiara, the brothers camped for four months in the no man's land between the Malaitan and Guadalcanalese militants. The *tasiu* negotiated for the release of hostages, they calmed bands of vigilantes, they sheltered refugees. They carried the bodies of the dead back to their relatives. They exhumed corpses from shallow graves so that murder victims could be identified. They marched into militant camps to press for peace.

"In the name of Jesus Christ we appeal to you: stop the killing, stop the hatred, stop the payback," went their official letter. "Those people you kill or you hate are your own Solomon Islands brothers. Blood will lead to more blood, hatred will lead to greater hatred and we will all become the prisoners of the evil we do."

Their prediction was accurate. Hundreds of people were shot, chopped or tortured to death, hundreds more were wounded and tens of thousands of people displaced. The country indeed became a prisoner of hatred. The killing did not ease up until the *tasiu* made their most famous stand, out past the airport on the Alligator Creek Bridge. Everyone knew the story: how the *tasiu* had walked right out onto the concrete stage of the bridge with their walking sticks; how, shielded from the bullets only by their holiness, they created a human barrier between the ignorant armies. The fighters saw that the *tasiu* were not hurt by their bullets. They saw that God disapproved of their violence. This was the beginning of the end of the war.

After the peace agreement was signed, members of the Melanesian Brotherhood led the ex-militants and their convoys of stolen trucks into Honiara and presided over the peace celebrations. For all their dashing back and forth amid the bullets, not a single *tasiu* was killed during the conflict. Most people agreed this was a sign of their special relationship with God.

Now, when people in Honiara wanted to forget their sad stories and push back the darkness a little, they talked about the Melanesian Brotherhood. The *tasiu* had pulled a demon from so-and-so's soul. The *tasiu* had used a dash of holy oil and a tap of a walking stick to extract a sickness-inducing stone from a man's wrist. The *tasiu* had rescued a bloodied victim from Harold Keke's boys and taken him to their base at Tabalia, where God had made him strong again then sent a single thunderbolt to illuminate the faces of the man's rescuers. Everyone had a story about the *tasiu*. There was the one about the truck that came under gunfire from some militants. The driver was so scared he burst into tears. Fortunately, he had a *tasiu* in the passenger seat who told the driver not to fear and who raised his walking stick out the window. That caused the bullets to lose momentum and fall harmlessly to the ground. After that, the militants hailed the truck to stop so they could apologize to the *tasiu*.

Guns were a problem. The Peace Monitoring Council had been attempting for more than a year to retrieve arms from all the ex-militants. But the boys liked their guns and did not want to give them up. The police weren't much help, largely because it was members of the Royal Solomon Islands Police who had stolen their own guns and distributed them to *wantoks* in the first place. The situation seemed hopeless. So a few months before my arrival, the government had asked the Melanesian Brotherhood to take over the job of disarmament. The *tasiu* formed a special unit to go out and ask for the guns back, in God's name.

The brotherhood's disarmament unit had already collected several hundred guns when news came of a shootout on the outskirts of Honiara. The *tasiu*, not the police, went to investigate. They drove to the house of the man responsible. He denied everything. The lead *tasiu* told him, "We know you were shooting a gun at your neighbours, and if you don't give us that gun, we will just have to wait here until you change your mind." They waited. The man sweated nervously in the sun. Minutes passed, maybe hours. Finally, a shadow appeared on the man's dirt floor. It slithered out into the sunlight. The man's son said: "Daddy! Daddy! Look at the snake!" The man tried to ignore the shadow, which continued to writhe threateningly in front of him. One *tasiu* said, "Don't touch it." Then he reached down and grabbed the snake by its head. The serpent stopped writhing. It became as hard as metal. The *tasiu* lifted the snake in the air, and it was transformed back into the machine gun it had always been. This is the kind of story they tell now in the Solomon Islands.

THE MELANESIAN BROTHERHOOD's headquarters at Tabalia was just west of Honiara, so the *tasiu* were everywhere in the city. I saw them each time I returned. Some wore the same humble black-and-white uniform I had seen Ken Brown wearing back in Vureas Bay. Others, the novices, wore electric blue robes with red sashes. They walked barefoot or in flip-flops. Their brass medallions glinted in the sunlight. They held hands and giggled like schoolchildren.

I had heard all the miracle stories and was drawn to the *tasiu*, but at first I had felt unfit to befriend them; surely they would sense my scepticism and know my questions were insincere. But my time in the lagoons had changed me. Now I was ready to believe.

When I returned from Langa Langa and found neither the *Temotu* nor the *Eastern Trader* in port, I was not surprised or upset. I went straight to Chester Rest House, a hostelry which happened to be run by members of the Melanesian Brotherhood. There were no guards at the rest house, nor was it wrapped in barbed wire like the Quality Motel. But it was the safest place to bunk in town. A rascal wouldn't dare enter the place and risk God's anger. I did not go to Chester for protection—Honiara was dangerous for everyone *but* foreigners—but because I imagined it would bring me closer to the brothers and to their magic.

The rest house stood in a grove of flowering trees on the hillside above the port. There were papayas in the garden and frangipani blossoms scattered in the dirt. There was a cement porch on which the brothers lounged, smoked, chewed their betel and guffawed at the world. These brothers were not at all like Tasiu Ken, that stoic dispenser of curses I had met on Vanua Lava. They nestled in each other's arms like children at naptime. They shrieked like birds when amused. They liked to tease the Sisters of Melanesia, who lived in a house just down the hill. The brothers became my friends.

A dozen *tasiu* lived in a communal household next door to the rest house. Seven times a day, a bell would ring and the brothers would disappear to the chapel inside their house to pray. That's what made the brothers powerful, people said. All that prayer. My first friend, little Brother Albert Wasimae, showed me the chapel. It was the size of a bedroom. There was a small wooden cross on the altar, and a picture of a pale, white Jesus wearing his crown of thorns. Also on the altar:

Two chicken's feet, bound together and caked in dried blood. The feet were a killing charm, surrendered by a man on Malaita.

A plastic vial of ground coral. You could kill a man, or at least give him insomnia, if you blew that powder at him.

A tongue of shrivelled ginger root, wrapped in a brittle leaf. You could use that root to spoil someone's brain.

A bullet, whose power was obvious.

Brother Albert told me that all of these bad things had been rendered impotent by prayer and a sprinkling of holy water, which was kept in glass jugs on the floor. The bad things had been gathered in the course of the brothers' Clearance Mission.

I had heard about this Clearance Mission. It was not the same as evangelical work; it was a campaign of direct action against black magic.

The *tasiu* would tour the countryside, making surprise visits to villages where people had complained of curses and sorcery. When they arrived, the brothers ordered the entire community to come to church. All the residents were then obligated to wrap their hands around one of the *tasiu*'s walking sticks and tell the truth about their own use of magic. People knew that *kastom* spells were no match for those walking sticks, just as the Egyptian pharaoh's magicians had not stood a chance against the staff of Moses. They handed over whatever charms they had. A liar would simply be unable to let go of the walking stick until he told the truth. The test left the worst ne'er-do-wells in convulsive fits. Sometimes, said Brother Albert, if the confrontation was with a *kastom devil*, the clash could be so explosive it would break a walking stick in two. So the *tasiu* carried spares.

By the door of the chapel, there was a corkboard. Tacked to it were dozens and dozens of notes written by people who wanted the brothers' help—or rather, God's help, which they hoped the *tasiu* would direct their way. People asked the brothers to pray for their careers, their marriages, their children's success in school exams. Some had attached money. A politician's wife complained that her husband spent too much time campaigning: could the *tasiu* pray for the politician to come home, or at least send money? One writer lamented that his daughter was having trouble becoming pregnant and explained that this was likely the result of a curse cast by angry in-laws. Another pleaded for the brothers to save him from the "green leaf with satanic power."

I WAS FASCINATED by the modern twist the brothers had given to the traditional concept of *mana*. Like the old *kastom* priests, the *tasiu* were credited with directing supernatural forces, but their power came from the same God I had learned about in Sunday school. I had been taught to see biblical miracles as educational metaphors. But the brothers had taken my family's Anglican God and wrestled him back down to earth, where he was behaving much like a Melanesian ancestor spirit. Here he was, allowing his power to be directed by incantations and walking sticks. Here he was, getting involved and taking sides, just like in the Old Testament.

I was ready for the brothers' magic. I wanted to witness the spectacle of the Clearance Mission, to see sorcerers squirm in church. But the brothers in Honiara had no idea which outstations were conducting clearance raids. They learned of clearance victories only after the fact (some ginger collected here, a sorcerer humbled there).

I also wanted to witness the Disarmament Mission, to see the brothers turn guns into snakes, or at least to see them strike the fear of God into the hearts of men like Jimmy Rasta. The disarmament crew was based in the Bishop of Melanesia's old house, where they had a television on which they watched American cop shows to hone their investigative skills.

One member of the team promised to take me along on a mission. Brother Clement Leonard was a great bear of a man with enormous hands and ruby-stained lips. "You stick with me," he said. Brother Clement had so much betel crammed into his cheek he could only slur. "I am your connection. I am your source. I will help you."

"There is urgency," I said. It was true. I was running out of money and time.

"I understand," said Brother Clement. But he must not have understood, because I didn't see him for days.

I could not get close to things. The adventure was always yesterday. The action was always beyond the horizon. In fact, receiving news of any action in the Solomons was a bit like looking at the night sky; you knew a star had been real at some point because its light reached you, but you also knew that the spark you saw was thousands of years old and that the star's fire might by now have died entirely.

I was waiting out the midday glare at Amy's Snack Bar on Mendana Avenue one afternoon when a man with pale skin and long legs strode by. I noticed white skin in Honiara because, like everyone else, I kept an eye out for my own *wantoks*. (After months alone, I was beginning to grasp the *wantok* concept. Nobody understands you like someone from your own island, or even better, like someone you can talk to without resorting to pidgin, which is nobody's mother tongue.)

The white man wore glasses and had an unruly shock of blond hair. He was smoking. That wasn't remarkable. This was: he wore a black shirt, black shorts and a black-and-white sash around his waist. I had never thought of asking the *tasiu* if there were any white men in their order. I couldn't imagine someone from my world falling so completely into the realm of miracles. I pushed my way onto the street and chased him down.

"Awright?" he said when I caught him. His accent oozed south London, but he had the bearing of an Old Etonian.

I knew of the brotherhood's vow of poverty and I had seen their diet of root vegetables and mush, so I knew the white *tasiu* would accept an invitation to dinner at the Hong Kong Palace, where the spring rolls were served with ketchup but the beer was cold.

"Brother," I said, after we had polished off a couple of SolBrew, "what the hell are you doing in that uniform?"

He laughed. "Sometimes I wake up and think I must be bonkers," he said, wolfing down the last of our chop suey. "I'm forty-two years old and I have no estate, no house, no money, no car, no material symbols to mark my existence ..."

"You are an ascetic," I said.

"Actually, yes."

Richard Carter was born in Gilford, a hamlet just south of London. His father was an Anglican priest. He had studied English and drama. He had always been a Christian, at least in a postmodern sense. He had thought that God was a good idea, that Jesus was a very good teacher. Christianity had seemed a useful religion.

The young man's view of the cosmos changed after he moved to the Solomons in 1987. He came to teach at the Church of Melanesia's Selwyn College. He saw things he had never seen in England, things that convinced him, just as they had convinced the Victorian missionaries, that the struggle between good and evil was something that could be seen and touched. Carter was ordained a minister in 1992. From the beginning, he was drawn to the *tasiu*, and they to him. He was captivated by their lives, by their meekness, by the tenderness and nobility of their community, by the holiness he saw in their poverty. The brothers invited Carter to join their order, and he became Brother Richard. Soon he was rewriting Christian parables as Melanesian dramas, which the brothers performed on tour throughout the islands.

"But what about the miracles?" I asked. Did he believe in the fantastical *mana*-ization of the brotherhood or in all that funnelling of divine power through walking sticks and holy water? Had the islanders wiped the rational scepticism from his English soul? I wanted him to shout yes.

But instead he smiled cryptically. "I have become more receptive to the mysteries of faith, to things that can't be explained simply . . ."

"Bending bullets?"

"No, I don't believe in bending bullets. But believe me, somehow this community of young men is able to do things that other Melanesians can't. And it's all through the grace of God. The brothers don't spend three or four hours a day in prayer for nothing, you know. Here, let me tell you a story.

"In my early days, I was on the *Southern Cross*, heading for the Reef Islands with the brothers. We heard on the ship's radio that a man back at Taroaniara, the ship's base, was possessed by some kind of evil. The poor guy had been foaming at the mouth, that kind of thing, and finally he had died. Well, by some miraculous coincidence, our first landfall in the Reefs happened to be this man's home village. We went ashore. The old folks gathered around and told us that the dead man had just been selected as their next chief. But not only that: they said that anyone they had ever chosen to be their chief had been afflicted by a death curse—there had been possessions, sickness, freak accidents, all kinds of stuff. It had been going on for decades. You could feel the darkness in the village. We were faced with an ancestral curse so strong it had cast a pall of darkness over the place. So the brothers sat down and decided to perform a clearance.

"The next morning we conducted a rousing service about the power of light over darkness. We reminded people that in the presence of God, evil is a non-reality: it cannot exist. We made a procession around the village with big pots of holy water. We went from house to house, driving out evil and praying while the brothers marked crosses in the sand. A lot of this 'driving out' involves using primeval symbols, you know: water, fire or marks in the sand to express spiritual truth. Anyway, this exercise was incredibly powerful. More and more people joined the procession. They followed the brothers around. They started singing hymns to the rhythm of *kastom* songs. Then, after the ceremony, all the people who had been pie-faced, dark and grey, they were suddenly light and cheery and laughing. You could feel the oppression lifting like a great weight from their shoulders! There was a physical sense of release from darkness. I felt it too, the darkness dissolving away. And, you know, the village has never been bothered by that curse again."

"And this is your big miracle?"

"Yes it is. I would probably explain those events differently than the Melanesians would. But their fears were real. The darkness that held them was not something you could simply dismiss. It was killing people, and the brothers helped put an end to it. I have no difficulty coming to terms with the miraculous aspect of what happened there."

The event did not seem like proof of anything other than the power of psychology to me. I wanted to ask him how miracles worked, what demons looked like, how he thought evil and goodness might interact with atoms and molecules in order to change events in the material world. What about the guns that melted into snakes, the helpful crocodiles, the walking sticks that hung in mid-air? Did he believe these things really had happened or not?

"Why can't you just let the stories be?" he asked.

"Because, I would like to *know* they are true."

"Ah," he said. "You want proof."

"I made it rain by blowing on a *kastom* stone," I offered, hoping to win his trust by showing I was a believer, too.

He sighed. "Look, our knowledge of truth, the truth about that which is life-giving and eternal, it exists beyond the bounds of rationalism. Faith carries us closer, but in the end we can't describe it. We just don't have words for it. At the end of the day, we are reduced to telling stories about that mystery. That's what I know."

"But guns turning into snakes . . ."

"Did Jesus actually walk on water? My answer would be yes he did, in his disciples' memory of him. He did in their faith experience. The walk on water could not be captured on video or analysed by a scientist, and yet it was profoundly true for those who witnessed it."

The white *tasiu* refused to take sides in the magic debate. He drifted between metaphor and an amorphous mysticism. It took many hours of conversation, and months of reflection, and the death of a friend, to understand his message. What I now think the brother was saying was that stories are containers for spiritual truths. What I think he was saying is that it was the apostles' faith in such miracles that enabled them to surmount fear and chaos in order to lay the foundations for their Church. The miracle was made true *because* it was believed. But did the miraculous moment lay in history, in imagination or somewhere in between?

The Canadian scholar Northrop Frye argued that it was a mistake for biblical scholars to attempt to divine the boundary between historical and mythical truth. Frye, who called himself a Christian, insisted that the key to understanding the Bible was to see it entirely as a work of metaphorical literature. Some parts of the New Testament may be historically accurate, but they are accurate *only by accident.* The Bible's writers—none of whom actually met Jesus—were not at all interested in historical reporting because they were tackling the much more important task of imparting a grand metaphor. And that metaphor was the life of their Messiah, who was, as they say, the *word* made flesh.

"Jesus is not presented as a historical figure," wrote Frye, "but as a figure who drops into history from another dimension of reality, and thereby shows what the limitations of the historical perspective are." The Bible, he concluded, was *more* true because of its counter-historical nature.

Frye could just as easily have applied his theory to Melanesia. If people used myth to express spiritual truths, then it made sense for miracles to be attributed to the *tasiu,* who embodied everything that Melanesians had come to see as holy. People felt their goodness, their glow. Stories about the *tasiu* began with observed events, but these were not always enough to convey the force of the holiness that people felt. So the storytellers dramatized the observed moment with symbolism. A bouncing bullet. A helpful crocodile. Whatever. They did what storytellers have done since the beginning of time: they embellished in order to elevate their formless truths and place their stories in the mythical realm.

The key to finding God, Frye said, was imagination.

This was certainly not the version of God that my great-grandfather had carried to Melanesia. He insisted that a man had no business serving as a religious teacher if he denied "the plain facts of the Gospel record." You could debate the minutiae of the scriptures all you liked, but the incarnation and the resurrection of Jesus were non-negotiable.

That way of thinking, that absolutism, had guided my journey too. Miracles occurred or they did not. There was no hazy middle ground. But unlike my great-grandfather, I did not carry enough faith with me to lend the supernatural the benefit of the doubt. I needed proof. I was greedy for more storms, more shark-like shadows. I wanted the *tasiu* to make their walking sticks hang in mid-air for me. I was not yet ready to consider the idea on which Frye and the white *tasiu* likely agreed: The measure of a miracle's truth was not the accuracy of the event so much as the quality of the faith it inspired.

Brother Richard said he disdained magic that did not lead to God. That is why he was so worried about the Melanesian Brotherhood. Some people's belief in the power of the *tasiu* and their walking sticks was verging on idol worship. They were forgetting that those walking sticks were merely symbolic. Some members of the order had even begun to believe they could direct supernatural power. All this talk of guns turning into snakes was causing them to develop a sense of invulnerability and spiritual pride. It was a trap, and it could only lead to more fear and superstition. What the islanders needed, said the white *tasiu,* was a new kind of story, one that would lead them closer to the transcendent vision of the New Testament.

I did not see the *tasiu* bend bullets or cast out demons. I did not see them ride on the backs of crocodiles. But I did see something of their power, which was not as I imagined. And I did see the beginning of a story that would carry them through a great darkness and back into the light, a story in which the brotherhood would give up their *mana* but be utterly reborn. And like the New Testament, that story would be about suffering as much as it would be about rebirth.

I WAS SITTING on the veranda at the Chester Rest House one morning when the MV *Temotu* appeared like a great white lie in the port. I saw her tie up to one of the cement piers. Then came the *Eastern Trader.* I ran down to swear at their crews. Tomorrow, they told me. They would be leaving for Santa Cruz tomorrow.

"Tomorrow, someday—or tomorrow, the day after today?" I asked.

"Tomorrow, tomorrow, of course."

I was about to leave when I spotted a burly *tasiu* climbing over the *Temotu*'s rails; it was Clement, the gun brother who had promised to be my source. He was lumbering towards a Toyota Hilux with a white flag mounted on the roof of the cab. The flag had a black cross stitched to it. There were more *tasiu* inside the truck. It was the disarmament gang.

"Where are you going?" I demanded.

"CDC-I," said Brother Clement. "Criminal activity. We're on a mission."

CDC-I was the nearest of the giant swath of plantations east of Honiara that had been run by the foreign-owned Commonwealth Development Corporation. During the tension, the company had evaporated and its Malaitan workers had been run off the island. Now the people who considered themselves to be the traditional owners of the plantation lands were fighting over the spoils. There had been half a dozen murders in the area in the last month.

"I'm coming with you," I said.

"Of course you are coming," said Brother Clement, as though he had planned it all along.

We stopped at the Sweetie Kwan store where I bought bread, peanut butter and sticks of tobacco for everyone. Then we were off: stereo blasting, cigarette smoke pouring from the windows, betel spit flying.

The driver, who would not tell me his name, threw on a New Caledonian reggae cassette.

"We will call him Driver X!" said Clement, who sat in the front seat, chewing and toying with his medallion. The necklace was strung with hundreds of tiny dolphin's teeth. I sat in the back seat, flanked by Brothers Floyd and Nicolas, who sang and giggled and tickled me until I had to slap them. Another brother huddled in the truck's box. I recognized him as Francis, the white *tasiu*'s best friend. He had the soft skin and straight hair of a Polynesian. I couldn't see his eyes through his wraparound sunglasses. He was very quiet. I concluded that he was not so important.

I wish that I had known then about the fate Brother Francis would meet on the Weather Coast. I wish I had known then that he was the beginning of a new story and the end of my own.

Driver X threw on a Bob Marley cassette and cranked up the volume. We rocked out of town, past the rusting remains of WWII Quonset huts, past the garbage mountains and the hundreds of betel-nut stands, past Jimmy Rasta's bottle shop and the airport. We crossed the Alligator Creek Bridge, which seemed to have forgotten the battle that had been fought across its span. Grass was beginning to sprout through the concrete.

We howled like teenagers. We sang along with the music: *Let's get together and feel alright.* There was trouble ahead, but we were blameless. It was a road trip. I felt as though we should have been drinking Slurpees spiked with vodka and throwing beer cans at street signs. None of the *tasiu* was over thirty.

There was no traffic after Alligator Creek, but sometimes we saw people on the road, hiking with gas jugs or plastic baskets on their heads. Driver X slowed to pick them up, but Brother Clement stopped him.

"No! Official business! Very important! Very dangerous!" bellowed Clement.

"Commando unit! Strike force! Bruce Willis!" shouted Floyd.

"Army! Army!" chanted Nicolas, poking me beneath the ribs and saluting. *"Yumi stap insaed long army!"—We're in the army.*

Brother Francis just smiled and waved at the foot travellers. We didn't stop for anyone.

Soon the countryside changed. There was nobody left on the road—which had once been a paved highway but was now disintegrating, clawed by great forests of grass and fern and woody shrubs pushing in from both sides. We passed the bullet-riddled shell of a gas station and later a health clinic, also abandoned. The journey began to feel less festive.

The next bridge required four-wheel drive. It had been bombed to stop the Malaita Eagles from getting too far out of Honiara, but the bombing had been half-hearted. The bridge had not been destroyed but had simply sagged into the riverbed. The midday air thickened. The air dripped with bad memories and a hazy, shapeless malevolence. The brothers stopped singing.

We approached what looked like a lemonade stand. Its occupant, who wore a camouflage sun hat, stood up, rubbed his eyes and motioned for us to stop. Clement spoke to him in mumbles, and the man waved us on.

"Which side is he on?" I asked.

"This week, he is Gold Ridge," said Clement.

A junction in the road and another guard hut. Men leaned against what looked like a giant outhouse, erected in the middle of a side track. Its walls were solid and windowless except for a horizontal slit in one wall, from which a gun barrel pointed. The shack gave off a puff of smoke, and then it lurched forward. The shack was not an outhouse. It was a homemade tank. Its gun barrel shifted and remained trained on our truck as we rolled away again.

The situation on the plantations was not simple, Clement said. Sometimes the plantation villages fought with each other. Sometimes they fought with a faction based at Gold Ridge, in the hills near the abandoned mine. Brother Clement wasn't sure why the Gold Ridge people were fighting with the plantation people, but the two sides had been alternately blocking roads and shooting at each other for months. The previous day, a boy from Matepona, a village just past CDC-1, had been taken by the Gold Ridge militants. We were here to rescue the boy, since the police were still too afraid to cross Alligator Creek.

We stopped at the boy's father's compound, a clutch of tin-roofed bungalows hopping with children and clucking chickens. The father was a weak-looking man with grey hair and glassy eyes. His name was Johnson.

"I was just working in my garden when they came to tell me my boy was dead. Where is Junior? Where is my boy?" Johnson said somewhat rhetorically, since by this point we had established that the Gold Ridge boys had kicked the shit out of Johnson Junior, then taken him back to their base. Why had they taken him? Johnson had no idea. His was a good Christian family. Clement tapped his feet impatiently as Johnson told us his story.

Johnson, his wife and his brother hopped in the back of the truck with Brother Francis, who smiled at them but remained silent. We headed east, past another roadblock, past rows and rows of oil palms, their shaggy tops casting mottled shadows on the jungle that had begun to rise, unchecked, beneath them. Bushy vines climbed up the palm trunks, arcing into the sky above the fronds. I once heard someone describe the Solomons as a green desert. Now I understood. Like the shifting sands, the jungle was always creeping closer, seizing on weakness, threatening to bury human industry in suffocating mounds, in an impenetrable, seething desolation of electric green.

We pulled into a clearing. There was a sign: Tetere Police Post. But there were no police. The lawn was overgrown. A crowd of men waited in the shade of an oak tree.

"The Gold Ridge boys," said Brother Clement.

Our arrival was not a surprise. That was obvious, because although the Gold Ridge militants were said to be well armed, no one in this crowd was actually holding a gun. (People were careful around the brotherhood. If a *tasiu* saw a gun, he would insist that it be handed over.)

The militants shifted nervously, glaring at Johnson like wolves assessing a wounded buck. Their leader was a fat man with silver aviator glasses.

"Now we will straighten things out," Clement whispered to me.

"Welcome *tasiu*, welcome," said the leader. "This is just a family problem. We are sorry to bother you."

"Yes, said Johnson, who was slouching deferentially behind Clement. "Just a small problem. I just want my Junior back."

"And we want our machine gun back," snarled the leader.

"And no more bombing," said a sinewy young man behind the leader, pausing to spit a great hork of betel into the grass no-man's land between us.

Machine gun? Bombing?

It was difficult to understand the exchange that followed. The militants were furious and Johnson was vague. But by the end of it, and with a bit of commentary from Clement, it became clear that Johnson and his boy were not as meek as they seemed.

Apparently, a gang from CDC-1 had blocked the road between Gold Ridge and Honiara. That was a month ago. The Gold Ridge gang was upset about this, even though they had blocked plenty of roads themselves—roadblocks were a convenient way of extorting cigarettes and petrol from travellers. The Gold Ridge gang had made a retaliatory sweep through the plantations, beating the odd settler and stealing the odd pig. But when they hit Johnson's compound, Johnson and his Junior fought back mightily, wrestling an SR-88 assault rifle from one of the attackers and sending the Gold Ridge gang running.

Then Johnson Junior acquired some explosives from the CDC-I gang and bombed a bridge on the Gold Ridge road. That's why the Gold Ridge boys had hunted him down, and why Johnson Junior was now bleeding in some shack behind the police station.

Nobody shouted. Johnson whimpered. At first the militants spoke in hushed, pleading voices. Clement tried to negotiate, but even as the militants deferred ("Thank you *tasiu*, yes, *tasiu*, we are sorry, *tasiu*"), they grew more agitated and shuffled forward. They hissed like snakes and quivered with quiet outrage. The militants stopped chewing their betel. Clement chewed faster. A drop of red foam boiled at the corner of his mouth. Perspiration beaded on all our faces. The tension was nauseating. I wished I had not come.

And then Brother Francis stepped forward. He wore a shy half smile. He pulled off his wraparound sunglasses. He did not look at Johnson or at the militants. He gazed at the trampled earth as though looking right through it, then towards the deep green folds of the highlands, then up at the sky, and then he bowed his head. The militants seemed transfixed by his movements, like charmed snakes. The bickering trailed off. Brother Francis spoke softly, and his voice was like a breeze blowing through the yard, rustling through the dry grass, easing the weight of the humid afternoon. I could barely hear him. At first I thought he was reasoning with the militants. But his murmurs were too melodic for that. I realized he was praying when I noticed all the other bowed heads. The militants unclenched their fists. Their leader removed his aviator glasses. An immense calm settled on them all.

Within minutes, the problem was settled.

We drove back to Johnson's house, where his wife and his sister served us great lumps of taro in coconut milk. Johnson beamed. "You know, my boy didn't blow up the bridge," he said cheerily. "He just made a little explosion to scare those Gold Ridge boys away."

"*Hem stret brotha,*" said Clement. "But we need the gun."

"The gun?" said Johnson, smiling weakly.

"The gun," said Clement, rolling a fresh wad of betel around his gums.

Johnson hummed and hawed. So did his brother and his wife. But they knew the game was up. Finally, someone produced a battered SR-88 assault rifle from inside the house. There was no ammunition. We took the gun with us. The agreement back at the Tetere police post had been for everyone to return the following day. The *tasiu* would bring the gun. The Gold Ridge gang would bring Johnson Junior, alive. There would be an even trade, and then they would all make a picnic together. (In fact, when the brothers returned the following day, they picked up Johnson Junior but informed the Gold Ridge boys that they were keeping the SR-88 so they could dispose of it in God's name. Who could argue with that? The militants didn't.)

We sang all the way home, and we stopped at the middle of the Alligator Creek Bridge so I could take a photo of the brothers. I wanted them to hold the gun above their heads. They refused, but they did pull out their walking sticks. I keep that photo on my wall. There is Driver X, running along the bridge railing. There is Brother Nicolas, beaming, and Brother Floyd, barefoot. There is Brother Clement, with his walking stick and his white cross-trainers. And behind them, squinting into the light, his lips pursed into that shy half smile, is Brother Francis, whose face and name have now been seared into my memory.

How could I have known that it was my job to remember more than I remember of Brother Francis?

How could I have known that he would go off to challenge the greatest darkness his country had ever seen and that he would be transformed by that journey? Would I have warned him? And if I had warned him, would he have sailed to the Weather Coast of Guadalcanal anyway?

How could I have known that I was destined to return to the day that Brother Frances had whispered and chuckled and remained very small, so small that I had decided he was not central to the story until the moment he stepped forward and radiated something so infinitely good and true that the tension was washed from the afternoon and the men with anger and guns were made humble? I did not yet know the significance of the moment. I did not yet know Brother Francis's place in the story. I did not yet know that after all the talk of miracles and magic, it was Brother Francis who would offer the answer that obscured all the rest. I did not yet know my own place in the story. That knowledge would take months to come to me, and by that time Brother Francis would be dead.

The last time I saw Brother Francis, he wrote in my notebook: *Believe.*

20

NUKAPU AND THE

MEANING OF STORIES

Behold, I shew you a mystery; We shall not all sleep, but we
shall all be changed, In a moment, in the twinkling
of an eye, at the last trump: for the trumpet shall sound, and the
dead shall be raised incorruptible, and we shall be changed.

1 Corinthians 15:51–52

MAPS INSIST that Nukapu is a real place. There
it is, a tiny speck on the northern fringe of the
Santa Cruz group. There it is, caught in the
cartographer's grid, 166 degrees east of Greenwich, 10 degrees south of the
Equator, 700 kilometres east of Honiara, beyond a vastness of sea and the
deep blue canyon of the Torres Trench. The island is real, but it is a pin-
prick compared to the geography of its imagined existence.

People in Melanesia all talked about Nukapu but nobody had been
there. They knew it for the act of violence that marked the frontier between the age of the ancestors and the age of the new god. They knew it
as the epicentre of the myth that bound them to their Church. For all this
knowing, the island remained wrapped in mystery: who had murdered
the first Bishop of Melanesia and why? Everyone had a theory about the
death of John Coleridge Patteson, whose bones still shifted at the bottom
of the sea off Nukapu's barrier reef. The island and its story had captivated

me from the moment I discovered that packet of sand back in Oxford. Nukapu. I couldn't shake the sense that it was the place where myth and history intersected. If I could just cross that reef and wade to its shore, if I could feel the island's certainty, I might be able to divine the space between all the old stories, and in that space find some truth about the idea that my ancestors had bowed down before, sacrificed to and carried around the world.

But Nukapu had begun to feel like more of an idea than a real place. Weeks had passed since the captains of the *Eastern Trader* and the MV *Temotu* had first promised a quick departure for the Santa Cruz group. So it was with no great expectations that, on the morning after my adventure in CDC-1, I packed my air mattress, stocked up on cookies at the Sweetie Kwan store and sauntered down to the port as I had done a dozen times before. I didn't get my hopes up even when I saw diesel smoke curling above my two ships and the pier between them seething with bodies.

A fierce, betel-stained drunk lurched out of the crowd towards me. *"Yu go wea? Fren! Fren! Yu go wea?"*

What eyes! What breath! What teeth! The man was a complete mess. I gave him the standard brush-off: *"Jes walkabaot."*

He grabbed me by the hand before I could escape. *"Yu no rememba mi?"*

There was something about his face, those broken teeth, the foam gathered around the edge of his lips. Of course! This was the man I had been harassing for weeks. It was the captain of the *Eastern Trader*.

"My friend, we are all fuelled up," the captain spat excitedly. *"By yumi go long Santa Cruz! Olgeta cabins booked-up nao. Sori! Sori! But yu savve slip insaed cabin blong mi!"*

The thought of bunking with the captain was horrifying. I knew the decrepit *Eastern Trader* would only be sailing if the MV *Temotu* was leaving, too—that way there would be a quick rescue if the old rust bucket foundered at sea. But was the captain drinking in celebration or fear? I shook free of his grip and lost him amid the hundreds of Santa Cruzians and big-boned Polynesians who crowded the pier. There was a desperate excitement in the air. Everyone was flush with compensation money. People climbed over the *Temotu*'s rails, tossing aboard sacks of rice, rolls of chicken wire and jugs of petrol. I joined them.

The *Eastern Trader* gave a wail and pulled bravely away. We all assumed the *Temotu* would follow, and there was much joyous smoking and spitting, at least until a loudspeaker crackled and hissed to life. "*Wantoks*, this is your captain," a voice boomed. "We should go now. We are ready to go now. But we cannot go now. I'm sorry *tumas*, but human life is too precious to risk. So we will try again at 10 a.m. tomorrow."

What had happened was this. The police had finally mustered the courage to confront Jimmy Rasta's boys over their pirating of the Langa Langa ship *Sa'Alia*. There'd been a shootout on the beach east of Honiara. The police had won. Five of the pirates had been captured and taken to jail, but Rasta had returned to his compound for cocktails, and everyone knew that when Rasta hit the booze he got angry, and when Rasta got angry he tended to steal ships and bludgeon people with his gun. The seas would be much safer when he was hung-over.

The loudspeaker crackled again: "I want to warn anyone who would steal any of the personal belongings left on this ship, especially the person who has lifted the calico, that we *tasiu* are here as God's witnesses. Think hard. If you want to enjoy the rest of your life, do not steal on this ship. God will punish you." It was Brother Clement.

When I returned to the port the next morning, the voice of the *Temotu's* captain was echoing off the warehouse walls. "If you don't come on time *wantoks*, how can we leave on time? I'm serious now! We're going home! Brothers and sisters, we're going home!"

I climbed aboard. The ship's pastor read a prayer, finishing it with an imploring, "Lord God, *olgeta laef blong mifala stap insaed long hand blong yu.*"

The lines were loosened and tossed aboard. The engine rumbled. I went to check on my berth. I had fought with the ship's agent until he had agreed to assign me a first-class berth. This, I now discovered, gave me the right to occupy a painted rectangle of floor, roughly the size of my inflatable air mattress, in a cabin with sixty other people. I had left a blanket on my square to mark it. Now the blanket was buried under a heap of bagged rice, Chinese noodles, grass mats and plastic buckets.

I squeezed between two families: on one side, a mountainous Polynesian matriarch whose children crawled over her breasts like ants on their queen, and on the other, a prematurely seasick woman with a gaggle of teens who took turns wiping the drool from her chin.

I ran into Brother Clement and remembered his vow of poverty. I invited him to my painted square for a picnic of crackers and peanut butter. He fell asleep on my inflatable mattress and stayed there for a day. I curled up on the linoleum with the Polynesians.

We sailed southeast, down the strait which separated Guadalcanal and Malaita. The sea was orderly. At dawn, we reached Makira. It was a dark spine of thick jungle skirted by jagged coral and pockets of black sand. Vines and shadows obscured the foreshore. The island was rendered especially hostile by the bruised folds of an approaching storm.

I wish I could say that I sat with my legs dangling over the bow, listening to tales of adventure and magic, experiencing the mariners' camaraderie and the exhilaration of the open ocean. But it was not like that at all, especially after we left Santa Ana, the last of the islets that trailed from the eastern tip of Makira. The wind picked up. The storm filled the sky. The waves grew beneath us, lost their form and became a mishmash of monstrous lumps, like giants writhing under a blanket. The ship vibrated and rolled. The cargo mountains collapsed and babies began to howl. The optimism of our departure evaporated. The cabin was transformed into an infernal daycare of screaming tots, glassy eyes, swollen breasts and bile.

Occasionally, the ship corkscrewed, sending cargo and babies and vomit buckets tumbling across the cabin and unleashing a chorus of, *"Oh, Jisas Krais! Oh, Jisas Krais! Oh, Jisas Krais!"* The cries sounded like accusations, as though God were letting us down horribly.

"Tasiu!" people shouted after one nasty lurch, as though Brother Clement could calm the tempest. But he snored through the night and into the morning, oblivious, on my mattress.

The thought of capsizing was never as immediate or unpleasant as the thought of remaining on board amid the sloshing vomit buckets and diesel fumes. And then there was the business of plumbing: the *Temotu*'s head was on the lower deck, which meant it was usually under 30 centimetres or so of water. Each time a wave peeled over the rails, a river of foam poured under the door, performing a kind of backwards flush on the toilet before seeping out again. Once you experienced that, you stopped eating and drinking. You prayed for intestinal paralysis and for land to appear on the horizon.

The *Temotu* was not graceful or elegant. It didn't deserve the feminine pronoun. But I suppose it did exhibit a rough integrity. It did push on, even after the *Eastern Trader* turned back to Santa Ana.

We crashed through another afternoon and evening. I could not sleep. Near midnight, I climbed to the top deck to watch the ship's dogsbody wrestle bucket after bucket of trash over the rails. "We must not carry this mess with us to paradise," he shouted cryptically, "so we must feed the sea, my friend. Ha ha! The sea will consume it!"

I watched the garbage disappear into the night. The storm had exhausted itself. A light appeared on the horizon just off the bow, a faint crimson glow. It grew and became not a fire but a damp reflection of fire, like a red spotlight projected up onto the belly of the clouds. My heart raced at the sight. The light could only be Tinakula, the volcano around which the Santa Cruz islands were scattered like the remnants of an ancient eruption. Tinakula! The volcano had inhabited my dreams for years.

It was Tinakula that had guided explorers and missionaries to their deaths for nearly half a millennium. There was poor Alvaro de Mendaña, the first European to find the Solomon Islands. The Spaniard had hoped to build a Christian colony on Nendo, which he called Santa Cruz when he reached it in 1595, but his dream became a nightmare of hunger, mutiny and disease. His soldiers and crew fought with each other and the natives. His ships began to rot at anchor. Mendaña was stricken with malaria and died on his ship beneath Tinakula's fires.

Then there was the Comte de la Pérouse. The French navigator had ably explored much of the North and South Pacific, but he was never seen again by Europeans after he left Australia's Botany Bay in 1788, bound for the Solomons. Nearly forty years later, Irish adventurer Peter Dillon discovered relics from la Pérouse's two ships on Vanikoro, a day's sail southeast of Tinakula. Islanders told Dillon that their ancestors had slaughtered most of the shipwrecked sailors and had retired their skulls to a local spirit house.

Then came the missionary martyrs. First to die were Edwin Nobbs and Fisher Young, the youthful Norfolk Islanders who rowed Bishop Patteson to shore at Mendaña's Graciosa Bay in 1864, only to be ambushed in a flurry of arrows. A decade later, the protector of the Melanesian Mission, British Commodore James Goodenough, sailed past Tinakula and waded ashore at Carlisle Bay on Santa Cruz. He walked from one village to a neighbouring settlement, leading to much confusion among the natives as to whose side he was on. To be safe, the locals again let fly their arrows. Goodenough was said to have recognized his diplomatic blunder. Before dying, he ordered his men not to bomb or burn the village in retaliation.

But these were not the ghosts that had drawn me into the volcano's orbit. The one who called to me was John Coleridge Patteson, the martyred bishop whose bones lay somewhere in the deep beyond Tinakula. The story of the bishop's death was more than a tale of missionary zeal or heroic misfortune. It gave the Anglican Church its first episcopal missionary-martyr, a shining archetype of Anglo-Catholic sacrifice. The story was pictured on stained-glass windows, carved into the stone of Exeter Cathedral and writ into Victorian children's books, place names and Sunday sermons. It was the inspiration for generations of seafaring missionaries, including my great-grandfather. It was remembered in the prayers of Melanesians and passed down in stories told by firelight from Tanna to Papua New Guinea.

I had found a dozen different accounts of Patteson's death in libraries in Oxford, London and Sydney. Some were the scribbled testimonies of sailors. Some were written years later by amateur evangelical historians. Some were fanciful reconstructions. Some were fabrications. These stories captivated me, but they also bothered me, mostly because the earliest versions were constructed and put to work even before the bishop's followers had figured out exactly what had happened to him. But Patteson's story did not require facts to survive. It lived independently of them. That is why I call it a myth.

My great-grandfather recounted Patteson's death in *The Light of Melanesia*, which he published to raise funds for the Melanesian Mission. His version ran close to earlier accounts. If you were to amalgamate them, the story would go something like this:

Bishop Patteson was never the same after the martyrdom of Nobbs and Young at Graciosa Bay. The strain of their deaths, especially that of

Patteson's favourite, Young, sapped him of his youth. Friends urged Patteson to return to England, but he was determined to crack the pagan shell of the Santa Cruz group. For nine years he tried to land there, and for nine years he was repelled. His work was made increasingly dangerous by the presence of labour recruiters among the islands. The natives found it hard to distinguish between the *Southern Cross*, which carried their children away to mission school, and the blackbirding vessels, which carried strong young men off to work on plantations.

"The exasperation of the Natives is very great," wrote Patteson. "Kidnapping is going on fast. Many quarrels have arisen; Natives are retaliating; And they can't always discriminate, you know, between a friendly and an unfriendly white man."

The bishop sailed towards Santa Cruz in 1871 in an atmosphere of foreboding. The *Southern Cross* had just completed a loop north through the Solomons to collect the evangelists it had deposited two months previously. The missionaries' reports were alarming. Natives had killed all the crew on at least two labour-recruiting vessels. At Nggela, Irish missionary Charles Brooke reported that blackbirders had kidnapped more than fifty men and killed more than eighteen others. He later wrote: "[The chief] Takua came to me, in alarm and anger, to say that the kill-kill vessel had anchored in the neighbourhood. Tomorrow she would be here, and what was he to do—'to kill, or to be killed? And how is it that *Bisopé* and you came first, and then these slaughterers? Did you send them?'" Brooke, outraged and fearing for his own skin, had advised the chief that if the recruiters attacked, then the people should rise up and "kill, kill utterly!"

Meanwhile, at San Cristobal (now Makira), the captain of the Fiji-based labour-recruiting ship *Emma Bell* bragged to missionary Joseph Atkin that his next hunting ground would be Santa Cruz.

All this bad news weighed heavily on Patteson, who expected to die on the islands but did not wish his followers to die along with him. The *Southern Cross* sped towards Santa Cruz but was becalmed near Tinakula, whose peak smoked and glowed like the fires of Sinai. The bishop fell into deep meditation. The crew mused that he was praying for the poor souls who still remained in ignorance and darkness. Patteson then wrote in his diary: "On Monday we go to Nukapu. I am fully alive to the probability that some outrage has been committed here. The master of the vessel whom Atkin saw, did not deny his intention of taking away from these or from any other island any men or boys he could induce to come on board. I am quite aware we may be exposed to considerable risk on this account. I trust that all may be well, and that if it be His will that any trouble should come upon us, dear Joseph Atkin, his father's and mother's only son, may be spared."

The bishop would be denied that last wish.

The wind picked up, and at midday on September 20, 1871, the *Southern Cross* hove to outside Nukapu's barrier reef. No canoes ventured out to greet the ship, so Patteson, despite his trepidation, decided to go ashore. The crew lowered a whaleboat, and Patteson set off with four rowers: Joseph Atkin, Stephen Taroaniara from Baura, and two youths from Mota. They paddled to the reef, where they were intercepted by several canoes from the island. The Nukapuans were friendly, but the low tide made it impossible for the whaleboat to cross the reef, so the bishop accepted a ride to shore in one of the canoes. The rest of the canoes remained with the whaleboat and its rowers.

The strangers chatted across the water. The missionaries and the Nukapuans watched the bishop land on the island and disappear into a hut. Then one of the Nukapuans stood up in his canoe and raised his bow.

"Have you got anything like this?" he asked.

What a strange question. Of course the missionaries did not carry weapons.

Then he shot his first arrow.

"This one is for New Zealand!" shouted another warrior.

"This one is for Mota!" shouted another.

"This is for Baura," shouted another.

And so on, until the air was full of arrows.

The missionaries beat a frantic retreat, but not before Atkin had been struck by an arrow in the left shoulder and one of the Mota boys had taken one in his right, and someone else had an arrow through his straw hat. The arrows were each a yard long, heavy and tipped with shards of human bone, designed to break in the wound. Stephen Taroaniara was hit six times: one arrow broke his jaw; another pierced his chest. The Nukapuans yelled and laughed at the fleeing missionaries, but they did not give chase.

When the whaleboat reached the *Southern Cross*, Brooke pulled five arrowheads from Taroaniara's body, but the sixth had lodged too deeply in his chest to be extracted. It was clear he would not live long.

As soon as his own wound was cleaned, Atkin climbed back into the whaleboat with four men and went to look for the bishop. When the tide rose, they crossed the reef and scanned the shore with a telescope. They saw two canoes put out from Nukapu, each with a solitary paddler. Near the middle of the lagoon, one paddler dropped a rock anchor, then climbed into his companion's canoe. The two men retreated back to shore, leaving the first canoe behind. Atkin and his fellows rowed towards it cautiously and peered inside. The canoe contained a large parcel wrapped in a fine woven mat. Poking out from one end of the parcel was a pair of feet in striped socks. They unrolled the mat to find the bishop otherwise naked. The right side of his head had been shattered. There were a few more light cuts here and there on the body, but it was clearly the blow to the head that had killed him.

And this: the Nukapuans had attached a palm frond to the mat, over the bishop's breast. Five of the frond's leaves had been knotted. Five wounds. Five knots. It must have been a message.

And this: the dead bishop was said to have been wearing a placid smile, which was also widely interpreted as a message.

As soon as Patteson's body had been lifted into the whaleboat, a hundred islanders poured onto the beach and let out a collective scream. The missionaries retreated to the *Southern Cross* and put her sail to the wind.

The next morning, Bishop Patteson's body was consigned to the deep. It took six days for tetanus to take hold of Joseph Atkin's nervous system. Taroaniara died two days later. The two were buried at sea before the ship reached Mota.

Against the protestations of Robert Codrington and others in the mission, the warship HMS *Rosario* was dispatched to Nukapu, where the commanding officer bombed the island, then sent a well-armed landing party ashore to teach the natives a lesson. They burned homes and canoes, and, according to the commander, caused "severe loss of life."

Years passed before the missionaries returned to the island and learned the details of Patteson's death, but that did not stop them from wrapping the tragedy in symbolism and political intent within weeks. The attack had not been an act of spontaneous passion. The Nukapuans, they noted, did not decapitate the bishop, nor did they eat him, as islanders had done to the Reverends Williams and Gordon on Erromanga. The Nukapuans knew the bishop was a big man among Europeans. They treated his body with respect, right down to its presentation in that woven mat. So why had they killed him? The murder was a message, and that message was crystal clear, at least to the missionaries. Five knotted palm leaves. Five wounds. Five islanders must recently have been killed or kidnapped by labour recruiters. This was more than revenge: it was a demand for white men to stop the kidnapping.

"There is very little doubt but that the slave trade which is desolating these islands was the cause of this attack," announced Codrington. "Bishop Patteson was known throughout the islands as a friend, and now even he is killed to revenge the outrages of his countrymen. The guilt surely does not lie upon the savages who executed, but on the traders who provoked the deed."

The missionaries, who had long fought with labour recruiters for the islanders' attention, now lobbied in England and Australia to restrict the blackbirders. Churches and newspapers across the empire joined the outcry. Queen Victoria expressed her disapproval, and early in 1872, the British Parliament finally passed a law to regulate the trade—all this before anyone knew exactly what had happened on Nukapu.

When the *Southern Cross* returned thirteen years later, some Nukapuans told the missionaries what they wanted to hear. Patteson had been led to the hut of the chief, Moto. The bishop was given a mat and lay down on it. Behind the bishop sat a man with a wooden club. All was calm. Moto left to find food. The bishop closed his eyes. The man with the club got up and with one blow smashed in the bishop's head. The bishop died peacefully. He never opened his eyes.

That much, all the Patteson stories had in common. But there are many stories and many more details.

Some islanders said the murderer was a relative of one of five men who had been kidnapped and taken to Fiji on a labour vessel. Some said the chief, Moto, had no part in Patteson's killing and was in fact so outraged by it that he banished the murderer from Nukapu. Some said the murderer later drifted from island to island like Cain, until he was finally shot by a chief on Santa Cruz. And those kidnapped men? One of them died on Fiji, but the other four, or perhaps only two of them, stole a boat and followed the stars west back to Nukapu.

Of course, all these accounts were related through interpreters, and the shell-shocked islanders were unlikely to contradict a tale that had already gained popularity among white men. The mission-friendly version also happened to give the islanders a convenient scapegoat for the crime. But as historian David Hilliard noted more than a century later, the story did not explain the obviously premeditated attack on the crew in the *Southern Cross*'s whaleboat. In fact, it was contradicted by the first missionary to actually live on Nukapu and become fluent in the language. He was told that Patteson was killed over nothing more than a social affront. This version did not carry the symbolism and power of the earlier myth. Perhaps that is why it was quickly forgotten.

Also forgotten was the missionary who reported it: Actaeon E.C. Forrest, the fly in this mythological ointment. The story of Patteson's martyrdom is only half the story of Nukapu's conversion. The other half of the story has been crumpled up and tossed into the dustbin of mission history. It is the tragic tale of a misfit whose life did not fit the missionary template. Forrest came to the Santa Cruz group on behalf of the Melanesian Mission sixteen years after Patteson's death. He was a lay missionary and small-time trader. It was Forrest who guided Henry Montgomery to shore on Santa Cruz in 1892.

"To step ashore at Santa Cruz! To sleep among people so famed for outrages committed in moments of excitement! The very thought was inspiring," gushed my great-grandfather, who was equally in awe of Forrest. He described how Forrest had heroically survived ambushes and assassination attempts. How Forrest had repeatedly dashed out between two parties of warring natives, determined to halt the whistling arrows and make peace. How Forrest had braved the seas by canoe to initiate the pacification of the Reef Islands, despite having once being capsized and stalked by a giant horned sea monster. How, despite the hostility of the warrior chief Natei, Forrest had survived by pluck and wit, built a school on Santa Cruz and finally begun to win over the hotheaded natives. "This gallant man," wrote Henry, "single-handed, is fighting our battles here in perils among waters, in perils among arrows, in perils among fever, and in loneliness." It was Forrest alone who had begun the Christian conquest of Santa Cruz.

A photo in *The Light of Melanesia* shows Forrest standing with a group of Cruzian men. The men are naked except for what look like woven handbags hanging in front of their genitals and, of course, their spectacular shell jewellery: wide hoops through their ears, moon-like discs strung from their necks. The men are stern and muscular. Forrest is bookish and shy among them in his white, three-quarter-length trousers and rolled-up shirt sleeves. He looks like a schoolboy hoping desperately to be chosen for the cricket team.

Forrest's name was not wiped from *The Light of Melanesia* because it was published before his downfall. The rest of Forrest's story has survived only in bits and pieces. I found scraps of it at Lambeth Palace, in the private correspondence of colonial administrators and church leaders. "Forrest ... the temptations on a desert island," was all I could discern from the scribbles of one distraught cleric. But in 1896, Cecil Wilson, the Bishop of Melanesia, alerted the Archbishop of Canterbury that Forrest and another teacher had fallen into very great sin. "They were both found guilty of indecency with the native boys," wrote Wilson, who elsewhere lamented that Forrest had shown a damning lack of remorse: "He says that [the natives] do not think much of his offence; if so, his work during the 9 years he has been here has been worth nothing." And Charles Woodford, the resident commissioner of the Solomon Islands, wrote that tales of Forrest's "sodomy" were a matter of common report among steamship crews.

Forrest was dismissed from the mission, but he refused to leave Santa Cruz and began a trading business. The missionary conqueror of Santa Cruz soon became the mission's greatest foe. Woodford wrote in 1899 that Forrest, who had more influence among the natives of Santa Cruz than any other living white man, had bragged about reducing the number of mission schools in Santa Cruz from six to one.

The Bishop of Melanesia was concerned about a scandal. He wanted to kick Forrest out of the diocese. But Forrest had become so popular among the islanders it took Woodford five years to convince anyone to testify against him. Finally, Woodford had a couple of men from Ulawa sign depositions accusing Forrest of cajoling them into bed some years previously, then trying to put his penis between their legs. Woodford took care to edit the depositions for clarity and word choice, then he declared Forrest "dangerous to peace and good order" and signed a warrant for his arrest.

Before he could make a dignified exit, Forrest was arrested by a passing sea captain and taken to Sydney. He escaped from custody immediately upon arrival and, using his cutter, *Kia*, established a trading base in the Torres Islands, south of Santa Cruz—just beyond Woodford's jurisdiction. Forrest settled down and adopted a young man, whom the natives referred to as his "wife." He lived in relative peace for nearly a decade. But this was the Victorian era. Once the albatross of unspeakable sexuality had been slung around Forrest's neck, he was doomed. It did not help that he warned the natives on his island not to be lured aboard recruiting vessels. When the recruiters complained to the government about this, they never failed to point out that Forrest's wife was clearly not a woman at all.

Forrest had one friend left in the mission, the Reverend W.J. Durrad, who also lived in the Torres Group. When one of Durrad's servants complained that Forrest had invited him to bed and sought his co-operation in an "act of indecency," Durrad informed Forrest that he intended to report the matter. It was now certain that if Forrest did not take drastic action, he would spend years behind bars. He wrote to the New Hebrides resident commissioner, vehemently protesting the accusation. He left instructions for his debts to be paid through the sale of his boat. He left gifts for his crew. He left his land and personal effects to his "adopted son," Barnabas Ditwia of Loh. He apologized for having troubled the resident commissioner. And then he committed suicide by drinking poison. The investigations into Forrest's character, his actions and his involvement with the Melanesian Mission were suspended, and he began to sink into the murk of history.

There was no place for Forrest in the Nukapu myth because evangelical myth offers no room for sex. In order for the Nukapu story to sanctify the mission and give Melanesian Christians their martyr archetype, it needed to remain immaculate, asexual and incomplete.

Sex: according to one English historian, it was very much a driving force behind empire-building, particularly in the famously repressive Victorian era. In the book *Empire and Sexuality*, which I carried to Santa Cruz in my knapsack, Ronald Hyam argued that imperial expansion was as much a matter of copulation and concubinage as it was Christianity and commerce. He pointed out that while Victorians exported their prudish sexual mores around the world (banning polygamy in Melanesia, for example), those who carried the torch of empire were frequently refugees from psychosexual tyranny at home. So it was that Indian Army regulars were serviced by licensed regimental brothels and high-ranking officials from East Africa to Malaya maintained "veritable harems of native women." Lawrence of Arabia had his masochistic fantasies fulfilled by whip-cracking desert nomads and later dedicated his *Seven Pillars of Wisdom* to the fourteen-year-old Hittite Arab lad with whom he had fallen in love. The Empire seethed with sexual possibilities, and its fringes were adorned with the finery of prostitutes, concubines and catamites.

(It was a world with which at least one member of my family maintained a conflicted relationship. Henry Montgomery's son, Field Marshal Bernard Montgomery, condoned the brothels that offered his troops "horizontal refreshment" in Egypt, India and France, but he was less effusive about other kinds of sex. The field marshal claimed, in a speech to the House of Lords, that to permit sodomy would be to "condone the Devil and all his works," and he proposed that the age of consent for homosexual relations be fixed at eighty years. But the field marshal's official biographer has since revealed he was a deeply repressed man whose greatest affections were reserved for adolescent boys, to whom he very much enjoyed giving baths.)

Melanesia was fraught with temptation, which the missionaries were not always able to resist. So it was that Charles Brooke was dismissed for some unnamed sexual impropriety just three years after he chronicled Patteson's paddle towards death. Arthur Brittain and C.D.G. Browne were sacked for their lack of self-control in the 1890s. And, according to Hyam, adolescent sex was "rampant" at the mission school on Norfolk Island: thirteen Melanesian recruits were suspended for sexual misbehaviour in 1899 alone.

Forrest had first defended himself by saying the islanders were not offended by his conduct. That was probably true. Early anthropologists reported accounts of homosexual behaviour all across Melanesia, notably in Papua New Guinea, Malaita and Malekula in the New Hebrides.

I can't help but be drawn to Forrest, whom I have decided to remember through the fog of history not as a sinner but as an irrepressible gay adventurer. Perhaps I am drawn to him for the tenacity with which he survived after being abandoned by his colleagues and peers—everyone who shared his skin colour. More likely it is because in all my months among the islands, through all those long nights, amid the sad whoosh of wind and waves, among men who would stand close, grasp my hand in their own strong hands for hours and gaze into my eyes without reservation or intent, I knew how Forrest must have felt. That loneliness. That longing. I could understand how Forrest, who had tried to reach for the infinite, was yet pulled by the desire for something closer, something like, but yet unlike, himself. It was the wrong desire for his times. It was even more wrong after Melanesia had been transformed into a twentieth-century holdout of Victorian sexual mores. But still it was there and I felt it acutely. The loneliness that wanted more than a firm handshake. The longing that did not seem to fit into any Christian myth and that was monstrous in the eyes of Melanesians—and also those of my ancestors.

And so the ghost of Forrest also travelled with me through the night, as present as Patteson and Codrington and my great-grandfather Henry, as present as a lingering doubt and the faint glow of Tinakula, which was now fading, drifting towards the stern of the *Temotu*.

We were turning, and a great shadow had grown from the sea to starboard. This was Nendo, the island that Mendaña and the missionaries had called Santa Cruz. The calm water that soon steadied the ship was Graciosa Bay, where Mendaña had failed. We steered towards a constellation of quivering flashlights. A hundred people waited for us on a rubbly pier.

Nobody wanted to unload cargo in the rain, so we stayed for two nights. I slept at the village rest house. So did the captain and crew of the *Temotu*, because there was a gas stove at the rest house and a woman who was a distant relative of a crew member, so could therefore be ordered to cook.

I ate with the crew of the *Temotu*. We found warm beer. The crew drank to get drunk. I drank to stop the world from swaying. It felt like we were still at sea.

"You go to Nukapu? I'm half-Nukapu!" said a thin man with an enormous, stretched mouth. He might have been the ship's engineer. "And I can tell you I am a proud man."

"Why do you happen to be so proud?" I asked.

"Because it was my people, my blood, who killed Bishop Patteson."

"Then perhaps you should be ashamed."

"Aha! Wrong. You know, the bishop predicted that he would die on one of our islands. And he said he would die for us. My people helped him achieve his destiny. We made him a martyr."

"Stronger in death . . ." I said.

"Yes, much stronger in death!"

"Just like Obi-Wan Kenobi," I said.

"Yes! Just like . . . *hao?*"

I told the crew the great tale of Obi-Wan Kenobi, the Jedi master from *Star Wars*. I liked the film because it was unambiguous. Kenobi was the wise man of the story and the keeper of sacred knowledge, like Patteson. I told the crew how Kenobi had confronted Darth Vader, the personification of darkness, in a lightsabre duel. Kenobi did not win by slaying his opponent. No. He warned the Dark Lord: "If you strike me down, I shall become more powerful than you can possibly imagine," and then he raised his lightsabre above his head and allowed Vader to cut him in half. But there was no blood. Obi-Wan Kenobi's body simply disappeared. The martyr's spirit lived on to inspire and guide the forces of goodness. There was also the part about the Force, which I said was something like *mana.*

"Oh yes, our story is like that exactly," said the Nukapuan. "Patteson is more powerful now than ever. You know what we call the spot where he was killed? We call it 'the Clinic.' Because if you are sick, you just go to the bishop's cross and pray, and you will be healed. Ah! And when cyclone Namu hit in 1986, the only place that wasn't drowned on Nukapu was the Clinic. Everyone gathered there and was protected from the waves."

The residents of Nukapu are now so proud of their place in history they stage a feast on each September 20, the anniversary of the bishop's murder. The next party would take place in four days. If I could reach the Reefs and find a canoe, I could get to Nukapu in time for the martyr's anniversary.

The *Temotu* set out again at dawn. Everything had changed. The ship was nearly empty. The cargo was gone. So was Brother Clement and so were all the vomiters. We followed the coast of Nendo, then turned north at a bearing nearly parallel to the swell, which had found its shape again.

I was standing by the rail on the ship's bow when John, the ship's dogsbody and garbage-dumper, gripped my arm, pointed north and squealed. "Look, Charlie!" he panted. "It's paradise, Charlie! Don't you see it?"

There was nothing to see but a frothy white line on the horizon. It looked like the first hint you get of the Rocky Mountains when driving west across the prairies: a ragged fringe of glaring peaks and cumulonimbus clouds. I peered and peered and saw only that mirage of snow. But by afternoon, a faint, dashed line had begun to appear amid the glare. It thickened into tufts of palm. The snow revealed itself as surf. A wall of foam, a thousand white bouquets of spray, exploded along a reef which stretched as far west as I could see.

John began to leap up and down like a child. A dozen other men climbed to the bow, and they too were all leaping and jigging on the shifting deck. They were Reef Islanders and they were coming home.

The Reefs: it was a good name for the collection of low islands among which we now drifted. They were as much shoal as they were island. It was as though a vast jigsaw puzzle of coral had been shaken and a few pieces had shifted and slid atop the rest. Some, with their palms and breadfruit and papaya trees, resembled flower baskets perched on black stone pedestals. The rest were like giant clumps of moss. None was as high as the mist that billowed from the breaking surf.

The sun fell into the reef. The palms were seared gold. The lagoon and the sky melted into shades of scarlet. John pulled a lever and the anchor rattled into the sea. Canoes came from every direction, like iron filings towards a magnet. At the helm of one of them was a white man. I knew this must be Ben Hepworth, because the Hepworths were the last of the old-time traders, and the only Brits left in the Reefs. Perhaps their life had once been a glamorous adventure, but those days were long gone. I could see it in Ben Hepworth's face when he motored up in his fibreglass runabout. His eyes were sunken and resigned. His hair wouldn't keep the neat part he had set for it. He shook my hand and ran me back to his trading post on Pigeon Island, which was the only shore not now veiled in darkness.

ON MY MAP, the Reef Group resembled a jellyfish swimming east. Its head was a cluster of flat islands, with great tentacles dragging behind. Some of those tentacles began as islets, but they all disintegrated into light blue tendrils and streamers, coral reefs which disappeared, appeared, zigzagged through the sea until the longest finally trailed off more than 30 kilometres west. Nukapu lay on its own, far beyond the last reef. It was not an easy place to reach. Fortunately, anyone heading for Nukapu was likely to first come to Ben's trading post and wake him by banging an iron rod against a ship's propeller that he had hung from a tree. Ben sold petrol.

Three men arrived with a boatload of mosquito nets. They were conducting an anti-malaria campaign. But they had also heard of the impending feast on Nukapu, and they liked the idea of free food. They agreed to take me with them in exchange for a few litres of petrol.

We left at dawn. The boat was a broad aluminum sled with a 40-horse outboard engine. The lagoon was so vast you could barely see its western fringe. But it was as warm and as calm as a bath. Sometimes the water was so flat and so clear that skimming across it felt like flying above a surreal blue desert. It glowed like the sky. Here and there, coral colonies rose beneath us like giant muffins or clouds. Sometimes they stood like castles. Parrotfish swirled around their ramparts like flocks of birds. Sometimes the lagoon showed the curve of the earth. Passing islands did not retreat into the distance but sank beneath the ice-smooth horizon. The last thing I saw of them was the shaggy top of a coconut palm. Sometimes I saw people and canoes on the horizon, stabbing at the water with spears. But the people were not in canoes. They seemed to be walking above the water. When we approached them, we found they were standing along the edges of barely submerged mesas of coral. Sometimes the water was so shallow we had to cock the engine, climb out of the boat and push, and then the reef was a miniature forest of grasping fingers, white twigs and brain-like stones. Orange anemones moved like animated shag carpet. The coral sliced into my ankles, and a flurry of tiny fish the colour of Bunsen burner flames rose to chase the trail of my blood.

We approached the northern lip of the lagoon and cut the engine again. The men used an oar to push through what looked like a field of sunken caribou antlers. Then the lagoon floor was cleaved open by a deep crevasse. We followed it as it widened into a canyon and then a valley, and finally a deep blue infinity of ocean. The sun and the stillness of the day had pressed the southeast swell into a benign, undulated smoothness.

We passed Pileni, where Henry Montgomery had landed with Forrest. A single cloud hung above it like a white umbrella. A few kilometres beyond Pileni was what appeared to be the last island in the world, a lonely white dune, bare except for a low fin of scrub and oak. The swell curled into long arcs around its reef. We skirted the reef, and I scanned the island for signs of life.

"Nobody stap long disfala aelan," said one of the mosquito men. What a thought. A desert island. I realized that I had not spent a night alone for four months. Solitude is strange to Melanesians, something less than human.

We switched fuel tanks and continued northwest. By midday, the horizon had been wiped clean of everything except Tinakula, which we could see if we stood up. The journey had begun to feel like a descent into a dream. The world was delicate and ethereal. It lost its solidity. We rode up gentle blue hills and down again.

These were our way marks:

A sunbathing turtle.

A leaping porpoise.

A flock of black gulls.

A single cloud grew in the sky to our west. We aimed for it. After an hour, palms rose out of the swell. Nukapu.

Nukapu looked just as it should, like the lithograph I had seen in the Melanesian Mission's annual report for 1878. Like a scrap of shag carpet. Like Gilligan's Island.

It was eerily familiar: there was the reef, which we poled across, and the lagoon. There was the sandy shore. There were the thatch huts, and there was the smoke that had twisted up from cooking fires for a millennium. There, on a raised terrace, was Bishop Patteson's iron cross, painted white and decorated with palm fronds. Behind the cross, presumably on the site where the bishop was killed, stood a rickety church. With its palm-thatch eaves, the church resembled the pool bar at a Club Med. The people of Nukapu clearly had Polynesian blood in them, with their delicate faces and teak-hued skin.

We were led to the chief's house, which was an immaculate, split-level thatch cottage. The ground level was lined with grass mats. On stilts, at waist height, was a sleeping room. The chief was away. A man who claimed to be the chief, but who was really only the assistant chief, came to greet us. Silas Loa was his name. He had thick jowls and tiny eyes. "You are on Nukapu now," he said, puffing his chest up under his floral shirt. "You will pray tonight. You will bow down before the bishop's cross before you enter church."

"Yes, of course we will," I said.

"Watch out for him," one of my friends whispered when Silas turned his back.

The village grew crowded. People arrived in dugout canoes and fibreglass long boats. There were church choirs in matching T-shirts and swaggering bêche-de-mer traders.

At dusk there was a memorial service. A choir from Pileni sang in exquisite harmony. People wore their best T-shirts. Some wore shoes. One boy had runners with LEDs imbedded in the soles. They flashed when he walked. The minister, who had come in a canoe from Nendo, retold the story of Patteson's death. "This is why you and I are Christians now," he said in Solomons Pidgin. "Because someone laid down his life for us."

Later, as the half moon crept up through the palms, we carried oil lamps to the clearing beneath the bishop's cross. The children performed a pageant starring a dreadlocked altar boy as Patteson. The old folks gathered around me and whispered their version of the bishop's death. The stories all conflicted. The murderer was a Nukapu chief, insisted one codger. No, the murderer was from Matema, hissed his wife. And so on. Nobody could imagine why a palm frond with five knots had been placed on the bishop's corpse.

"What about Mr. Forrest?" I asked.

Nobody had ever heard of a Mr. Forrest.

What people agreed on were the details of Patteson's supernatural legacy. The ocean floor where the bishop's body had lain for decades was moving, heaving, pushing the bishop's bones towards the surface. "The bishop wanted us to remember where he was buried, so he made a reef," said Silas solemnly. "We call it Patteson Shallows," said an old woman.

Then there was the site of the bishop's murder. It had been rising every year too. It was the highest spot on the island. The iron cross that stood on that mound was the nexus of the bishop's power. "If you lose something in the bush, just go ask at the cross and you will find it," advised the old woman.

"Once a missionary told us that we did not need to go to the hospital if we were sick. We just need to go to Bishop Patteson's cross," said a man.

"The old, the sick, we just take them there," said another.

"You must hold the cross and also hold the sick part of you, then ask for help," said another. "There are special prayers for healing . . ."

"For example," interrupted Silas, "one catechist had ten or twelve kids and they were all dying, all in the space of a few weeks."

"Malaria?" I asked.

"No. A *kastom* sickness, which came because he had been fighting over land. So when the man had but one son left, he took the boy and pushed him underneath the cross. He said, 'All my *pikinini* are dead, please, bishop, let me keep just this one. And if my boy lives, he will work for God.' That boy was saved. Now he is a catechist in the church."

It seemed the bishop's ghost was being treated much like Melanesians had always treated their ancestor spirits. He was, indeed, becoming stronger in his death. His cross oozed *mana*. Why not? The Bishop of Malaita, who had railed against the *mana*-ization of Christian symbols, would not have approved, but it didn't seem like such a bad thing for Patteson's ghost to exert a benevolent influence. Especially if it worked.

Silas moved closer. "You understand it was God's plan for the bishop to die here, not ours."

"Okay."

"And you see that we have helped you," he said. "So now you must help us. We want to find Bishop Patteson's family. His grandsons."

"Tell them we are Christian now," pleaded the old lady. "Tell them we know the Master now."

"We want to build a special house for the cross," said Silas. "And we want to put a computer in it, so we can be on the Internet."

"For tourists," added someone else.

"You would need electricity for a computer," I said, "and a telephone line . . ."

Silas was not listening. He leaned in towards me and lowered his voice. "And you should help me, too. The bêche-de-mer trader has a crate of beer in his canoe. You should buy me some beer."

At about ten Solomon dollars a can, beer was fantastically expensive for islanders. When they got their hands on it, they drank as much as they could as fast as they could. To buy a crate of beer would be to catalyse an evening of chaos and tears. And besides, I didn't like Silas. I didn't like his bulging, suspicious eyes, or the way he took care to stand slightly higher than everyone else, or the way he pushed his face into mine.

I assured the people I would try to help them, and then I retreated to the real chief's house. Silas followed me. I felt his hand on my shoulder just as I was about to duck inside.

"Did you know that sometimes a column of light shoots up into the sky from the bishop's cross?" he said.

"I'd like to see that," I said, pulling away.

"Of course it takes weeks of prayer to bring the light." Silas tightened his grip on my shoulder. His breath was heavy with betel.

I waited.

"A storm is coming. You are in danger," he said. "But I can help you in your journey. I can keep you safe. I am very powerful, because the bishop, the patron saint of Nukapu, gave me his power."

I did not want to hear this. It was not the end I wanted for my story.

"Bishop Patteson came to me in a dream once. He told me not to be afraid. He told me he would take special care of me. There was light shining from his face. Ever since, I have been able to use his power."

"Sure," I said. "You heal people."

"More than that."

Silas stepped between me and the door of my hut. "Suppose I get in a fight with some man. Maybe he has hurt me or done something bad. I always warn him first: I tell him watch out, now something bad will happen to you. And then in a day or two, he will fall down, or cut himself, or get bitten by a shark. That's the power the bishop gave me."

"That doesn't sound very Christian to me."

"Ha! Don't you worry. You have promised to help us. So tomorrow I will pray under the cross for the bishop to protect you. Then, sometime— I can't promise you when—he will come to you in a dream. He will make you safe. He will bring you success."

"Thank you," I said, straining to free my shoulder from his grip.

"But remember your promise. You must find the bishop's grandchildren. You must tell them to send money. If you do not do that, something very bad will happen to you."

He squeezed harder. "Something very, very bad. Maybe you drown."

The three-quarter moon had climbed to its apex. It cast the village in silver light. Our shadows were sharp and black beneath us. Silas's eyes glistened. I despised him for what he was doing to Patteson's myth. A century after their conversion, the Nukapuans were now converting Christianity: Patteson had not banished the *tindalo*, the powerful ancestor spirits. He had become one. And here was Silas, threatening me with an invocation of the martyr's ghost. Patteson would surely be rolling in his saltwater grave. I crept inside and waited until the sound of Silas's footsteps faded away. One of my friends stirred on the floor.

"Don't worry, Charles," he whispered. "That man is a liar."

NUKAPU WAS spoiled for me after that. I couldn't wait to get off the island.

The feast day was searingly hot. Silas seemed to be everywhere. There he was announcing the Pileni Youth for Christ dance group (they wore grass skirts, waved their arms like the dancers at the Waikiki Hilton and sang, "We are dancing in the light of God"); there he was doling out food (the feast consisted of parcels of leaf-wrapped pork and sweet potato, baked in an earthen oven, and they resembled the remains of little Christmas presents after a house fire); there he was ordering people to sit down at their banana-leaf placemats and eat. Silas was always barking at people. And he always seemed to be watching me with one eye. He insisted I make a speech, so I stood up and told the people that Nukapu was *"wan gudfala Christian paradaes."*

But when I saw the bêche-de-mer trader loading his boat, I collected my things and threw them in.

As I said my hurried good-byes, an old lady, who turned out to be Silas's grandmother, pulled me aside. The sun-baked skin on her face and arms was covered in tattoos. There were fish bones and stars, and on one arm, a name: Steven. Her earlobes had been stretched into long, flabby rings. She pulled the pipe from her mouth and hissed at me in her own language.

"She is telling you to remember that we are not heathens any more," said the girl beside her. "We are Christians. You must not be scared. We won't kill any more white men."

The woman thrust a woven handbag into my arms and peered at me imploringly.

The trader pushed his boat free of the sand. I waded into the sea behind him. Silas charged into the water behind me.

"My friend. You won't break your promise, will you?" he said. "Because if you do . . . Ha! Ha!"

He slapped me on the back. I scowled at him and hopped into the boat.

"Mi funi nomo!"—*I was only joking!* Silas shouted over the roar of the outboard as we pulled away. But he wasn't smiling.

I turned to the sea and did not look back.

I ASKED THE BÊCHE-DE-MER trader to drop me on the deserted island I had seen near Pileni. All the boats returning from Nukapu would pass near it when the feasting was over in a day or so. I could just flag down one of those boats, I said, imagining it would be like hailing a cab. I wanted to be alone.

It was a foolish idea. The trader agreed to drop me only because he knew the island was not actually deserted.

To my dismay, a fisherman and his family were standing on the beach when we crossed the reef. They had paddled over from Pileni in dugout canoes loaded with water jugs, cassava and babies, a portable stereo and a shoebox full of gospel cassettes. They had built huts from sticks, palm leaves and plastic bags. Now the music was blaring, the babies were bawling and the white sand had been transformed into a minefield of buried shit. The men were tired. They had spent ten nights diving in the lagoon for bêche-de-mer. The slugs were now shrivelling on racks above a fire tended by the fisherman's wife. They felt like rubber and smelled like urine. Their insides oozed out like pus.

The fisherman offered me a shell full of turtle soup. I ate with him in the shade, but then I told him I wanted to be alone. This made him sad, but still he ordered his two sons to carry my backpack away from their camp, through the young palms and oaks to the south end of the island, which he called Makalom.

The island was a temporary place, a perfect teardrop of sand that would surely disappear with the next big cyclone. A strong man could throw a coconut across its widest point. I had brought a tent. I pitched it where I could see the surf breaking on the reef, the smoke curling from Tinakula and the palms of Pileni trembling like a clump of dandelions on the southern horizon. If I climbed a tree I could probably see Nukapu too. But I didn't do that, and I tried not to imagine Silas, who would surely still be licking the pig fat from his fingers and bragging about the special magic he had inherited from the martyred bishop.

I watched the family from my tent as daylight bled from the sky. After dark, the fisherman and his sons pushed their canoes out from the beach and drifted silently across the lagoon. They slid into the water, shattering the reflection of the moon. Their flashlights glinted, glimmered and faded with each dive, illuminating the surface of the water from below. Beyond them, the surf burned white on the edge of the reef like a phosphorescent brushfire sweeping back and forth across a dark plain. Thunderheads boiled silver in the distance. Tentacles of vapour were reaching north across the sky. A storm was approaching.

I waited hours for the men to paddle back to their camp. When they did, I listened for their murmurs to cease, for the last gospel song to finish, for the babies to stop crying. Through the trees, I watched their fire spark and flicker and finally settle into an untended glow. I knew the fisherman and his family said their prayers. They thanked God, and probably their ancestors too, implored them to bring more slugs and to keep the storms at bay for just another week.

Now, for the first time in months, I was alone, facing the sea. A breeze sent shivers across the lagoon.

From the moment I had spotted Makalom, I had imagined ending my story there. I had imagined myself alone, knee deep in the lagoon, understanding the weight and truth about stories and gods and ancestors. But it would not work. The story could not end with Silas's threats still rippling across the water. It was not the concept of the dead bishop's power that troubled me. It was the idea of Silas using Patteson's spirit like a curse-dispensing *kastom* stone, the idea that God could be reversed and reduced to a weapon. No. It wouldn't do.

The central struggle in Melanesia was no longer the fight between Christian and pagan mythology. The Christian God had pretty much won the battle. Paganism was on its last legs. The old spirits survived only in a few last pockets of resistance, like the wounded remnants of an army at the end of a long siege. Even in the Kwaio hills, Christian soldiers were hammering at the battlements of pagan ritual. But the old way of thinking, the way of *mana*, had survived and flourished within the Christian Churches. The real fight now was the tug-of-war between *mana* and mysticism; between those who tried to claim and direct supernatural power, like children throwing rocks at their enemies, and those who were certain that the heart of their Christian myth was self-sacrifice and divine love. It was between Old Testament thinking—which was very much in keeping with *kastom* ideas about *mana* and which was increasingly popular among Christian evangelicals—and New Testament thinking, which rejected sorcery and magic in favour of a transcendent kind of vulnerability. The Church of Melanesia claimed to have oriented itself unambiguously towards the mysticism of the New Testament. It was a profound distinction. The key to this philosophy was not commandment, reward or punishment. It was not the directing of thunderbolts towards one's enemies. It was not the prophet Fred draining the lake on Tanna Island. And it was certainly not Silas invoking the spirit of the bishop to bring bad luck to his neighbours. It was not magic as technology, nor was it a sorcerer's stone. The key, which you do not have to be Christian to appreciate, was Jesus without his miracles, trudging out of Jerusalem with his cross on his back, towards death and rebirth. It was the shedding of power and worldly wherewithal. It was love. But most of all it was a story whose power came only through faith and its sister, imagination. Silas had gotten it wrong, and so, in my hunger for magic, had I.

It can take years for miracles to become true. That is how it worked for my great-grandfather, who was not quite the great adventurer I had invented in my childhood. Henry Montgomery sailed through the islands for only three months, then refused all attempts to appoint him the next Bishop of Melanesia. He returned to Tasmania and then to London, where, as secretary of the Society for the Propagation of the Gospel, he devoted nearly two decades to the mundane tasks of mission administration. In his old age, he sat in the garden of the family estate in Donegal, Ireland, and he thought, and he prayed, and he wrote books for his children, and in those books he laid claim to the narrative of his life, investing it with sweeping mysticism. The miracles of his faith were made manifest. Satan appeared to him directly. And so did God, who arrived one Easter morning in that garden above the shining Lough Foyle, in something like a dream.

First came the ghosts of his ancestors, tramping one by one through the foliage. They spoke to Henry approvingly. Then a mist-like veil settled upon the garden. Flowers and shrubs began to stir as though murmuring in their own secret language. Henry's ancestors raised their faces and their hands to an unseen spirit, and they urged him to follow it into the church they had built amid the oaks. He crept to the church door, pushed against its worn grain and slipped inside. That's when he felt his Lord looking down on him. He fell to the stone floor, covering his eyes. God asked Henry as he had asked Abraham: "Lovest thou me?" Henry did not reply. He could not bring his lips to form words. All he could do was weep with shame and awe, and know that the Lord would accept that as his answer.

This was the miracle Henry had waited for all his life. He awoke with the light of Easter morning, feeling a new vigour for the pilgrim path he intended to follow all the way to heaven.

MY STORY IS DIFFERENT. The last pieces of it came to me months after I left Melanesia.

I was sitting at my desk on the far side of the Pacific Ocean, thinking about the day I had joined the *tasiu* on their mission to rescue Johnson Junior. I was considering Brother Francis—how he had murmured and chuckled and remained very small, so small that I had decided he was barely worth noticing until he stepped between the militants and broke the tension with that whispered prayer—when I received the news I had been fearing for months.

After I left the Solomons in November 2002, the country began to fall deeper and deeper into darkness, despite all the Melanesian Brotherhood's efforts at disarmament and peacemaking. There was the corruption, of course, and the failed economy, and a general lawlessness. But these were nothing in comparison to the storm of violence that was building on the Weather Coast of Guadalcanal, where the warlord Harold Keke had gone berserk. Keke, the only militant leader not to have signed the peace accord in 2000, knew that his former allies in the Guadalcanal Liberation Front were joining forces with the police and that they intended to catch him, dead or alive. Anger, jealousy and paranoia—and perhaps the bullet he had received in his skull back in '99—had pushed him beyond the bounds of sanity. Keke imagined treachery in every face. He had razed villages and murdered dozens of people, including some of his own followers. A wave of refugees poured north from the coast to report the atrocities. One man, who had escaped by trekking 50 kilometres through the mountains, told a reporter that every house in his village had been burned to the ground and that Keke's lieutenants had taken three men to the beach where they were forced to parade naked and were beaten until all their bones were broken. Then the men were decapitated. Others were kidnapped and carried to Keke's mountain camp, where they were tied up, beaten with sticks and also dismembered. Heads, arms and legs were dumped into mass graves like mannequin parts.

Keke escorted former allies to the altar of his village church, where he demanded that the congregation deliberate on each victim's loyalty before he cut off their heads. The blood trickled in the unceasing rain, through the soot-blackened mud of incinerated villages on darkness's darkest coast, barely a mountain away from Honiara.

In April, a pair of *tasiu* journeyed to the Weather Coast, bearing a message to Keke from the head of the order, the Archbishop of Melanesia. Only one of them returned. The other died after three days of torture. The Melanesian Brotherhood was shaken but still not afraid. Brother Francis, along with five others, set out for the Weather Coast to retrieve the body of their dead comrade. The mission was a last chance to confront the warlord and convince him to return to the light before his fury spilled beyond the coast and infected the rest of the islands. The six brothers left their canoe on a beach near the village of Babanakira and hiked into the dripping jungle to search for Keke's base.

It was said that Keke had taken the six *tasiu* prisoner. It was said that they never stopped praying for their captor. It was true that, directed by the white *tasiu*, Richard Carter, thousands of Anglicans around the world began to pray, not just for the release of the captive brothers but for the return of Keke and his followers to the way of light.

People were confident the brotherhood would triumph, as they always had, through their God-given *mana*. But weeks and months went by. Keke captured five more brothers and two of their novices, and the kidnappings became a wound in the soul of an already weak nation.

By July, the government had given up. With even the Melanesian Brotherhood failing, it was time for foreigners to come and save Solomon Islanders from themselves. An Australian-led coalition of more than two thousand troops and police landed in Honiara. Keke welcomed the foreigners and invited the new acting police commissioner, an Australian, to meet with him. Keke informed the Australian that his men had already executed Brother Robin Lindsay, second-in-command of the *tasiu*, and young Brother Patteson Gatu-Young, who had once welcomed me to Tabalia with a song, and quiet Brother Alfred Hilly, who had unlocked the door for me late each night at Chester, and Brother Ini Ini Partabatu, who had confronted the Royal Solomon Islands Police for their beatings and extortion, and Brother Tony Sirihi, who had no parents. And Keke had also killed one more: Brother Francis Tofi of the half smile, of the whispered prayer among the militants, of the calming breeze at the Tetere police post.

What do you do when you learn something like this? What can you do but look out your window and watch the buses and bank towers disappear behind a haze of tears, and wonder whether you are crying for the dead, for yourself, or for something shining and good that once called to you, dared you to believe and then was gone again?

What can you do but rise above your doubt and let the heroes and their faith have their moment? What can you do but return to the story and give it the power it demands?

The Bishop of Malaita had told me he was concerned about the brotherhood. The *tasiu* were the bridge between the old religion and the new. They represented Melanesians' ideas of holiness, but they also embodied their belief in *mana*. The bishop worried that all their alleged miracles—not to mention the sickness and death that sometimes befell those who challenged the *tasiu*—lured them towards the old thinking, the thinking of shamans and sorcerers, and away from a more mystical relationship with God.

Beyond my grief, which is shapeless and confusing, I have decided to believe that, on this mythological level, the brothers' deaths were a kind of triumph. They knew Keke was mad. They knew he had already killed dozens of civilians, one government minister and at least one *tasiu*. And yet they journeyed alone to the darkest edge of their world. And there, far from home and light and love, under the unceasing rain, amid the mud and the squalor, under the gaze of an illiterate psychopath, they had offered themselves up as martyrs.

Their deaths would mirror those of their heroes, of Bishop Patteson, Stephen Taroaniara, Edwin Nobbs, Fisher Young and all the other fallen missionaries of Melanesia—and of Jesus. In one audacious leap, the brothers moved from *mana,* the hoarding of personal power advocated by the old cosmology, to self-sacrifice, the transcendental love and martyrdom of the new. And in their sacrifice, surely they would become more powerful, more illuminated, than they had been in their lives. That is the way martyrdom works. That is the geography of the hero's journey.

Richard Carter had tried to chart the brothers' mystery for me. He had tried to explain that the stories which surrounded them were people's attempts to get at the truth of things, truths which were so profound and elusive, so beyond language, that storytellers were forced to fall back on miracles to represent them.

There is truth in myth; not just allegory but a hint of the divine we cannot name—I'm sure that's what the white *tasiu* meant. If this is so, then imagination is more than the ability to produce fiction. It is the expanse between the shores of historical fact and the truths of the soul. Mythmaking, then, is the journey between those truths: an expedition to chart the hidden geography between matter and spirit. Miracles *do* contain truth, though as Northrop Frye tried to explain, these were truths, above all, of the soul's relationship with the universe. The story itself becomes a communion, because the story itself is the journey.

It has always been the storyteller's role to claim the lives of heroes, squeeze them into form, polish them and adorn them so that they achieve a kind of mythic luminescence—not to turn them into fairy tales, but to allow the ideals they represent to shine more brightly. It is what the missionaries, including my great-grandfather, did for Bishop Patteson: "He died with a smile on his face," said those who were not there to see Patteson's last gasp. It is what mythmakers did for Joan of Arc, what Steinbeck did for Zapata, what an entire nation did for John F. Kennedy, sweeping away his sexual adventures, amplifying his speeches. It is what the world is doing now for the Dalai Lama, what we will one day do for Nelson Mandela. Isn't it my job to do the same for Brother Francis? It is hard, when you are caught in the tide of the moment, to feel otherwise. I am close to understanding these things.

I would like to exchange my vision from the bottom of the Langa Langa Lagoon, trade the shark boss and his circling shadow, for a clearer image of Brother Francis. I wonder, if I returned now to the Tetere police post and the shade of that huge oak tree and the tension that showed in the twitching muscles of the young militants, if I returned to the very moment when Brother Francis stepped forward, removed his wraparound sunglasses and began to pray, would it be wrong for me to paint a faint, saintly glow around his head? It would be like the halo that surrounds the moon on a humid night, so faint it would be easy to believe I had imagined it. And the militants, did they not remove their sunglasses too, and did they not wipe tears of shame from their eyes? And the cicadas, did they not cease their incessant whirring for the first time in months? And the wind, did it not rise? Did the wind not tear at the grass and lift the dust so it swirled in a circle around Brother Francis, never quite touching him, and did the wind not wail and whistle, not to obscure but to strangely amplify his whispered prayer? And were we all not lifted? Did we all not hover there, for a moment, just above the rustling grasses, at once humbled, helpless and yet buoyed by holiness? Would it be wrong for me to tell the story that way? Because that would be closer to the truth of things. That is a story I could claim as my own.

Four days after admitting he had killed my friends, Harold Keke released the rest of his hostages and gave himself up. His followers turned in their machine guns. Keke's enemies among the police force and various militias also handed over hundreds of shotguns, pistols and SR-88s to the Australian-led intervention force. Even Jimmy Rasta surrendered his arsenal. Within weeks, the country was proclaimed gun-free. It was the beginning of peace. There was dancing on Mendana Avenue. At Saint Barnabas Cathedral, where the knotted palm leaves from Bishop Patteson's death shroud were still kept in a glass case, thousands of islanders gathered to mourn and praise the fallen *tasiu*.

Richard Carter, now chaplain to the Melanesian Brotherhood, told the crowd that the *tasiu* had been instrumental in manifesting the new peace. It was the brothers' captivity that had precipitated the foreign intervention. It was the influence of the second group of captured brothers that had softened Keke's heart and encouraged him to surrender. God, said the white *tasiu*, was pouring out his grace through the martyrs' deaths. The curse of violence had been lifted from the nation. Meanwhile, the brotherhood itself had been transformed by the ordeal. The *tasiu* had been humbled and purged of pride. They had been allowed a glimpse through the mystery of things to the promise of the eternal.

Through their sacrifice, the martyrs had offered their country the greatest gift of all. They had laid the foundations of a new story, one far more potent, far deeper, than tales of bouncing bullets or magic walking sticks, one that reaffirmed the truths they had been telling each other for a century.

The specifics of the martyrs' final days were vague. People wanted details. They wanted pieces of their new myth. So the white *tasiu* shared with the crowd at the cathedral a tale that reflected the order's holiness. The story had come by e-mail, from a Canadian traveller. It described a tense negotiation between militants at a police post on the plantations east of Honiara; how one quiet *tasiu*, who seemed at first not at all powerful or charismatic, had stepped forward and brought the two enemy groups together in a whispered prayer. "He radiated something so good and true and bigger than the moment, and the tension was washed from the afternoon, and the men with anger and guns were made humble."

When I read a transcript of Carter's eulogy and recognized my own words in it, I realized that, regardless of what had really happened at the Tetere police post, Brother Francis's myth had begun its journey, and that if we told it well, it would grow through the decades and the centuries until it was unquestionably true in its transforming power, as grand and shining as *The Light of Melanesia*. The story itself would be the miracle.

21

INTO THE STORM

Do thou draw the canoe, that it may reach the land;
speed my canoe, grandfather, that I may quickly reach the shore
whither I am bound. Do thou, Daula, lighten the canoe,
that it may quickly gain the land, and rise upon the shore.

Florida Islanders' invocation of a frigate-bird tindalo, in

R.H. CODRINGTON, *The Melanesians*

Y DAWN the storm had engulfed Makalom. Oaks
groaned in the wind. Palms hissed. The surface
of the lagoon vibrated with exploding raindrops.
The wall of surf that marked the fringe of the reef had grown, and so had
the swell in the open ocean beyond. The sandbar that trailed from my side
of the island had been consumed. I stood knee deep in the water and
scanned the blackened swell for boats, but the world had disappeared.

The fishermen's sons yelled at me from shore. "Nobody will leave
Nukapu until the storm has passed. Nobody will rescue you!" The boys
were drenched, grinning. "You will stay on Makalom many, many days,
unless!" bellowed the elder of the two above the roar of the storm.

"Unless what," I shouted back. I wanted to get as far as I could from
Nukapu.

"*Unless yumi padel long Pileni,*" shouted the younger. He said there was
a village on Pileni, and a longboat with an outboard engine that could
ferry me back to the trading post at Pigeon Island.

"But how will we find Pileni?" I asked. "We can't even see past the edge of your reef."

The boys shifted in the sand, conferred with each other, considered the sky, then clapped their hands. "The waves will tell us which way to go!"

We pushed the fisherman's dugout canoe out into the shallows. I jammed my pack into the bow, and the boys passed me a crude, hand-carved paddle.

The surf had now wrapped itself around Makalom, rendering even the sheltered lee side treacherous. Each approaching wave sucked the reef plateau almost bare before rising to curl and collapse across the exposed coral. To linger in the shallows before a wave set would be to risk being crushed. We measured the rhythm of the swell.

Three rollers, then two calves, then a set of seven.

A lull.

We charged, paddling for all we were worth across a sheet of foam, cutting diagonally over the collapsing shoulder of the next wave and high along the crevassed edge off the reef; on over the abyss, rising, falling, rising again through the foothills of the Pacific. We left the scant shelter of Makalom's wind shadow. The first gust hit us like an explosion, transforming the ocean into a confused stampede of chop, whitecaps and spindrift.

"Pull, Charlie!" yelled the elder. "Pull!"

I pulled. So did the elder, and his exhalations were like the snorting of a bull. The younger, wide-eyed and delirious with the excitement of the moment, held his paddle like a rudder at the stern. The wind may have come from the southeast. The waves may have come from the east. They peeled over the bow, filling the canoe with warm water. It rolled but it did not tip.

We sliced through the folds, keeping them at an angle.

We pulled until my shoulders ached, until blisters rose on my hands and knees.

We pulled until Makalom became a silhouette behind us, then a phantom, then nothing but a memory.

The sky collapsed. The horizon was lost in vapour. The universe was reduced to the roll of the canoe, the plunging of our paddles and the swell, which came from beyond the edge of the world, and which existed to guide us. The rest was uncertain. The shifting sands, the white cross of Nukapu, the sun-bleached skulls, the charms, the Bibles, the machine guns, the magic walking sticks, the igneous fires of Tanna—all the things I had seen or touched now seemed formless, malleable. They could have been fiction. And the things that I had called myth—the curses of sorcerers, the revelations of prophets, the bouncing bullets, the *mana* of stones, the circling shadows, the god of my ancestors—they too lurked, unreachable beyond the veil of mist and spray yet now somehow possible, pregnant with potential. In the fullness of the storm it was easy to imagine they might allow themselves to be gathered, squeezed and moulded into a shape that made sense. The shape would be a story. It would begin with a grain of memory, a packet of sand, perhaps, but it would end with imagination. A sign from beyond, yes, and an island conjured by faith and will from the immensity of the sea.

A NOTE ON LANGUAGE
AND SPELLING

OST CONVERSATIONS relayed this book were conducted in Bislama or Solomon Islands Pidgin. Many of those exchanges have been translated into English to avoid confusion. I was assisted in the translation, and also in correcting the spelling and syntax of Bislama and Solomons Pidgin, by Helen Tamtam of the University of the South Pacific and Richard Carter of the Melanesian Brotherhood. However, I have deviated from their advice in several respects and have certainly introduced errors along the way.

I have generally used the most common (and mostly phonetic) modern spelling for Bislama and Solomons Pidgin words, but in some cases I have fallen back on the spellings used by earlier traders and travellers. For example, I use *rubbish* instead of *rabis* or *ravis,* to mean "of bad character," to reflect that word's metaphorical origin. I use *savve* to mean "to know/to be able to" rather than the now more popular—yet confusing for English speakers—*save.*

When the same words appear in both Bislama and Solomons Pidgin, I have stuck with the first Bislama spelling, rather than switching to the Solomons standard, for consistency. For example, the word "you" is spelt *yu* throughout the book, rather than switching to *iu* once we reach the Solomons.

My apologies to those who are working to standardize both languages.

SELECTED BIBLIOGRAPHY

MANUSCRIPT SOURCES

Harold Turner Collection on New Religious Movements, University of Birmingham, Selly Oak, England. Essays and papers on Pacific cults and millenarian movements, missiology and religious syncretism.

Lambeth Palace Library, London, England. Archbishops' Papers (Benson, Davidson, Tait, Frederick Temple); *Church Times* 1895–1901 and other miscellaneous papers.

Mitchell Library, Sydney, Australia. Western Pacific High Commission Archives, Patteson Memorial Endowment Fund of the Melanesian Mission, Papers, 1871–1906.

Rhodes House Library, Oxford, England. United Society for the Propagation of the Gospel Archives, Codrington Papers, Patteson Papers, reports from missionaries, Wilson letters to Montgomery, 1894–1906.

Viscount David Montgomery Private Collection. Notes and diaries of Bishop H.H. Montgomery.

SOUTH PACIFIC JOURNEYS

Lord Amherst of Hackney and Basil Thompson, eds. *The Discovery of the Solomon Islands by Alvaro de Mendaña in 1568*, vol. 2. London: Hakluyt Society, 1901.

Coates, Austin. *Western Pacific Islands.* London: Her Majesty's Stationery Office, 1970.

Davidson, J.W. *Peter Dillon of Vanikoro.* Melbourne: Oxford University Press, 1975.

Edwards, Philip, ed. *Journals of Captain Cook.* Abridged.. London and New York: Penguin, 1999.

Jack-Hinton, Colin. *The Search for the Islands of Solomon, 1567–1838.* Oxford: Clarendon Press, 1969.

London, Jack. *Cruise of the Snark.* New York: Macmillan, 1919.

McAuley, James. "Captain Quirós" in *Collected Poems.* Sydney: Angus & Robertson, 1971.

Markam, Sir Clements, trans. and ed. *Voyages of Pedro Fernandez de Quirós, 1595 to 1606,* vol. 2. London: Hakluyt Society, 1904.

Montgomery, H.H. *The Light of Melanesia.* London: Society for Promoting Christian Knowledge, 1896.

Shineberg, Dorothy, ed. *The Trading Voyages of Andrew Cheyne: 1841–1844.* Canberra: Australian National University, 1971.

Theroux, Paul. *The Happy Isles of Oceania.* New York: Ballantine, 1992.

HISTORY OF THE MELANESIAN MISSION

Hilliard, David. *God's Gentlemen: A History of the Melanesian Mission, 1849–1942.* St. Lucia: University of Queensland Press, 1978.

Macdonald-Milne, Brian. *The True Way of Service: The Pacific Story of the Melanesian Brotherhood 1925–2000.* Leicester: Christians Aware and the Melanesian Brotherhood, 2003.

Sarawia, George. *They Came to My Island.* Sioata, Solomon Islands: St. Peter's College, 1996.

Whiteman, Darrell. *Melanesians and Missionaries.* Pasadena: William Carey Library, 1983.

Williams, C.P.S. *From Eton to the South Seas.* London: Melanesian Mission, n.d.

SOLOMON ISLANDS

Bennett, Judith. *The Wealth of the Solomons.* Honolulu: University of Hawaii Press, 1987.

Honan, Mark, and David Harcombe. *Lonely Planet: Solomon Islands.* 3d ed. Hawthorne: Lonely Planet, 1997.

Hviding, Edvard. *Guardians of Marovo Lagoon: Practice, Place, and Politics in Maritime Melanesia.* Honolulu: University of Hawaii Press, 1996.

Kabutaulaka, Tarcisius Tara. *Beyond Ethnicity: The Political Economy of the Guadalcanal Crisis in Solomon Islands.* Suva: Australian National University, 2001.

Keesing, R.M., and Peter Corris. *Lightning Meets the West Wind.* Melbourne: Oxford University Press, 1980.

Tippett, A.R. *Solomon Islands Christianity: A Study in Growth and Obstruction.* London: Lutterworth Press, 1896.

VANUATU

Adams, Ron. *In the Land of Strangers: A Century of European Contact with Tanna, 1774–1874.* Canberra: Australian National University, 1984.

McClancy, Jeremy. *To Kill a Bird with Two Stones: A Short History of Vanuatu.* Port Vila: Vanuatu Cultural Centre, 1985.

Paton, J.G. *John G. Paton, Missionary to the New Hebrides: An Autobiography.* London: Hodder & Stoughton, 1893.

Rice, Edward. *John Frum He Come: A Polemic Work about a Black Tragedy.* New York: Doubleday & Company, 1974.

Rush, John, with Abbe Anderson. *The Man with the Bird on his Head: The Amazing Fulfillment of a Mysterious Island Prophesy.* Seattle: YWAM Publishing, 1997.

Tryon, Darrell. *Bislama: an Introduction to the National Language of Vanuatu.* Canberra: *Pacific Linguistics,* 1987.

ANTHROPOLOGY, MYTHOLOGY, THEOLOGY

Arens, William. "Rethinking Anthropophagy" in *Cannibalism and the Colonial World,* ed. by F. Barker, P. Hulme and M. Iversen. Cambridge: Cambridge University Press, 1998.

Bidney, David. "Myth, Symbolism and Truth" in *Myth: A Symposium,* ed. by T. Sebeok. Bloomington: Indiana University Press, 1974.

Brunton, Ron. *The Abandoned Narcotic: Kava and Cultural Instability in Melanesia.* Cambridge and New York: Cambridge University Press, 1996.

Campbell, Joseph. *Myths to Live By.* New York: Bantam, 1972.

Carter, Richard. *Liturgy Beyond Words: Symbolic Exchange with the Transcendent God.* Leeds: University of Leeds, 2001.

Codrington, R.H. *The Melanesians: Studies in their Anthropology and Folklore.* Oxford: Clarendon Press, 1891.

Evans-Pritchard, E.E. *Theories of Primitive Religion.* Oxford: Clarendon Press, 1965.

Frazer, James. *The Golden Bough: Abridged Edition.* New York: Macmillan, 1940.

Frye, Northrop. *The Double Vision: Language and Meaning in Religion.* Toronto: University of Toronto Press, 1991.

Kulick, Don, and Margaret Willson, eds. *Taboo: Sex, Identity and Erotic Subjectivity in Anthropological Fieldwork.* London: Routledge, 1995.

Leenhardt, Maurice. *Do Kamo: Person and Myth in the Melanesian World.* Chicago: University of Chicago Press, 1978.

Lévi-Strauss, Claude. "The Structural Study of Myth" in *Myth: A Symposium,* ed. by T. Sebeok. Bloomington: Indiana University Press, 1974.

Loeliger, Carl, and Garry Trompf, eds. *New Religious Movements in Melanesia.* Suva: University of the South Pacific and the University of Papua New Guinea, 1985.

Michaud, Jean. "Ethnological Tourism in the Solomon Islands: An Experience in Applied Anthropology." *Anthropologica* 36:1 (1994).

Obeyesekere, Gananath. *The Apotheosis of Captain Cook: European Mythmaking in the Pacific.* Princeton: Princeton University Press, 1992.

————. "Cannibal Feasts in Nineteenth-Century Fiji: Seamen's Yarns and the Ethnographic Imagination" in *Cannibalism and the Colonial World,* ed. by F. Barker, P. Hulme and M. Iversen. Cambridge: Cambridge University Press, 1998.

Rivers, W.H.R., ed. *Essays on the Depopulation of Melanesia.* Cambridge: Cambridge University Press, 1922.

Sahlins, Marshall. *Islands of History.* Chicago: University of Chicago Press, 1985.

Worsley, Peter. *The Trumpet Shall Sound: A Study of 'Cargo' Cults in Melanesia.* London: Schocken, 1968.

HENRY MONTGOMERY AND FAMILY

de Montgomery, B.G. *Origin and History of the Montgomerys.* Edinburgh and London: William Blackwood and Sons, 1948.

Hamilton, Nigel. *The Full Monty, Volume I: Montgomery of Alamein, 1887–1942.* London: Penguin, 2001.

M.M. *Bishop Montgomery: A Memoir.* Westminster: Society for the Propagation of the Gospel on Foreign Parts, 1933.

Montgomery, Brian. *A Field-Marshal in the Family.* London: Constable, 1973.

Montgomery, H.H. *Foreign Missions: Handbooks for the Clergy.* London: Longmans, Green, 1904.

————. *Life's Journey.* London: Longmans, Green, 1916.

————. *Mankind and the Church: Being an Attempt to Estimate the Contribution of the Great Races to the Fulness of the Church of God.* London: Longmans, Green, 1907.

————. *Visions.* Westminster: Society for the Propagation of the Gospel in Foreign Parts, 1910.

————. *Visions: Third Series.* Westminster: Society for the Propagation of the Gospel in Foreign Parts, 1915.

OTHER SOURCES

Conrad, Joseph. *Heart of Darkness with The Congo Diary.* London: Penguin, London, 1995.

The Holy Bible, Authorized King James Version. London and New York: Collins' Clear-Type Press, 1928.

Honigsbaum, Mark. *The Fever Trail: In Search of the Cure for Malaria.* New York: Farrar, Straus & Giroux, 2002.

Hyam, Ronald. *Empire and Sexuality.* New York: Manchester University Press, 1990.

A Melanesian English Prayer Book with Hymns. Honiara: Church of Melanesia, 1965.

Niutestamen: The New Testament in Solomon Islands Pijin. Suva: Bible Society of the South Pacific, 1993.

Said, Edward. *Culture and Colonialism.* New York: Knopf, 1993.

ACKNOWLEDGEMENTS

I OWE FIRST thanks to my mother, my favourite storyteller, for keeping the old myths alive, and to my family and friends, for encouraging, forgiving and supporting me through my geographical and emotional absences.

Many people shared their homes and their lives with me in England, Fiji, Vanuatu and the Solomon Islands. I hope this story respects their truths. In the Solomons, thanks go especially to the members of the Melanesian Brotherhood, and in particular: Brothers Harry Gereniu, Albert Wasimae, Clement Leonard, John Blythe and, for help with pidgin and other mysteries, Brother Richard Carter. Thanks also to Bishop Terry Brown and his household, David MacLaren, Geri and Alvin Gaines, Roni Butala and his *wantoks,* John Palmer, Grant and Jill Kelly, John Roughan, Ben Hepworth, Robert Iroga, Henry Isa of the National Museum, Johnson Honimae, Morris Namoga and Andrew Nihopara at the Solomon Islands Visitors Bureau. In Vanuatu, I was assisted by the Anglican Diocese of Banks and Torres, Jirus Karabani, Alfred of Mota, Don Fockler, Rona Dini, Sabine Hess at Vureas Bay, Eli Field, Ralph Regenvanu at the Vanuatu Kaljoral Senta, and Linda Kalpoi and Natasha Motoutorua at the Vanuatu Tourism Office. The wise and patient Helen Tamtam of the University of the South Pacific taught me Bislama and performed triage on my translations. Laura Palmer and Alex Wolf offered refuge in Fiji. Alastair Macaulay saved me from the wilds of North London.

I was assisted in research by the shining Catherine Wakeling, archivist for the United Society for the Propagation of the Gospel, John Pinfold at Rhodes House Library, Richard Palmer at Lambeth Palace Library, Allan Anderson at the University of Birmingham, Fergus King, Ben Burt, David Hilliard, Robert Withycombe, Thorgeir Storesund Kolshus, Viscount David Montgomery, Tarcisius Tara Kabutaulaka, Manfred Ernst and Adele Plummer.

Support from the following magazine editors opened doors for me across the Pacific: Jim Sutherland at *Western Living*, Matthew Mallon at *Vancouver Magazine*, Chantal Tranchemontagne at *enRoute*, James Little at *Explore*, Anne Rose at *WestWorld*, Ian Hanington at the *Georgia Straight* and Aryn Baker at *Time Asia*. Crucial support also came from Air Pacific, Solomon Airlines, Air Vanuatu and VanAir.

Friends, family and colleagues read and critiqued my early proposal and various chapters of the book. Thanks to Michael Scott, Carol Toller, Daffyd Roderick, Erik Lees, Andrew Mayer, Michael Prokopow, Edward Bergman, Kevin Griffin, Jeff Hoover, Deborah Campbell, James MacKinnon, Brian Payton, Alisa Smith and, in particular, Chris Tenove, who offered regular doses of savage and necessary criticism. The Vancouver FCC kept the creative fires stoked. Jorge Rivero-Vallado showed me new ways to imagine language and stories, and his counsel is still missed.

I am grateful to Scott McIntyre for giving me the benefit of the doubt. My editor, Saeko Usukawa, led me down a trail of cookie crumbs towards an infinitely stronger manuscript. My agent, Anne McDermid, worked miracles on two continents. The journey was kick-started with financial support from the Canada Council for the Arts and the B.C. Arts Council, but I would never have considered it without constant encouragement and badgering from Michael Scott, who was the first to believe.